D0846322

the Gospel and Human Destiny

Institute for Ecumenical Research

Strasbourg, France

The Gospel Encounters History Series

Edited by Vilmos Vajta

In cooperation with: Günther Gassmann, Marc Lienhard, Harding Meyer, Warren A. Quanbeck, Michael Rogness, and Gérard Siegwalt

Other Series Volumes

The Gospel and Unity

the Gospel and Human Destiny

Edited by
Vilmos Vajta

Augsburg Publishing House
Minneapolis, Minnesota

THE GOSPEL AND HUMAN DESTINY

Copyright © 1971 Augsburg Publishing House

Library of Congress Catalog Card No. 79-159013

International Standard Book No. 0-8066-9431-9

All rights reserved. No part of this book may be used or reproduced in any manner whatsoever without written permission
except in the case of brief quotations in critical articles and re-
views. For information address Augsburg Publishing House, 426
South Fifth Street, Minneapolis, Minnesota 55415.

Scripture quotations unless otherwise noted are from the Revised
Standard Version of the Bible, copyright 1946 and 1952 by
the Division of Christian Education of the National Council of
Churches, and are used by permission.

Manufactured in the United States of America

Contents

Preface 7

Part One   The Acts of God in Creation and History   9

Chapter 1

Creation and History in the
Old Testament—Claus Westermann 11

Chapter 2

The New Testament Witness to the
Cosmic Christ—Roy A. Harrisville 39

Chapter 3

The Cosmological and Anthropological
Significance of Christ's Redeeming Work—
Lars Thunberg 64

Chapter 4

The Presence and Acts of the Triune God in
Creation and History—Joseph Sittler 90

**Part Two   The Acts of Man in
Creation and History** 137

Chapter 5

The Dialogical Character of Human Existence—
Wilhelm Dantine 139

Chapter 6

Man as Responsible Co-worker with God in a
Dynamic World—Gyula Nagy 178

Chapter 7

Political Responsibility as the Obedience of
Faith—William Lazareth 218

List of Authors 271

Preface

This volume of essays is the continuation of a project initiated by the Institute for Ecumenical Research in Strasbourg, France. A first volume, *The Gospel and Unity*, examined the problem of Christian unity in the contemporary world.

The present, second volume deals with another area of basic theological and ecumenical reflection: the question of the destiny of man in history and in the world. The problem is approached both from the perspective of God's activity in time and space (creation and history), and from that of man's involvement in that activity. More concretely, the first half of the volume relates to the discussions which, since the World Council of Churches New Delhi Assembly, have not ceased to animate ecumenical discussion. The idea of the "Cosmic Christ" binds together the problems of creation and salvation in a unity, and conceives man's role in the world in a specific way. The second half of the book, relating to social-ethical problems, investigates the fundamental theological reorientation applied to concrete human existence in the contemporary world. The basic statements of the Second Vatican Council, the World Council of Churches, and the Lutheran World Federation are critically examined.

The editors hope that these essays will contribute to a creative dialogue by opening avenues for a clarification of central and burning issues, as well as for closer ecumenical understanding. The present volume itself represents the continued efforts of the Institute to strive toward a theology in dialogue. It was possible to gather all but two of the authors of this volume at the Institute for a consulation on the projected essays. Through this fraternal dialogue the variety of theological thinking was encouraged and at the same time further clarified and more properly related.

Warren A. Quanbeck carried special responsibility for the English edition of this volume, with Russell Norris and Ulrich Reetz acting as editorial assistants.

THE EDITORS

Part One

The Acts of God in Creation and History

Chapter I

Creation and History in the Old Testament

THE ACTING OF GOD IN CREATION

The Old Testament speaks about the creator and creation especially in three contexts: In the narratives of primeval history (Gen. 1:1-24a; 2:4–3:24; and in several passages in Gen. 5-11), in conjunction with the praise of God as the praise of the creator (above all in the Psalms, in Deutero-Isaiah and Job; and in the predications of God as the creator throughout the Old Testament), and in the Wisdom literature.[1] If one views all of these individual texts and larger contexts, it is clear that this way of speaking is an essential element of speaking about God, and is found in all parts of the Old Testament: in the historical books, the prophetic books, the Psalms, the Wisdom literature. In no part of the Old Testament is this way of speaking wholly lacking.

The special place of speaking about the creator and creation is the primeval history (Gen. 1-11). If one views this special place in the Bible as we have it, then speaking about the creator and creation forms the beginning, the introduction, the overture. If one, however, views the construction of the Pentateuch, which begins with the creation stories, in its historical process, then the primeval history to which the creation stories belong forms the outer-most horizon; the Pentateuch grew out from its center, from the account of the deliverance of the people out of Egypt. Around

11

this center was added the story of the patriarchs (Gen. 12-50) and as the outer-most circle, the primeval history Gen. 1-11.

1) That speaking about the creator and creation in the Old Testament belongs to primeval history means that the Old Testament does not speak about creation simply as of a beginning of history or the acting of God at the beginning of history. It consciously sets creation apart from history and the acting of God in history as a primeval event. That means as an event inaccessible to human experience and comprehension. A number of features indicate that the first 11 chapters of Genesis speak differently about reality than the presentation of historical events beginning with Gen. 12. In setting aside the first 11 chapters as primeval history, the Bible will say that the beginning, like the end of time (the primeval history corresponds to final history), is not accessible to human experience and comprehension in the same way as the time we count as history.

That creation belongs to primeval history also means that it can only be understood in conjunction with the whole primeval history (Gen. 1-11). In the tradition of the church, the first three chapters have almost always been removed from their context, interpreted for themselves and held as the essence of the primeval history. This separation of chapters 1-3 is exegetically impermissible. If Gen. 1-3 are interpreted within their broader context of Gen. 1-11, important shifts in meaning and changes over against the previous interpretations take place. A consideration of this broader context shows that:[2]

a) To creation in primeval history belongs the blessing bestowed upon all living things through which the life given in creation is carried on from generation to generation. The blessing bestowed on man at his creation *takes place* in the passage from one generation to the next, as is pictured in the genealogies of the primeval history (Gen. 4:1-2, 17-26; chapter 5; chapter 10; chapter 11:10-32).

b) To creation belongs the limitation of the creature. Over against the creation of the world, the flood is the possibility of the world's end (Gen. 6-9); over against the creation of man stands his limitation in death and fallibility. This limitation is not only described in Gen. 3, but also in 4:2-16; chapters 6-9; 9:20-27; 11:1-

9. Fallibility and the threat of death in their many possibilities and forms belong to the world and to man as God created them.

c) To creation in primeval history belongs the commission to subdue the earth (cultural work), for which man is created. To man's being belongs his relationship to God, human fellowship, language and cultural work. These are elements of man's being according to the opinion of the creation narratives; human existence cannot be abstracted from them. The blessing bestowed on man pertains also to his work; the progress of work in discoveries and achievements is grounded in the blessing (Gen. 4:17-22; 9:20; 11:1-9; and individual passages). Cultural work is so closely connected with the creation of man in Gen. 1-11 that this context forbids a theological or philosophical definition of the "nature of man" which abstracts man from his work.

2) The way in which western theology speaks about the creator and creation is characterized by an abstract concept of creation which is far removed from biblical speech. The Bible does not first have a comprehensive concept of creation which then can be filled with different objects (heaven, earth, animals, man); for the Bible, rather, each act of creation is an individual, complete event, and each can also be expressed with a different verb. The most important difference lies in the fact that in the Old Testament a distinction is made between the creation of the world and the creation of man. Both go back to different historical origins and are transmitted in different lines of tradition. That means that Gen. 1:1—2:4a (P) and Gen. 2:4b—3:24 (J) are not, as almost everyone has held up to now, two parallel creation narratives, the one younger, the other older. The older (2:4b—3:24) is a narrative of the creation of man, the younger (1:1—2:4a) a narrative of the creation of the world. (Here it is still clear to see that the part about the creation of man, 1:26-30, is presented differently and differs from the other works of creation. It was originally an element of an independent tradition.

Both creation narratives in Gen. 1-3 have a long previous history. Both were given their final form in Israel and according to a theological conception formed in Israel. But both show that it was the intention of their authors to pass on and preserve the old, polymorphic tradition of speaking about the creator and creation. Both creation narratives show that the Bible speaks about the creator and creation only as part of a series of different representations of God's work of creation. This intention is especially evident in the presentation of the creation of the world by P. His special way of presentation is that of the creation of the world through the commanding word of God. The manner of presentation is seen in the series of identical or almost identical sentences which present in their order the issue and execution of the command. But P combined this with another, older manner of presentation, which speaks of making, dividing, setting, calling. These verbs point to an older manner of presentation which P combined with his own. Just as here in *one* presentation different kinds of creating are combined, so a survey of all statements about creation in the Old Testament shows a series of quite different ways of presenting creation in the different traditions. The most important, clearly recognizable kinds of creating are:

> Creation through birth or through the descent of birth
> Creation resulting from a battle or victory
> Creation through acting or working
> Creation through a word [3]

If the Bible speaks about the creator and creation only in the multiplicity of different presentations of creation set one beside the other, then it is not possible to ground a doctrine of creation on the Bible which overlooks these differences and presupposes that there is only *one* valid presentation of creation in it. The intention of speaking about the creator and creation in this multiplicity is to preserve reverence toward the work of the creator. The Bible makes clear that we have no access to the act of creation itself. Creation is a primeval event in the very fact that it, unlike history, cannot be witnessed to. There were no witnesses of creation and thus there can also be no witness to it. It is thus impossible to say that the one presentation of creation is true and the other is false. The multiplicity of presentations points to a divine work of creation which in its real course remains a mystery. The basic theological tendency in all speaking about the creator and creation is to call the creature to reverence toward his creator and to the acknowledgement of God as the creator. This is indirectly expressed in the creation stories at the beginning of the Bible in the tendency to indicate step by step that the work of the creator is inaccessible for human understanding.[4]

This basic tendency receives its direct expression in the praise of the creator in the Psalms. It has its place in the descriptive praise of God (hymn). The descriptive praise of God lauds God in his majesty and in his goodness. This polarity characterizes all praise of God in Israel. The praise of God's majesty is developed in many Psalms in two directions: God is praised as the creator and as the Lord of history. That the praise of the creator in the Psalms is a praise of God's majesty can be seen in the fact that the Old Testament does not want to speak factually about the creator and creation; it does not seek to establish what took place in the beginning nor explain how it took place. Its basic tendency is rather to honor God as the creator, to articulate in the praise of the creator the relationship between creator and creature.

A peculiarity of the way the Old Testament speaks about the creator and creation is that it makes no attempt to fully integrate the statements about creation into the acting of God in history.[5] Throughout the whole Old Testament the being and acting of God as creator is regarded as something essentially different from his saving and judging acts in history. This demonstrates that the redeeming action of God which began with his intervention in history is set over against the work of the creator which is not redemptive, not a special work aimed at a special people and a special history, but a universal work. The whole primeval history has this universal character. Because creation has to do with the universe, the world, and mankind, speaking about creation takes part in this universal character. The primeval history in Gen. 1-11 shows sentence by sentence that it does not want to be a specifically Israelitic account, that the statements about creation as such are also not specifically Israelitic statements. All the peoples known to Israel spoke of creation; Israel knew that the creation traditions it took up reached back thousands of years into the past. These are traditions of all peoples which as such are bound to no special people or culture.

It is then quite natural that nowhere in the Old Testament are there so many parallels from other religions and cultures to biblical texts as in the texts of Gen. 1-11.[6] The history of the interpretation of these first 11 chapters of the Bible has encountered such parallels in ever increasing number. This has led to the question, which for a long time stood in the center of the discussion of whether literary dependency of biblical on nonbiblical texts could or must be assumed. Especially controversial was the question whether or not the creation story in Gen. 1 is dependent upon the creation story in the Babylonian epic Enuma elish, and whether or not the biblical flood narrative in Gen. 6-9 is dependent on the Babylonian narrative in the Gilgamesh epic. In recent research, the question of literary dependency has receded in importance. It has been recognized that the relationships among the different creation stories can not be decided on the basis of the literary period of the tradition's history alone. This literary period comprises only a very small part of the total history of speaking about the creator and creation; the main part of this history lies in its oral period. The Babylonian epics are late products of that culture, whose previous history—especially in the Sumerian myths—is now well known to us. It is also no longer possible to limit the previous history of the creation motifs to the immediate surroundings of Israel; both the Egyptian and the Mesopotamian creation mythologies show that many motifs originated not in the high cultures, but in the primitive ones. It is an astonishing fact that in the early period of mankind, in the high cultures as well as in the primitive ones, there are not an infinite number and variety of ways of speaking about the creation of the world and man. Rather in the history of man there are only a very limited number of creation motifs which appear again and again around the world and at quite different times. To these belong, for example, the notion that the creation of heaven and earth took place as a separation of heaven and earth. To these belong also the notion that man was formed by the creator from earth or clay. Since notions appear across the face of mankind, the question of literary dependency loses its meaning; it is seen, however, that speaking about the creator and creation really has universal character and that the biblical primeval history in Gen. 1-11 also cannot be taken out of this universal context.

In view of this, speaking about the creator and creation within the primeval history in Gen. 1-11 receives an importance for the whole of the Bible which has not yet been sufficiently acknowledged by Christian theology: the special history of God with his elect people which began with the calling of the one man Abraham and the forefathers of the one people Israel is grounded on the universal, primeval acting of God, as the introduction to the history of the patriarchs in Gen. 12:1-3 clearly shows. Only in this way is it possible that the special history of God with his elect people can flow into a final event which again widens into the universal end history of mankind and the world. The so called salvation history can then never be seen apart from the universal acting of God. That God is creator then also means that as creator he continues to work in the world and in mankind even outside the people of God and without visible connection with his action in salvation history. God remains the Lord of mankind, the Lord of history, the Lord of the cosmos; the history of the believers is not identical with the history of God with his creation. In order that both merge again, the end history belongs to the Bible.

The universal character of the Old Testament accounts of the creator and creation is also shown in the fact that in the strict sense of the word it does not become a statement or confession of faith. This is seen in the striking fact that a) speaking about the creator never became part of a "credo" in Israel; the summaries of Israel's faith were limited from beginning to end to the *"historical* credo" (G. von Rad). It is first with the Apostolic Creed of the Christian church that speaking about God the creator is united in a confession of faith with speaking about God's saving acts. b) The other fact is that the Old Testament never speaks of faith in the creator or in creation. The word faith never appears in connection with a speech about creation or the creator. The simple reason for this fact is that Israel in this regard saw no alternative; *not* to believe in the creator or creation was impossible. The idea that the world and man were created by God was for the people of the Old Testament something like a presupposition of all thought. Another possibility for the origin of the world and man could not be conceived. If one considers this fact, it becomes clear that the whole controversy between belief in creation and a scientific explanation of the origin of the world and mankind is based on a false pre-

supposition. The Old Testament statement about the creator and
creation does not an any way exclude a scientific explanation of
the beginning of the world and mankind.[7]

This fact gains a special significance for the situation of contemporary thought. It has been self-evident for the whole of western theology that the biblical speaking about creation is a theological speech in the strict sense; there was no question that as a
speaking determined and shaped by faith and revelation, it was
necessarily and principally different from every other speaking
about the world and mankind. It was an indisputable presupposition that only theology was competent to speak about the origin
of the world and the origin of mankind. All that is changed when
it is seen that the language of the primeval history, the language
of the Bible in the first 11 chapters, is still prior to the later separation into theological and nontheological, spiritual and worldly,
sacred and profane language. The Old Testament speaks about
creation in such a way that in this speech—as seen by us—theology,
philosophy, and science are all inseparably bound together. That
the world and mankind are God's creation is a presupposition of
thought that is universal in a twofold sense: it is true for Israel
just as for all peoples in Israel's surroundings; within Israel it is
true for all realms of life and for all possible reflection about the
world and man.

3) Speaking about the creator and creation itself has undergone
an historical development in the Old Testament. The presupposition that the world and mankind are created by God does not
mean that something like a doctrine of creation existed; it does
not mean that a certain idea about creation dominated from the
beginning to the end. If one asks what the whole Old Testament
says about creation, one discovers a multitude of quite different,
essentially divergent presentations of creation. I will select three
points from this history.

a) Characteristic for the creation of the world as presented by
the Priestly writing in Gen. 1 is the creation through the word of
God. The first chapter of the Bible receives its peculiar, strong
rhythm in the alternation of the creation—word and the creation—
work resulting from this word. Creation is also presented in many

other places of the Old Testament as creation through the word, e.g. Psalm 33:9: "For he spoke, and it came to be; he commanded, and it stood forth." This special way of presenting creation is found not only in the Old Testament. It is often found in Babylonian hymns and in a very pronounced form in the so-called Memphistic theology in Egypt, here very similar to the presentation in Gen. 1.[8] But the fact that creation through the word also appears outside the Old Testament is not yet the decisive point. That is first seen when one views the creation story in the first chapter of the Bible in its own context, i.e. as the introductory chapter of the large Priestly writing.

If one views Gen. 1 in this broader context it is clear that the special aspect of the creation story in Gen. 1 does not lie in creation through the word. The special aspect is rather the peculiar construction in which the elements of a commanding, a creation-commanding, form the framework for the presentation of creation: God said . . . let there be . . . and there was . . . and God saw that it was good . . . and there was evening and there was morning. . . . Now this basic structure is found not only in this chapter, but characterizes the Priestly writing as a whole. The structure of the points just mentioned applies, of course, only to creation; but even in history only one thing is decisive: that all that takes place arises out of the command or commission of God. Thus, for example, by the theophany on Sinai the command of God goes forth to Moses to build the tent of meeting. The following part reports of the execution of this command. In and with this, history moves forward. It is thus a certain, fundamental conception of event itself that lies at the basis of the special presentation of creation by the Priestly writing in Gen. 1. It is not simply creation through the word, but creation through a creation-command of God, a command that brings forth being, as it then also grounds and determines all history. It thus becomes clear how the manner in which the Priestly writing presents creation is indissolubly connected with its conception of history. The Priestly writing thus speaks of creation in the same way in which creation is seen and understood in the total conception of this work.

b) The work of the Jahwist also begins with a creation story.

This creation narrative is already a wholly other kind of speaking in that it centers on man. This narrative stands in the very old tradition, found the world over, of telling about the creation of man. The line of tradition in which the Jahwist stands also tells about the creation of man in terms similar to all the other traditions. It is immediately understandable that the Jahwist begins his work precisely with a narrative standing in the tradition of the creation of man, when one traces the intense interest in man which runs through the whole of his work—in man in his heights and in his depths, in his astonishing capabilities and possibilities as well as in his limitations in guilt and sorrow. The special aspect of the Jahwist creation narrative can be seen in the genial fusion of two originally independent narratives. The one told of the creation of a man which was not yet good when God formed man out of earth to a living being; he first became man in a real sense after God created the partner who corresponded to him; man in the real sense is first the man in fellowship, only so is he the man who has a history and with whom God has a history. The other narrative begins with the garden and with the command not to eat from the tree in the middle. It tells that man who was created, cared for, and cherished by God succumbed through the entice-ment to disobedience and therewith had to be removed from the presence of God. Man so removed from God is man who is limited in fallibility, sorrow and death. With the fusion of these two narra-tives to a single narrative in which the junctures are scarcely visible, the Jahwist combined the two basic statements about man as God's creature: the man whom God created for the earth and the culture of the earth, for fellowship and for history, is at the same time the man to whom offense and disobedience, to whom limita-tion through death and sorrow belongs. It is not difficult to see how also in this historical writing, creation—here the creation of man—receives its special form in the larger context of the whole work which tells of God's history with *this* man.

c) The prophet Deutero-Isaiah in Babylonian exile does not speak about the creator in order to point to creation as such, to creation as an event in the far past, but rather he places the work of the creator immediately in the context of the present situation of the people in exile. In order to make it clear to the tired and desperate people that in spite of their apparent hopeless situation deliverance is a possibility of God lying before them, he reminds them of God's work of creation in which this possibility is given. He awakens in them again the praise of the creator once raised in the services of worship in their lost homeland in order, in this way, to make the acts of God real for them—acts which recall in their oppressed situation a universal, unbounded power (Isa. 40:28-29):

> Have you not known? Have you not heard?
> The Lord is the everlasting God,
>   the Creator of the ends of the earth.
> He does not faint or grow weary,
>   his understanding is unsearchable.
> He gives power to the faint,
>   and to him who has no might he increases strength.

Here then, speaking of the creative work of God is set in direct connection with the announcement of a new saving act. In order to gain attention for this message of salvation, in order to render faith in deliverance possible, the horizon of this saving act is widened all the way to the universal work of the creator God. The realization of deliverance which had become wholly uncertain received a new ground of possibility in the work of the creator God which is essentially a work of unlimited power, a work of unlimited possibility. The reference to the creator in Deutero-Isaiah receives a wholly new meaning in the fact that God's act of deliverance will be different from all previous acts; the creator of heaven and earth is able to carry out this deliverance through a non-Israelite, through the heathen king of the Persians, Cyrus (Isa. 45):

> Thus says the Lord to his anointed,
>   to Cyrus,
>   to subdue nations before him
>   and ungird the loins of kings,
>   to open doors before him
>   that gates may not be closed . . .
> I am the Lord, and there is no other,
>   besides me there is no God.
>   I gird you, though you do not know me . . .
> I form light and create darkness,
>   I make weal and create woe,
>   I am the Lord, who do all these things.

We can observe in Deutero-Isaiah that speaking about the creator and creation is so merged with speaking about God's saving deeds that its own meaning recedes in favor of its new function in relation to the saving deeds of God.[9] The New Testament mentions the creator and creation in many passages in a self-evident manner, without making God's work of creation its specific theme.

Finally a word about God's work as creator.

When the Old Testament speaks about creation, it speaks about reality. To speak about God means to speak about reality, for God is the creator. To be real in the Old Testament is identical with being created; reality is creaturehood. That is just as true for the world as for man. When in the Old Testament the tradition of speaking about the creation of the world and the tradition of speaking about the creation of man are still distinguishable, then that also means: it can still be recognized that in very early times being or reality could only be grasped in view of man's being. Connecting the creation of the world with the creation of man meant that now reality encompasses man and the world, that it was only as a creation of God that the world could be comprehended as reality. Thus man and the world find their reality in like measure as created beings; there is here neither a reality which is conceivable other than or apart from being created, nor an independent reality which thought or faith must first set in relation to God.

This means that the Christian-medieval doctrine of God as the *summum ens* is not compatible with biblical speaking about the creator. All being, like all that exists, is created; were God an *ens*, even the highest, then he would be created, not creator. Where being and existence are no longer identical with being created, God is no longer the creator as the Bible understands this word.

Because, however, being is identical with being created and reality with creaturehood, speaking about the creator in the Old Testament is necessarily universal in character. All universalism in the Bible, i.e. every speaking in which the work of God is directed at the universe, is based in God's being as creator and in the fact that the world and man are created. That is the reason that the Bible begins and ends with a universal action of God. Because God is the creator the beginning of his work is universal and the conclusion of his work is universal. The Old and the New Testament belong together also in the fact that only in the succession of these two parts can the whole scope of God's work from a universal beginning to a universal end be made very clear.

This raises the question of the *creatio continua*. How does God continue to work on his creation after creation in the real sense has been completed? It is important to see that this question arose only in later reflection. It is never asked in the Bible. The doctrine of the church speaks here of a *creatio continua* or of preservation. Both concepts are unsuitable. As creation is something absolutely unique, the formulation *creatio continua* is a contradiction in itself.[10] While this concept says too much, the concept "preservation" says too little. For the work of God on his creation is not just an act of preserving it in the state it once reached; it is much rather dynamic, manifold, and rich in contrast, which the term "preservation" fails to convey. The Bible does not by any means use a single comprehensive term to designate God's continuing work on his creation. Because God is the creator, *all* that happens is effected by him; there is no realm of existence in which everything that takes place could not be attributed to him. Because God is the creator, there is also no sharp division between nature and history. The realms of human life, nature, and cosmos belong together in the fact that together they form the *one* realm of creation. All that happens belongs together in the fact that God acts in it.

With that the question about preservation or *creatio continua* leads over to the second part, the acting of God in history: the separation of creation and history in the Old Testament is not such that one could speak of an acting of God in history *alongside* a work of God in his creation or in nature; God works in all that happens—that is what is meant by saying that God is creator. That, of course, does not exclude a relative independence of that which we usually call nature and history; but the Bible repeatedly breaks through the dividing line between these two realms. When God comes to help his people, his coming causes the surrounding nature to tremble; when Israel forsakes its God, heaven and earth are called upon as witnesses; when the congregation in worship sings to the praise of God, the whole creation is called to praise (Psalm 148):

> Praise him, sun and moon,
> praise him, all you shining stars!

God is acknowledged as creator precisely in the fact that all that exists and all that happens is explained from him, derived from him, and understood in connection with him. All that happens comes from him and all that happens leads to him (Rom. 11:36).

THE ACTING OF GOD IN HISTORY

The acting of God in creation and his acting in history stand in relation to one another in the Old Testament; the one is not without the other. That is seen above all in the descriptive praise of God (hymn), throughout which the praise of God's majesty is developed in such a way that God is praised at the same time in his work as creator and in his acting in history (so, e.g., in Psalm 33 and 136). Both belong so closely together that God's divinity can only be seen in both together; were God's acting limited to mankind, he would lose his divinity for the Old Testament way of thinking. It is only worthwhile to speak of God for the Old Testament when his acting encompasses creation and history. God's acting in history is prior to his work as creator insofar as it is history in which God confronts his people and Israel its God. God received his name in connection with an historical deed. The primeval confession of Israel speaks of this event, the covenant is grounded in it. The praise of God in Israel began with narrative praise; in it God is extolled for his great deeds, i.e. for his acts in history. But it must be immediately added: History cannot be understood in terms of our modern concept of history which stems from the 19th century. When we apply this concept of history to the Old Testament it must be expanded in two directions: It can only mean events in which God and his acting and speaking are not excluded but included; it can only mean events in which man principally belongs together with all the rest of creation.[11]

1) Thus history, as it is understood in the Old Testament, cannot be centered solely in political events or even limited to them.

It is also not possible to make a distinction here between political history on the one hand and individual-private occurrences on the other. History, as understood in the Old Testament, consists of many layers. That can best be seen in the contribution of the Pentateuch. The Pentateuch, which for ancient Israel was something like a Bible within the Bible, is divided into three parts in such a way that these three parts correspond to the three layers of the Old Testament concept of history. The third part, from the departure out of Egypt to the beginnings of the occupation of the land, deals with history as we understand it, i.e. with national history or political history; strictly speaking, however, this third part of the Pentateuch (from Exodus to Deuteronomy) only introduces the political history which begins in the land.

The second part of the Pentateuch, Gen. 12-50, is family history; the real subject of what takes place is the family or tribe. In all later history, this subject remains a part of history as a whole, above all of political history. To what extent family occurrence can participate in political events, to what extent they are interwoven in political events, can be seen especially in the history of the Davidic succession. In many ways it corresponds closely to our concept of historiography,[12] but then again it is typical of the Old Testament in the fact that the political history of David as king and the history of David as the father of his sons are inseparable. The family thus always remains an essential element of history: what occurs in the family is not "private," but eminently political.

The first part of the Pentateuch (Gen. 1-11) deals with primeval history; here man in the world is seen in his mere individual state, prior to any communal existence. That is: the essential elements of human life are presented—elements which are the same the world over and belong to man's being as long as he exists. This element of basic humanity belongs necessarily to history as it is understood in the Old Testament. If history is presented, it cannot be overlooked that the essential elements of human life—as for example that man's existence is limited by death, that male and female belong together, that man is fallible or that envy has a deadly power—are always in play even in political events.

If the Old Testament understanding of history contains these three levels that means that a separate political realm does not yet exist. Political events are still inseparably interwoven with the elements of family happenings on the one hand and with the elements of the humanum on the other. These three levels of event are held together in the fact that in each of these realms man is seen in his relationship to God. A separate political realm does not yet exist here, i. e. politics is not yet something abstract following its own rules, above all because political events also have to do with God. That can be seen in Israel especially in the time of the holy wars and of the kingdom. In like manner, a family occurrence takes place over against God, from and to him. The concept which holds the family stories together in Gen. 12-50 is that of the blessing; God's blessing causes the family to grow, and its wholeness and peace depends on it. But also man's being as such, the humanum, is seen as something that is only possible and conceivable in relation to God. The elements of man's being arise from his being created, which is true not only of man in Israel and not only of those who believe in Jahweh, but of man in general, at all times and in all places.

2) The understanding of history characteristic of the Old Testament can be seen in the presentation of the saving deed of God at the beginning of Israel's history.[13] It is most characteristic that during the many centuries in which this event was passed down it never became an "objective historical fact" in the sense that it was transmitted as a mere datum of history. No report of this event can be found in the Old Testament in which God is not seen as its subject; it is passed down as God's deed and only as such. Correspondingly, the elements of the presentation of the event describe a reciprocal action between man and God, a dialogical event then, which takes place neither in an "historical," nor in a "theological" realm, but from man to God and from God to man. These elements can be listed:

a) The cry out of the depths is the starting point of the event. This cry out of the depths is something like a primary datum. It is not asked what went before. It is also not asked if one caused the trouble or not. It is presupposed here that God hears the cry of the suffering creature and has mercy upon him unconditionally.[14]

b) The saving or deliverance from trouble is announced by a

messenger, a mediator of the word who tells the people that God has heard the cry of the oppressed. With that the message of redemption, of salvation, begins and moves from this announcement of deliverance at the beginning through the whole of the Old Testament, reaching over into the proclamation of the good news in the New Testament.[15] But in a broader sense the history of the divine word also sets in here, the history of the word that goes forth from God to his people. The deliverance is announced in a word; the departure for a new land on the basis of this announcement requires faith.[16]

c) For the proclamation of this message of deliverance a word-mediator, a messenger of God is needed. With that the history of the mediator sets in, which, starting with Moses, also passes on through the whole history of the people of God.[17]

d) The deliverance is realized in the coming of God who descends to liberate his people, who comes to help his people. The saving God is the coming God, the reality of this God is experienced in his coming. From this point on, the experience of the coming God always remains connected with his saving deeds: "Our God comes and is not silent!" In this coming he is the future God. God's future, however, remains indisposable; an "eschatology" which knows and disposes over the future of God, is not possible here.[18]

e) The deliverance is experienced as a wonder; the wonder of the deliverance awakens the praise which answers it. The event began with the cry out of the depths. In the praise which answers the deliverance it reaches its goal. It is thus from beginning to end a dialogical event. God's saving deed is not complete in itself; it first becomes complete in the praise which answers it.[19] Only in this context does it become clear what the Old Testament understands as wonder. Wonder here is an absolutely personal, dialogical event. It can only be experienced by one who experienced the deliverance; it can only be expressed in the answering praise of the delivered (Psalm 78:1-7). A wonder cannot be confirmed on the basis of its outcome; it has nothing to do with the difference between natural and supernatural effects.[20] In the praise of the delivered, the wonder of the deliverance is given expression;

through this praise it continues on, and in it lies the core of that which is handed down of the great deeds of God.

These are the elements then, which characterize the saving acts of God upon which Israel's history is grounded. It is understandable in view of this structure that it is presented as one *single* line of events. From the promise of deliverance out of Egypt to the entrance into the promised land, a succession of events is presented which as a whole—despite the differences of the individual events—presents the *one* saving deed of God; it was thus possible in the so-called historical credo (G. von Rad) to summarize the historical epoch of the origins as a unified event, as is the case, e.g., in Deuteronomy 26 or in Psalm 80.

The core of this creed is a confession of praise; the Pentateuch, at whose center the account of the deliverance out of Egypt stands, is a broad development of this confession of praise. If the Pentateuch contains the real "saving history" of the people of Israel, it is precisely because of the structure of the confession of praise which holds the individual facts together, from the cry of the oppressed to the praise of the delivered.

3) But where the answer of praise ceases, where the people "forget" God and his saving deeds, there God's work of judgment begins. It is introduced by an announcement of the acts of judgment and carried out in blows that strike the people, and finally in the blow which brings the history of the people to an end.

Here the commission of the judgment prophecy in the Old Testament is grounded. Prophecy is a feature of God's acting in the history of the people of Israel which is not present in the same way in the other religions. The significance of prophecy in Israel lies in the fact that the God of Israel is *one* God (cf. p. 30). Because his whole being and acting is turned toward his people, he takes his work of judgment so seriously that before he strikes the punishing blow he warns his people over and over again through the mouth of his messenger. The indictment which accompanies the announcement of judgment—a social, political, and cultic-theological indictment—seeks to wrest an acknowledgment of guilt from the people.

The proclamation of the prophets showed Israel's history as one long series of merciful acts of God: the indictment of the prophets contrasted Israel's present disobedience to those past saving deeds of God for his people (so, e.g. Amos 2 and Isa. 5); Hosea used the picture of marriage which was broken by Israel, a picture which shows the continuity of the whole relationship between God and people in an especially pointed way.

The proclamation of the prophets also showed the connection of Israel's history on the horizontal plane: above all in their social and political indictments, the prophets passionately fought against the isolation of different realms of existence, as if only certain areas of life stood in relation to God. The decision between the Yes to God and the No to God—so they said—is not made in a worship service isolated from the rest of life, but rather in the daily social and political life.

A final effect of the prophet's proclamation was the acceptance by those who remained that the political and cultic collapse of Israel—the divine judgment announced by the prophets—was necessary and meaningful because it confirmed the prophetic message. That formed a point at which a new beginning could be made following the collapse, and so the proclamation of the prophets made a continuity possible which lasted through the collapse.[21]

The judging work of God on his people could only be seen and presented in review, when those who were left acknowledged those blows as God's judgment upon his people. In the Deuteronomistic historical work (Joshua to 2 Kings), the history of Israel's apostasy is presented up to the destruction of the nation. This presentation is grounded in a confession of guilt which reveals the past to those spared by the judgment as a line of events which reaches from the (at first conditional, then unconditional) announcement of judgment to its final fulfillment. Now not everything that takes place in this long period of time is influenced by this one line of events; at the beginning beside the announcement of judgment stands the old line of the promise of salvation which continues on for a long time; this long period of time is marked, however, by the fact that with the entrance into the land the two possibilities of blessing and curse stand before the people (Deut. 27 and 28), and that in review the fulfillment of God's judgment is recognized as the close of this whole epoch.[22]

Correspondingly, the history of Israel from the deliverance out of Egypt to the destruction of the kingdom and the temple is summarized in two historical works: in the Pentateuch, based on the confession of praise, and in the Deuteronomistic historical work, based on the confession of guilt. The whole presentation is characterized by the polarity of God's saving deeds and his work of judgment. This historical presentation in the great historical works of the Old Testament represents a unique phenomenon. At no other place in the ancient Oriental world was an historical work produced which covered such a long period of time and at the same time possessed such an inner consistency. The reason for this lies in the fact that the God of Israel is *one* God. *All* that happens takes place here between God and his people, and in a wider sense between God and man. Where the gods can only be spoken of in the plural, it is quite natural that the emphasis lies on that which takes place *between* the gods. It is precisely this that is expressed in myth. For this reason the myth gained no importance for the people of Israel and is virtually absent from the Old Testament. The understanding of history in the Old Testament is thus grounded in the fact that the one God with his whole being and acting and planning is turned alone toward the world, man, and his people. That is the basis for the intensity and inner consistency with which the Old Testament speaks of history.[23]

4) What has been said so far about God's action is, however, not yet sufficient to describe his acting in history. Beside the polar works of saving and judging, the Old Testament knows a wholly different kind of divine acting in history: a constant acting not manifested in momentary events, namely God's work of blessing. Blessing really means the power of fertility. God's blessing causes a developing and growing, a ripening and fruit-bearing, a silent advance of the power of life in all realms.[24] The relationship between the momentary and the constant acting of God can best be seen at the beginning of the book of Exodus. At this point the history of the patriarchs, characterized by the blessing, passes over into the beginning of the history of the nation, characterized by the deliverance out of Egypt. The exposition of the dramatic story of the exodus is based on the fact that the descendants of

the family of Jacob had become a great people in Egypt. It is this divine work of blessing that was promised in the history of the patriarchs (promise of fruitfulness), and it is the same growth of a people that sets the drama of oppression and exodus in motion.

a) The history of the patriarchs is an account of the blessing (Gen. 12-50). The decisive theological concept in Gen. 12-50 is that of the blessing (Gen. 12:1-3). Abraham and his descendants are promised a blessing; this promise extends beyond him to "all the families of the earth." The history of the patriarchs is family history: in family history the blessing takes the form of being blessed with children, i.e. in the continuance of the race from the parents to the children (Gen. 12-25); of being blessed with possessions, whereby rivalry between the brothers arises (Gen. 25-36); of being blessed in the permanence of the extended family, the close fellowship in which peace goes hand in hand with blessing (Gen. 37-50, breaking and restoring the peace).

b) Deuteronomy reports the blessing on the people who are settled in the land. God's work of blessing is just as central in this book. The blessing bestowed upon Israel in its land is manifested in the gifts of the land. Thereby in a bitter struggle, Jahweh, the saving God from the wilderness, takes the place of the gods of the land; he alone bestows the blessing (Deut. 26, by the offering of the first fruits). The gift of blessing is the fulfillment of the promise made to the patriarchs (Deut. 6:10). This blessing, however, is now only spoken of as a conditional blessing; it is bound on the obedience of the people (Deut. 7:12f).

c) The kingship also stands in the context of God's work of blessing. The king, although at first sent to Israel as deliverer, is mainly the bearer and mediator of the blessing. The Nathan-promise, 2 Samuel 7, assures continuance and duration; it is the steady action of God that is manifested in kingship; anointment is something like a blessing for the king and grants him a steady character. The continuity of the dynasty is the continuity of a family in which the promise given the kingship is passed on from father to son. The prayer of consecration for the temple of Solomon,

1 Kings 8, shows the significance of the king in preserving the blessing for the people and land.

d) The place where God's work of blessing is mediated is the temple service of worship. The priest blesses the people at the close of the service, the pilgrims come to the temple to receive the blessing. There were many ritual acts of blessing, as well as a blessing of the individual, as Psalms 91 and 121 show. The importance of the blessing in the temple worship service is shown in many ways in the Psalms. The destruction of the temple also meant the destruction of the place where the blessing was mediated.

e) Finally the blessing has an essential significance for speaking about the future. A distinction must be made between the promise of salvation which assures the help of God in a certain situation, the proclamation of salvation which announces a certain saving *act,* and the description of salvation which portrays the coming time of salvation as a lasting condition. This state of salvation is presented in the language of blessing. Unlimited blessing and unlimited peace are characteristic of it. This description of salvation then became especially important in apocalyptic.[25]

Because God's acting on his people and God's acting in history are bound together, the Old Testament does not know a one-track, all-encompassing concept of history. The concept "salvation history," so popular in the past decades, leads to the misunderstanding that the Old Testament presents events consisting essentially of a series of saving deeds of God. Apart from the fact that in the Old Testament these saving deeds exist only in connection with God's judging works, which already shows the onesidedness of the concept of "salvation history," this term blurs the difference between God's work of salvation and his work of blessing. "Salvation" is usually understood as meaning both, although this is usually not made explicit. Decisive for the Old Testament's understanding of history is precisely the fact that history remains in the tension of God's saving and judging acts on the one hand and of his momentary and constant acting on the other. This history cannot be reduced to a single concept, certainly not to the concept of salvation history.

The history of which the Old Testament speaks has a beginning and an end. History as the history of mankind thus corresponds to the "history" of the individual which reaches from birth to death. The primeval events and the final events, however, differ from what we call history. Whereas with Abraham the particular history of the chosen people begins, the primeval events which precede him are universal. In like manner, in the final events as presented in the apocalyptic, the history of the people of God flows into universal history. The beginning and the end have to do with mankind and the cosmos in their origin and goal.

The history which takes place between the primeval events and the end events is divided into periods which are history in a different sense of the word, and in which the work of God is each time essentially different, above all in relation to the different communal forms in each period. Only the middle period, from the formation of the nation to the destruction of the Northern and Southern Kingdoms, is history in the sense of political history. The previous history consists of the period of family history (including the history of the clan and tribe) and the period of the nomadic group; the following history consists of the period of servitude in exile and of the post-exilic cultic community. That which remains the same in these periods is the never-ceasing acting of God on his people. But as the object of this acting changes drastically in different periods, the manner of God's acting changes also.

The decisive change in the way God acts on his people lies in the fact that only in the middle period, from the conquest of the land to the exile, does God save his people through their victories over their enemies. Only in this middle period does God act on his people through the military deeds of Israel—not before and not afterwards. This middle period is brought to a close with the promise—following the collapse and exile—of Israel's deliverance from the Babylonian captivity which the prophet Deutero-Isaiah sees taking place through a military deed. However it is no longer a military deed of Israel, but of the Persian king Cyrus who is appointed by God and who in this connection can even be called Jahweh's anointed. With that, God's saving work on his people is severed from acts of political and military power; it takes place from now on without political power and without the weapons of Israel.

In connection with this severance of political and military power from God's acting, a change in the work of the mediator can be observed. For the first time a single person is appointed to mediate God's acting through a mediating act of suffering. But the "servant" who suffers on behalf of the others (Is. 53) is no longer spoken of as an historical figure with name and date; his historical place remains remarkably undecided. In connection with that, Israel's relationship to the nations was decisively changed through the announcement that God's saving work was expanding beyond Israel to include the nations (Isa. 45:20ff). But it is here no more than an announcement.

At this point God's history with his people Israel is clearly open to the future. In these two facts a basic change is announced, but the realization of this change is no longer reported. Both points, however, are determinative for the New Testament account of the work of Jesus of Nazareth. A third point comes in: the new saving deed is principally an act of forgiveness; upon it the history of the new people of God is grounded (Is. 53; Jer. 31:31-34).[26]

To understand the New Testament as the fulfillment of the Old Testament it is, however, necessary above all to understand that the Old Testament history, which reaches its goal in the events of the New Testament, is the history of the *whole* Old Testament. The account of Jesus of Nazareth, understood as fulfillment, presupposes the history reported in the Old Testament which leads to him as its goal; this history, however, stands in the broader horizon of the history of mankind and the history of the cosmos between creation and consummation. Creation and history arise out of the same origin and move toward the same goal.

—Translated by Donald Dutton

NOTES

1. A short survey, together with parallels from other religions, is given by W. H. Schmidt, *Die Schöpfungsgeschichte der Priesterschrift*, 2nd ed., 1967. The statements about creation in Deutero-Isaiah and in the book of Job stand in relation to those in the Psalms as do most of those in the other prophetic books. Thus by far the majority of the statements about creation in the Old Testament stand in connection with the praise of God. That is also the case with the divine predications as, e.g., Gen. 14:19, 22; 24:3, 7; Jer. 10:12, 51:15; Amos 4:13; Ps. 121:2, etc.

2. The following is dealt with extensively in my Genesis commentary, *"Einleitung zur Urgeschichte,"* Biblischer Kommentar. Altes Testament, ed. by M. Noth, I, *1 Genesis,* Neukirchen, 1967 (hereafter abbreviated BK). This also gives a list of the literature as does the book by W. H. Schmidt, cf. note 1.

3. Explained further in my commentary BK I, 1, pp. 36-57.

4. For that reason a *creatio ex nihilo* cannot be found in or derived from Gen. 1; this concept goes beyond that which Gen. 1 intends; more about this in my commentary.

5. Otherwise G. von Rad, *Old Testament Theology,* Vol. 1, pp. 126ff.

6. The most important literature is listed in BK, I, 1, pp. 97-101 and pp. 248, 284f., 288f., and C. Westermann, *"Neuere Arbeiten zur Schöpfung,"* *Verkündigung und Forschung,* 11, 1969, pp. 11-28.

7. Important here is that the presentation of creation in P already shows the beginnings of a scientific understanding of the origins, especially in the creation of the plants and animals each according to its kind; so G. von Rad, *Genesis,* p. 64; C. Westermann BK I, 1, pp. 242ff., W. H. Schmidt, *op. cit.,* pp. 181-185.

8. K. Koch, *"Wort und Einheit des Schöpfergottes in Memphis und Jerusalem,"* in: *Zeitschrift für Theologie und Kirche,* vol. 62, 1965, pp. 251-293.

9. This is especially emphasized by G. von Rad, *"Das theologische Problem des AT-lichen Schöpfungsglaubens,"* *Beihefte zur Zeitschrift für alttestamentliche Wissenschaft,* Vol. 66, (1936) pp. 138-147 and R. Rendtorff, *"Hermeneutische Probleme der biblischen Urgeschichte,"* *Festschrift F. Smend,* 1963, pp. 19-29.

10. See also A. Loretz, *Schöpfung und Mythos,* Stuttgarter Bibl. Studien 32, 1968, p. 97.

11. O. Plöger, *Geschichte und Geschichtsauffassung I im AT* in Die Religion in Geschichte und Gegenwart [3], Vol. II, col. 1473-1476, more literature there. Hereafter abbreviated RGG.

12. L. Rost, *Die Uberlieferung von der Thronfolge Davids,* 1926, reprinted in L. Rost, *Das kleine Credo,* 1965, pp. 119-253. G. von Rad, *"Der Anfang der Geschichtsschreibung im AT,"* in: *Theologische Blätter,* vol. 8 (1958), pp. 148-188.

13. G. von Rad, *"Das formgeschichtliche Problem des Hexateuch,"* in: *Theologische Blätter,* vol. 8, 1958, pp. 9-86; M. Noth, *Überlieferungsgeschichte des Pentateuch,* 1948, esp. p. 7; E. Rohland, *Die Bedeutung der Erwählungstraditionen Israels,* 1956. Over against the custom of calling the accounts of the exodus out of Egypt and the conquest of the land "election traditions" (cf. K. Galling, *Die Erwählungstraditionen Israels,* BZAW 48, 1928), it must be said that this concept stems from a later interpretation (it is found frequently in Deuteronomy). The older accounts and the songs do not speak of election, but of God's salvation. That is important because salvation is something everyone knows and can experience; only the later theological interpretation says that in this event Israel is elected by God. The event that grounded and formed the *history* of Israel was the *experience* of salvation, *not* the election.

The same is true for the concept of the covenant. Such a concept does not really designate an historical event, but *interprets* this event. The covenant designates the context derived from the events at the beginning of Israel's history. Hence, the covenant refers to the constant relationship between Jahweh and Israel grounded in these events, and not to the events themselves.

14. This cry out of the depths is therefore an essential element of the presentation of the event which takes place between God and man throughout the whole history of Israel. It does not belong to "religion" or "piety," but to history insofar as in history man and the community remain in relationship to God. In view of this, the close connection of the psalms of lament with history can be understood, e.g. C. Westermann, *Vergegenwärtigung der Geschichte in den Psalmen*, Theolog. Bücherei, 24, 1964, pp. 306-335. Hereafter abbreviated as ThB.

15. The announcement is one of the most important functions of the divine word in the Old Testament; it has fundamental importance for the Old Testament understanding of history. "If we survey the whole Old Testament, then we find ourselves placed in a great history of the movement from promise to fulfillment" (W. Zimmerli, "Verheissung und Erfüllung," 1952, in: *Probleme alttestamentlicher Hermeneutik*, ed. by C. Westermann ThB 11, 1960, pp. 69-101) and G. von Rad, *Theology of the Old Testament*, vol. 2, Part 3, more literature there. The history of the word of salvation moves through the whole Old Testament, wherein its different forms each have their own function, cf. C. Westermann, "The Way of the Promise through the Old Testament," in *The Old Testament and Christian Faith*, ed. by B. W. Anderson, 1963, pp. 200-224; and "Das Heilswort bei Deuterojesaja," in: *Evangelische Theologie*, vol. 24, 1964, pp. 355-373. It is, however, necessary in this regard to see the history of the word of salvation in connection with the history of the word of judgment; in the Old Testament the announcement as well as the occurrence of what is announced encompass saving and judgment.

16. The word "faith," "believe" is found much less frequently in the Old Testament than in the New Testament, because faith is mostly that which is self-evident. In the Old Testament the normal response to the word of God that goes forth on men is a speaking (the praise of God) or an acting (obedience). Both imply faith. Only in the later reflection is it said that man believed God; so in obedience, Gen. 15:6, and in praise, Ps. 106:12: "Then they believed his words; they sang his praise."

17. Here it is important that the function of the mediator of salvation does remain the same throughout the Old Testament, but changes with the historical epochs: at the beginning Moses is presented as the mediator of word and deed (leadership, but not battle); then the office of the mediator splits into the mediator of the deed (charismatic leader and kings) and the mediator of the word (prophets); in the servant of God in Deutero-Isaiah both lines come together again, but his role is suffering and not deed.

18. That the saving God is the coming God is presupposed in every petition directed at God; therefore petition in the Old Testament (more exactly: a fervent call for help) always has two parts: the petition for God's intervention is preceded by the petition for his coming. The coming of God

is presented, among others, in the epiphany, which describes it (e.g. Judg. 5:4-5; Ps. 18:8-16). This coming of God has a specifically historical character in the fact that it is always a coming in a certain situation of distress for an individual or a group.

19. Such a praise answering the saving action of God is found therefore also in the historical books, e.g. Ex. 18:10: "Blessed be the Lord, who has delivered you out of the hand of the Egyptians" or 2 Sam. 5:20 etc. This descriptive praise in its simplest form is the origin of the descriptive psalm of praise on the one hand, and the historical account on the other.

20. Concerning the biblical understanding of wonder, cf. C. Westermann, *Our Controversial Bible,* Minneapolis 1969, pp. 34-39.

21. Concerning the prophecy, cf. the articles in: *Die Religion in Geschichte und Gegenwart,* ed. by K. Galling, 3rd ed., Tübingen, 1957; *Evangelisches Kirchenlexikon,* ed. by H. Brunotte and O. Webber, 2nd ed., Göttingen, 1961; and G. von Rad, *Theology of the Old Testament,* vol. 2, and H. W. Wolff, "*Hauptprobleme AT-licher Prophetie,*" in: *Theologische Blätter,* vol. 22, pp. 206-232.

22. Concerning the Deuteronomy, cf. M. Noth, *Überlieferungsgeschichtliche Studien,*[2] 1957; A. Jepsen, *Die Quellen des Königsbuches,*[2] 1956; H. O. Steck, *Israel und das gewaltsame Schicksal der Propheten,* 1967, more literature there.

23. It is perhaps possible in the light of this to explain a certain development in theology in the church of the early centuries. It cannot be explained out of the Bible itself why theology in this period was not so much concerned with that which takes place between God and man as rather with that which takes place by God himself, in his divine realm. Correspondingly, the interest in Christology was not primarily in Christ's acting toward men, but in the relationship between God and man in Christ himself. This dominating interest both in the doctrine of God, the doctrine of the trinity, and in the doctrine of Christ in the inner-divine occurrence presents a remarkable parallel to one of the basic characteristics of polytheistic thought. Only in polytheistic thought is the primary theological interest in that which takes place by or between the gods themselves; over against that, interest in the action of the gods on man is secondary. It is conceivable that it was the Greek language and the Greek thought inherent to it through which this dominating interest in the inner-divine occurence found its way into Christian theology. The basic impulses of the doctrine of the trinity as well as of Christology in the theology of the first centuries could then be understood in terms of a mode of thinking which is nearer to polytheism than to biblical monotheism.

In any case, one fact could be explained from this. The Old Testament understanding of history is dependent, as we saw, on the basic presupposition that God is only one, that all divinity is concentrated in the one person of Jahweh. On the other hand, where the emphasis lies on that which takes place between the gods, that which takes place between the gods and man can never have such a great importance. Now there is no question that the interest in history in the ancient church receded in the same degree as theology concentrated on questions of the inner-divine occurrence. This went hand in hand with a growing neglect of the Old Testament in the ancient church. The allegorical interpretation of Old

Testament texts led precisely to a loss of their historical character. This loss of historical understanding in the ancient church could then be explained by the fact that the concentration of theology on inner-divine occurrence, exactly as in polytheistic thinking, suppresses a genuine interest in history.

24. C. Westermann, *Der Segen in der Bibel und im Handeln der Kirche,* 1968.
25. That which is touched on briefly in points a) to e) is discussed in detail in the book listed in note 24; literature is listed there for the individual points.
26. C. Westermann, *The Old Testament and Jesus Christ,* Minneapolis, 1970.

Chapter 2

The New Testament Witness
to the Cosmic Christ

THE PROBLEM

For a decade, discussion of the New Testament view of God's activity in creation and history has centered about soteriology and its relation to the cosmos or physical world, construed not merely as the arena or stage of the drama of personal redemption, but as in some fashion constituting a realm of grace. The debate has thus narrowed itself to a single, ancient theme: *Christus Pantocrator*, the "cosmic" or "pleromatic Christ."

There are two reasons for this phenomenon. The first is that the Christian community, confronted with the unprecedented yields of human reason which now assigns to technical development, political action, or humanitarianism what once was assigned to God, has felt itself called to "recapture" nature, bringing it once more within the scope of God's redeeming work. The second reason emerges from out of specific insights into the church's missionary task gleaned by the Christians of Asia who are in search of a theology which has breadth sufficient to meet the challenge of newly-awakened religions attempting to furnish a universally valid solution to the human dilemma.

Alongside this preoccupation with "cosmic Christology," and intimately related to it from its anthropological side, is the current discussion arising from the recognition of atheism as a world-wide historical and sociological phenomenon which can exact a mere external allegiance and thus leaves open the possibility of belief in God. Since Vatican II, which enunciated the principle that not every positive atheism is the result or expression of an individual's personal guilt, Roman Catholic and Protestant scholars alike have inquired whether a man whose atheism is the product of his social situation and thus merely "explicit," may not "atheistically believe in God." [1] If, according to Rudolf Bultmann and Friedrich Gogarten, atheism ending in nihilism is the consequence of the secularization process,[2] then we have the gospel to thank for creating a situation in which such belief is possible.

THE SOLUTIONS

To the question concerning the shape or form such a "cosmic Christology" might take, the following answers have been supplied, each of them related and corresponding to the concerns noted above:

In his now famous address to the World Council of Churches at New Delhi in 1961, Professor Joseph A. Sittler stated that the Christian community had no effective response to the "vision and promises of the Enlightenment" which had come to such strange and awesome maturity in our time. He then appealed for reintroduction of the theme of the "cosmic Christ" in terms of a *"Christic view"* of the physical world, a "daring penetrating, life-affirming Christology of nature" by which all is claimed for God, contending that since the same grace of God sustains nature even in its fallen state, nature's "residual goodness" can be regarded as an anticipation or foretaste of salvation.[3]

In face of their missionary task, the churches of Asia, attempting to view the revolutionary turn of events in their societies in light of evangelical truth, have come to an appreciation of the "cosmic Christology" as constituting a "new apology," by which the revitalized non-Christian religions may be viewed as an *"anticipation of the faith"* and their prevailing philosophical and religious ideas pressed into the service of the gospel.[4] In other words, cosmic Christology makes possible an extension of the concept of the "preliminary," according to which a man, centuries "after Christ" from the historical perspective, can still live in a history "before Christ." [5] This concern of the Asian churches was echoed at the New Delhi Council which asserted that conversation about Christ with men of other religions, in the consciousness that Christ encounters us in them, is legitimized by the fact that the Spirit of God already works among men and prepares them for the coming of the gospel. [6]

To the question concerning a possible "atheistic belief in God," the Jesuit Karl Rahner has given positive reply in his exposition of "anonymous" or "implicit Christianity." [7] Appealing to the Thomistic premise that every moral act has a supernatural formal object whether recognized or not, [8] Rahner has urged that a "categorial" atheism, in which the content of a moral act may be insufficiently or falsely interpreted, can be coexistent with a "transcendental atheism" or experience of God, in which the content of that act is already a "given" within a man's conscious obedience to his conscience. [9] In dependence upon the conceptuality developed by Martin Heidegger in his *Being and Time,* Rahner then describes that "given" as the "supernatural existential," the "objective" constitution of human existence by the Christ-event, and prior to its appropriation. [10] Since the universal saving will of God always precedes the preaching of the gospel; since man is thus always referred to God whose love makes its appearance with every man, even if unnamed; then positive obedience to conscience in a concrete act of love sets a man within a situation of grace, apart from any conscious recognition of the work of Christ. [11] In this fashion, the relation of faith to God is conceived in analogy to interpersonal relationships, actualized above all at the point of *Mitmenschlichkeit* or mutuality. [12] Beyond Trent's "baptism of desire" and Pius XII's *votum Ecclesiae,* Rahner has thus proceeded to a description of faith as "implicit" in the given situation. [13] Rahner's position has gained support from Protestant theologians who assert that faith, though retaining its position as ultimately related to an act of consciousness, can under certain circumstances be an event independent of reflection—the interior realm, the community of believers acknowledging its head, while the other exterior realm is ignorant of it. [14] Indeed, the comments of a few New Testament scholars suggest that transcendence is not merely encountered at the point of *Mitmenschlichkeit* or the mutuality of historical existence,[15] but that such mutuality in some fashion constitutes or creates transcendence.[16]

THE BIBLICAL BASIS

The biblical basis for these thrusts toward a "cosmic Christology" or an "implicit Christianity" is gleaned from the Christological hymn of Ephesians 1:9-10, but particularly from that of Colossians 1:15-20, which now become the *locus classicus* of modern ecumenical theology.[17] The passage reads:

> [15]He is the image of the invisible God, the first-born of all creation; [16]for in him all things were created, in heaven and on earth, visible and invisible, whether thrones or dominions or principalities or authorities—all things were created through him and for him. [17]He is before all things, and in him all things hold together. [18]He is the head of the body, the church; he is the beginning, the first-born from the dead, that in everything he might be pre-eminent. [19]For in him all the fulness of God was pleased to dwell, [20]and through him to reconcile to himself all things, whether on earth or in heaven, making peace by the blood of his cross. (Revised Standard Version)

Though almost none of the principal advocates of "cosmic Christology" or of "implicit Christianity" has undertaken examination of the Colossians passages, choosing rather to base his argument upon work done by others, the following interpretation of the hymn may fairly be assigned to them.

To begin with, the hymn is construed in ontological fashion, that is, as descriptive of reality or existence as such. The "world-all" (vss. 16 and 17) or "fulness of being" (vs. 19)[18] inheres in Christ. "Fulness," then, is not construed as a *nomen actionis* but rather as that state or condition of being filled. Next, the "body" of vs. 18 is interpreted cosmologically. Christ is "head of the body" because of his organic connection with the cosmos, specifically, because of his mediatorial role in the creation of the "All"—"for in him all things were created . . . and in him all things hold together." Accordingly, "body" and "church" are not understood as coterminous. "Church" rather represents the place at which what has occurred to the body construed as world, as cosmos, has been concretely actualized. Finally, because the mediator of creation has reconciled the "All"— "and through him to reconcile to himself all things"—the act of redemption and existing reality coincide. What remains of the subjection of the All to Christ may conceivably be interpreted in terms of a "cosmic ripening" or, in the language of a Teilhard, of a cosmic tendency toward supreme personalization in the God-Man. The similarity of this interpretation with Heinrich Schliers' exegesis of the Ephesians hymn,[19] to which Karl Rahner makes specific appeal,[20] merely indicates that a number view the two hymns in tandem, the one (in Ephesians) more from an ecclesiological than a cosmological point of view.

THE BIBLICAL-THEOLOGICAL DEBATE

The Redactions-Historical Question

From an examination of the current exegesis of the Colossians hymn, it is immediately clear that a considerable portion of the biblical basis for a "cosmic Christology" is open to serious doubt. There is first of all the literary-critical question concerning the authorship of Colossians as a whole. The majority of New Testament scholars tend to deny Paulinicity to the epistle.[21] But assuming for a moment the epistle was penned by Paul, does it necessarily follow that he himself was author of the hymn? As early as 1912 Eduard Norden, denying Paulinicity to Ephesians but not to Colossians and noting the "liturgical" character of the hymn,[22] suggested that its source lay in a writing no longer preserved to us in which the Logos idea was treated from the standpoint of the old covenant.[23] In 1930 the Yale scholar Frank C. Porter, who also conceded Pauline authorship to the epistle as a whole, denied Paulinicity to the hymn because of its lack of correspondence with the apostle's thought elsewhere and concluded that Paul "might have quoted a current Logos Hymn to Christ which was not his own." [24] Scholars who deny Paulinicity to the epistle as well as to the hymn are not agreed on the nature of its source. Rudolf Bultmann and Ernst Käsemann assign the hymn to a non-Christian source,[25] specifically to a Jewish-Gnostic milieu which cultivated mythical cosmologies and Logos-Wisdom speculation of a type which ultimately penetrated Hellenistic Christianity.[26] According to this view, early developed by members of the History of Religions school,[27] the hymn, which originally identified the cosmos with the body of the cult's "redeemer" and interpreted his redemption as reconciliation of the All,[28] was accommodated to Christian tradition by the final redactor,[29] though the original cosmology remained more or less intact.[30] Käsemann contends that the reference to the church in vs. 18 and the phrase "by the blood of his cross" in vs. 20 are glosses which interrupt the hymn's original theme—Christ, mediator of creation, risen or exalted one [31]—and for the sake of accenting the cross-event.[32] In any event, Käsemann insists that the ultimate consequence of the Christian editing of the hymn is to give a paraenetic or ethical thrust to what was once construed ontologically or sacramentally,[33] however distant from Paul the final redactor may otherwise have stood.[34] On the other hand, Eduard Schweizer, also tracing the hymn to the Jewish-Hellenistic idea of the world-soul mediated through the Wisdom literature,[35] challenges the assumption of a pre-Christian, Jewish-Gnostic hymn.[36] He contends rather that an originally *Christian* exaltation-Christology, according to which the ascension of the redeemer was mythically conceived as restoring the connection between earth and heaven, has been corrected by the author of Colossians (and Ephesians) so as to harmonize with the thought of Paul, a revision which Schweizer assumes also for the Epistle to the Hebrews.[37]

In light of this redactions-critical debate, Käsemann's question to Schlier [38] as to whether or not the latter is justified in assuming, on the basis of the hymn's present form, that the intention of its religious-historical material has remained unchanged,[39] is a serious threat to the ecumenical theologian's use of the hymn in undifferentiated fashion as Pauline.

The Question of Scopus

As indicated above, the popular interpretation of the Colossians hymn conceives its scopus or aim as expressing Christ's reconciliation of the All by virtue of his mediatorial connection with the cosmos. To this view the majority of interpreters are opposed, whatever their position regarding the redactions-historical question. They note, first of all, that outside the hymn itself Colossians does not refer to the significance of Christ for the world-all.[40] Secondly, they contend that in its present form the hymn does not construe the term "body" as mystical event in any ontological or cosmological fashion, but rather as denoting the community of believers, the "church." [41]

For the majority, then, the hymn in its present shape does not intend to describe Christ as Pantocrator, but rather intends to give precision to his position toward the "powers" as well as toward the company of the redeemed. To a threatened community, in danger of exchanging the one mediator of redemption for a number of despotic powers, the hymn announces that those powers are mere creatures of the one they would repress. They have thus been removed from their venerated position in a radical way.[42] Further, the same Christ who is lord of the "powers" is also "head" of the church,[43] the accent then falling neither upon the cosmos nor upon the church, nor upon their relation to each other, but solely upon the preeminence of Christ who is Lord of the one and head of the other.[44]

That which the majority of commentators describes as securing to Christ his preeminence is the historical event of the cross—"by the blood of his cross," vs. 20—which dethroned the powers and wrought the radical change, and from which the life of men is constituted anew by incorporation into the body of the one crucified for them.[45]

To the question why the final redactor of the hymn retained the concept of the "body," an idea so liable to misunderstanding,[46] contemporary scholars respond by pointing to its facility for accenting the eschatological. Käsemann states that the term "body" contains more than can be expressed by the original, Pauline idea of a "people," viz., the idea of a new world or new creation.[47] Schweizer speaks of the "body" as "growing." [48] From this point of view, the new creation is actualized in the missionary function of the church.[49] Thus the intention of the editor to give a paraenetic or ethical turn to the hymn is preserved and the hymn's connection with Paul's own view of his mission among the Gentiles as of a piece with the "end time" is retained—by its obedience to Christ, its growth and mission, the church constitutes that place at which

Christ penetrates the cosmos and insofar rules it as Cosmocrator.[50]
What the ecumenical theologian thus refers to essence, a majority
of New Testament commentators refer to the soteriological function
of Christ or to the eschatological mission of his community.[51] To
this view, Bultmann and Conzelmann furnish the exception. While
both agree that the hymn is not concerned with the structure of
the cosmos, they nevertheless define its scopus in terms of "self-
understanding." Thus the hymn's use of cosmic, dualistic mythol-
ogy is for the purpose of expressing an understanding of existence
as "historical," [52] or as establishing the common life of the believers
in a "freedom" disclosed through faith.[53]

The Theological Question

Opponents of the popular use of the Colossians hymn state that
an interpretation made to serve a Christology of nature alters the
point or object of the hymn's orientation—faith is now directed to
the heavenly figure of the exalted Christ (the original object of the
hymn in its unedited, unrevised form). Rahner's statement to the
effect that by his death Jesus is freed from the limitations of his
earthly existence and established in a "lasting relationship to the
universe" is a case in point.[54] The result of such an interpretation,
the critics contend, is that the incarnation and thus the historical
character of the redemption is in danger of being obliterated or
reduced to a mere intermezzo,[55] the redemption then occurring
because Christ is mediator of creation, not because he is "the first-
born from the dead," having fulfilled the reconciliation on the
cross.[56] This same tendency in the direction of the spatial versus
the historical may be noted on the part of scholars who advance
Mitmenschlichkeit as the locus of transcendence.[57] Whether or not
such criticism is justified, it is true that cosmic Christology and its
anthropological counterpart, "implicit Christianity," tend to describe the *decision of faith* less in terms of a contingent act of God
than in terms of "mutuality." Again, Rahner speaks of man's "spiritual transcendentality" reflected in his intercommunicative existence
which is always confronting him for acceptance or rejection.[58] This
intercommunication, Rahner continues, actually furnishes the "exis-
tential-ontological" presupposition for the mediatorship of Christ.[59]

From this point of view, the moment a man acknowledges his existence as intercommunicative and gives it expression in a concrete act of love, he not only stands in an "altered situation," but his act becomes mediatory for all others.[60] In such fashion, Rahner gives theological-philosophical legitimation to the mediatorial role of Mary.[61] At any rate, though fixed in the saving will of God, the decision of faith occurs in that either-or between egoism and love. Dorothee Sölle's comment that Christology is carried on as anthropology, since God can "occur" among men in that "you did it to me" (Matthew 25:40), appears to represent a similar position, in contrast to the more radical view of transcendence as constituted by mutuality.[62]

From such language, the opponents conclude either that a most ambiguous *Christus in nobis* has been assigned what can only be attributed to the *Christus extra nos*,[63] or that the New Testament concept of man as himself reconciled and transformed is exchanged for a physical or metaphysical event in which man remains a mere object since not he, but only his situation or "living room" is changed.[64]

The critics have given attention to the presuppositions underlying cosmic Christology and its relative. Some state that contrary to its avowed monism [65] such Christology actually has its home in Greek dualism, since it maintains the conquest of a previously existing separation and thus does not proceed from a total view.[66] This suggests that of the alternatives of a boundless plurality or a boundless identity, cosmic Christology has chosen the latter, the alternative of mysticism,[67] an implication which Ott's tracing of Bultmann's and Rahner's theology to the conceptuality of Heidegger tends to reinforce.[68] Others maintain over against implicit Christianity or anthropological theology that the clear witness of the New Testament and the common confession of Christianity is obscured by a philosophical scheme of thought according to which the ontological dialectic of history and address is appropriated *en toto*.[69]

That which draws the critics' heaviest fire, however, is that cosmic Christology and implicit Christianity appear to give new life to a counter-reformation theme. To Schlier's exegesis of the Ephesians hymn Käsemann responds:

> The Reformation's witness for the prosecution is now hauled
> out as defense attorney for a Pauline exegesis with a counter-
> reformation drift . . . this would not have been possible had
> not the doctrine of justification already been made a side-issue
> . . . in Protestantism itself.[70]

Indeed, when loosed from his construct of the all-embracing saving will of God, Rahner's statements regarding the "content" of
faith as an action in harmony with "moral conscience"[71] appear
to give cause for Käsemann's complaint. Or again, when Sölle's
emphasis upon the apocalyptic though hidden character of the
redemption is overlooked, her reaction to faith as ideology and
insistence upon ethics as the goal of Christianity[72] raises the suspicion that theology has been absorbed in a legalism which makes
monotonous and perennial demand for unconditioned love.[73] The
proponents of ecumenical theology naturally deny such charges—
Fuchs writes that faith is recognized in the capacity to love, in a
selflessness which may appear to be demand but which in reality
is the gift of God's grace[74]—but at least one of their number has
noted the danger. Smith writes that Paul van Buren's *The Secular
Meaning of the Gospel* indicates how great is the threat of substi-
tuting a "welfare Protestantism" for the "culture Protestantism" of
the previous century, and chides van Buren for too naively and
undialectically reducing faith to an "infection" with the freedom
of Jesus.[75]

A SURVEY OF THE EXEGESIS OF
THE COLOSSIANS HYMN

From the vast store of exegetical comment on the Colossians
hymn, advocates of a cosmic Christology or an implicit Christianity
appear to derive only minimal support.

Following the sub-apostolic age, in which clearly ecclesiological
conclusions were drawn from the hymn,[76] the Greek fathers, prior
to the Arian controversy, applied the passage to the deity of Christ.
As is well-known, Colossians 1:15 was a favorite with Origen who
referred the term "image" to Christ's pre-existence. When Origen's
"image-Christology," which assigned a certain subordinate role to
the Son as distinct from the Father of whom he is the image, could

not endure the stress of the Arian debate, the orthodox reinterpreted the hymn either in terms of Christ's pre-existence, roundly rejecting any subordinationist implications, or in terms of the incarnation. Thus Chrysostom writes:

> The image of the invisible is itself invisible, and equally invisible. Otherwise he [Paul] would not say "image." And with us too, image, according as it is image, is identical to God.[78]

Chrysostom adds that the term "first-born" in vs. 18 of the hymn is not a title of dignity or value, but rather one of time, denoting Christ's antecedence.[79] Similarly, Basil and Gregory of Nazianzus define "image" in terms of the Son's identity or consubstantiality with the Father.[80] On the other hand, Cyril of Alexandria writes that Christ is called "first-born,"

> Not because he is first in order or is before the creation in time, nor because he is preeminent over things created, but on account of his descending to the created order and thus his likeness to us. For it was necessary that the Son of God, having the preeminence by nature, should not lose this when he became man.[81]

From such an interpretation as Cyril's, it was only a short step to identifying the "creation" in vs. 15 of the hymn with the "new, spiritual creation"—a commonplace among catholic expositors of the fourth and fifth centuries.

In view of their preoccupation with the question of Christ's deity, specifically with the question as to whether such terms as "image" and "first-born" could be construed of antecedence or consequence,[82] the Greek fathers gave little or no attention to the object of Christ's reconciliation, viz., to that "all things" in vss. 16, 17 and 20 of the Colossians hymn. And though Chrysostom and Severianus hardly form a majority, from their comments on the passage in Ephesians 1:9-10, in which they identify "all things" with men and angels or Jews and Greeks,[83] it may be inferred that for these two ancients, at least, the same identification applies to the passage in Colossians.

The all but exclusive application of the Colossians hymn to Christ's deity prevailed in the exegesis of the Latin fathers and of the Middle Ages as well. The comment of the Fulda monk, Walafrid Strabo, is thus as representative as any other. Of the term "first-born" *(primogenitus)* in vs. 18 Strabo writes:

> Just as he was born of God before all things that he might create all things, so he appears as the first man, that he might restore (all things), with the result that he is always first and chief.[84]

Strabo concludes from vs. 20 that Christ "opens to man an entrance to heaven," but does not define the "celestial and terrestrial things" which have been reconciled so as to make such entrance possible.[85]

In the exegesis of the Reformation and post-reformation years, themes struck earlier are resumed. The Socinians, just as their ancient counterpart, the Arians, interpret "image" and "first-born" in such fashion as to indicate Christ's subordination to the Father.[86] The Arminian J. J. Wettstein expresses the same point of view when he writes that "first-born" is no doubt to be construed in imitation of the interpreters of Homer, viz., as denoting "the first to have been born, that is, to have been made the creature," and identifies the "creation" in vss. 15 and 16 of the hymn with the "new . . . constitution of the world through the advent of Christ and the preaching of the gospel."[87] In opposition to such a view, the majority construes "image" as denoting Christ's essential oneness with the Father.[88] And, though often insisting upon the metaphorical or metonymous usage of the term "first-born,"[89] the "orthodox" nevertheless interpret it of the eternal generation of Christ or of the incarnation, and without intimating subordination.[90]

That which is new in the exegesis of this era, however, is the attention given the interpretation of the "all things" in the hymn. The troublesome *ta panta* and its modifiers are variously identified. John Davenant and Hieronymus Zanchi interpret the phrase "all things . . . in heaven" of angels and the blessed, i.e. by way of metonymy; Davenant then describes "all things . . . on earth" of things on the surface or in the vitals of the earth, or of things in the sea. Together with Wilhelm Estius and Zanchi, Davenant interprets the term "visible" in the same verse (vs. 16) of stars, plants, animals and all other bodies, and "invisible" of incorporeal creatures such as angels and the souls of the blessed. The terms "thrones," "dominions," "principalities," and "authorities" in vs. 16 are defined either as denoting the entire human family[91] or empires[92] with their kings, princes, prefects and inferior powers,[93] or as denoting the entire heavenly realm,[94] specifically angels,[95] according to their various offices or orders,[96] to which correspond the patriarchs in the church.[97] Wettstein insists, in light of Romans 8:22, that "all creation" does not always include the totality of things, but either the human genus, or the qualities furnished the reason. He adds that the Colossians hymn does not read "the heaven and earth were created" but rather "all things," by which are denoted the inhabitants which are reconciled. "In short," Wettstein concludes, "it reads . . . *ta panta* . . . both angels and men." [98]

Thus, with the exception of the comments of Davenant, Estius and Zanchi on the phrase "all things . . . on earth, visible," little support for a cosmic Christology can be gleaned from this period.

Not until the modern period is the reconciliation of "all things" hymned in Colossians plainly and unequivocally applied to the universe as a whole. Whether or not the English prelate and interpreter, Joseph Barber Lightfoot (1828-1889), is the first to make such application,[99] in no other commentator up to the present is such clear and sustained support given a cosmic Christology. Lightfoot's translation of the most salient portions of the hymn reads:

> He is the perfect image, the visible representation, of the unseen God. He is the Firstborn, the absolute Heir of the Father, begotten before the ages; the Lord of the Universe by virtue of primogeniture, and by virtue also of creative agency. For in and through Him the whole world was created. . . . All powers in heaven and earth are subject to Him. This subjection extends even to the most exalted and most potent of angelic beings. . . . Through Him, as the mediatorial Word, the universe has been created; and unto Him, as the final goal, it is tending . . . in Him, as the binding and sustaining power, universal nature coheres and consists.[100]

Stating that the author's (i.e. Paul's) teaching is an enlargement upon the Judeo-Alexandrian representation of the Logos as the divine mind energizing the rational world, the exception being that now the Logos is no longer a philosophical abstraction but a divine person,[101] Lightfoot describes the "Eternal Word" as the meeting point of "all the laws and purposes which guide the creation and government of the Universe;" [102] as "the principle of cohesion," impressing upon creation a unity and solidarity which makes it a cosmos and not a chaos. So, for example, "the action of gravitation, which keeps in their places things fixed and regulates the motion of things moving, is an expression of His mind." [103] That eternal word is also the goal of the universe which "must end in unity, as it proceeded from unity." [104] Thus, according to Lightfoot, the intention of the hymn is to sound the "absolute and complete reconciliation of universal nature to God, effected through the mediation of the Incarnate Word." [105] In striking contrast to his predecessors and contemporaries who establish some connection between the reconciliation of "all things" and the historical event of the cross,[106] the only event in the life of Christ to which Lightfoot links the reconciliation is the resurrection, and this only by indirection, since the resurrection is discussed only as the guarantee of Christ's title as head of the church.[107]

The rather curious fact that Lightfoot, never known to have done his work in a corner, has had next to no influence upon current theological discussion of the acts of God in creation and history [108] —a discussion which might have gleaned considerable harvest from his studies—renders him a most apt paradigm of the fate endured by all his kind, and allows us to draw at least one conclusion from our brief survey: current preoccupation with cosmic Christology or implicit Christianity has been less influenced by specific exegetical work done in the past, ancient and late, than by a general reading of the Pauline corpus (reinforced by only the most recent biblical scholarship) in light of the history of theology and modern philosophy.[109]

EVALUATION

Whatever position be adopted with reference to the authorship, redaction, and source of ideas of the Colossians hymn, it is certain that the ideas there expressed do not render the hymn unique. This most disputed of all the Christological utterances in the canon has its parallels if not its equivalents in the unchallenged Pauline epistles and elsewhere in the New Testament. Nor are the parallels confined to Christ's pre-existence or his reconciliation of the *kosmos noetos* or "rational world." They treat of the cosmic process as a whole. The same claim which Colossians makes for Christ as medi-

ator, center, and goal of that which is created is made, e.g., in 1
Corinthians 8:6:

> For us there is one God, the Father, from whom are all things
> and for whom we exist, and one Lord, Jesus Christ, through
> whom are all things and through whom we exist.

Years ago, the Tübingen biblicist Adolf Schlatter wrote of these
lines that both the eye turned to the world and comprehending
everything in a unity and the eye turned inward and sensing the
movement of its own life give content to the name of God, and
concluded that in Christ's activity and mission by which he was
made Lord of the church, "God gave notice that everything came
into being and will come into being through him." [110] Whether
such claims are made on behalf of the Father, as in Romans 11:36,
Acts 17:25, 27, and Hebrews 2:10, or on behalf of Christ, the concept of a cosmic, creation-wide deliverance is native to the New
Testament. Long-standing neglect of this truth, or its reinterpretation in terms of private existence drives a wedge into what the
New Testament does not separate—the creation's "eager longing"
and the "revealing of the sons of God;" the cosmos' deliverance
from "bondage to decay" and the "glorious liberty of the children
of God;" the creation's "groaning in travail" and our waiting for
"adoption" (Romans 8:19-23).

At the same time, the cosmic dimension cannot be loosed from its
true context. The apostle or his successor does not identify redemption with existing reality, nor does he wait for the subjection of the
All in terms of an ecclesiastical [111] or natural process of ripening—
the "Omega Point" is not the last member of an evolutionary
chain [112]—but, as Theodore of Mopsuestia acknowledged long
ago,[113] an eschatological event. And that event cannot be construed in terms of some "eternal now." For if the activity and mission of Jesus are that place at which God chooses to bind himself
to us, then the future for which the creation waits is God's future
as well. Then there is something toward which even God strains,
something which he will do, will be, which he has not yet done,
not yet been. Nor can that event be defined as a phenomenon
which "becomes an event repeatedly in preaching and faith." [114]
This would mean simply that the resurrection of the dead and the

life everlasting occur in the moment of self-recognition—when I come to myself, when I allow the anxiety that life is somehow slipping through my fingers to drive me to abandon the attempt to secure my own existence and to live in openness to the future. To all such theology of subjectivity,[115] the New Testament replies that final things have to do with man's environment as well.

Nor can eschatology be defined as the unfolding of what has already happened—a particular kind of history, a "salvation history" without connection with the rest of world or human happening and to which revelation merely furnishes the clue. For revelation is no mere key to something which has already occurred and which looks to nothing but its unfolding. The Lamb in the last book of the Bible breaks the seven seals in chapter five and the horsemen in chapter six ride, the multitude in chapter seven sings and the trumpets in chapter eight begin to blow. With all the kaleidoscopic imagery of that puzzling book, it clearly shares one thing with all the rest: revelation sets history in motion, gives it "legs," drives it onward toward something qualitatively new. Lastly, the end of all things cannot be interpreted as already anticipated in the resurrection of Christ. It is not merely that our future corresponds to his as to a *prolepsis*. He *is* our future, for he is the resurrection and the life, and therefore waits—for that moment "when all things are subjected to him," when "he will also be subjected to him who put all things under him, that God may be everything to every one" (I Cor. 15:28). For, "we do not yet see everything in subjection to him" (Heb. 2:8)—Christ is not yet Pantocrator.

Indeed, the New Testament speaks of God as the same, as a God whose "years never end" (Heb. 1:12), of Jesus the "same yesterday and today and forever" (Heb. 13:8), and consequently of last and final things as having already occurred in the mind of God, "before the foundation of the world" (Eph. 1:4). But the context or locus in which such utterances have their home is that of promise. And we did not require an Albert Schweitzer or a Johannes Weiss before him to tell us that it is that context which has the priority.[116]

But if the context of the eschatological is the context of promise, then it is also one of hiddenness, and the same judgment pronounced upon revelations—purism and positivistic preoccupation with the self as a taking flight back of Hegel, back of the ambiguity

and pain,[117] must be levelled at the "salvation-optimism" of a
Rahner [118] and its Protestant version, "atheistic belief in God,"
which attempts a synthesis of the world as it is and the deliverance
of God. For that anachronistic insertion in 1:20 of the Colossians
hymn—"making peace by the blood of his cross"—whether by the
hymn's author or its redactor, fingers the ambiguity of existence
rooted in an entropy which marks the life of God himself.

The point has been well made, viz., that the conceptuality with
which a Paul or his successors came to the hearing of the gospel
was that of Jewish apocalyptic, and that the hallmark of that con
ceptuality was visibility, or, as Wilckens puts it, "historical veri-
fiability." [119] But the biblical witness also supports the fact that
the death of Jesus forced the apostle and his companions to a drastic revision of their pre-understanding; that their conceptuality
was not merely *confirmed* by the resurrection—the death, consequently, constituting a mere temporary reversal, "an unfortunate
event which nevertheless, in view of the resurrection, need not be
an obstacle to faith." [120] Thus the discontinuity between the historical Jesus and the kerygmatic Christ lay in the fact that although
Jesus may have raised no explicit claim to Messiahship, he was
nevertheless crucified as Messiah, and as a result his death became
the content of the gospel *par excellence*.[121] The cross made totally
unobservable and incapable of historical verification any qualitative
change, in history and nature. For Paul, the collapse of apocalyptic
conceptuality took the shape of that doctrine of ambiguity, reflected in a dialectic style so common to him: "We are treated as
imposters, and yet are true; as unknown, and yet well known; as
dying, and behold we live" (2 Cor. 6:8). And the drastic revision
of Paul's pre-understanding was necessitated by the fact that God's
victory had occurred under the sign of its opposite—defeat, tragedy
and death—clear only to those willing to fly in face of the empirical
evidence: "The righteousness of God is revealed through faith for
faith" (Rom. 1:17). The difference between the gospel and the
Jewish hope was not that Paul, or his imitators for reasons of apolo-
getic, were unable to adhere to their conceptuality and so left their
theology in a tension [122]—the difference lay in the collapse, in the
fracture of their conceptuality as a coherent scheme.

Qumran proclaimed two Messiahs—the one a king who would

exercise lordship over the people of God; the other, the anointed of Aaron who would cleanse the community. Qumran could not wed the two any more than normative Judaism could marry reigning to suffering. It could assign no *endzeitgeschichtliche* significance to death as such and thus could give no eschatological significance to a suffering, dying Messiah. Beyond a few heroic utterances, the idea of the meaninglessness and absurdity of death is an ever-recurring theme in the Old Testament. Death and the consequent ambiguity of existence devastated Israel. This gives the explanation to its concept of the future without which, indeed, the idea of resurrection-exaltation might never have emerged, but also gives the reason for its rejection of a crucified Christ. Death and resurrection have little in common in Judaism, and such as they have must be assigned not only to late Judaism but to the outermost periphery of its thought. That ancient aversion to the movement from death to life, to hiddenness, is something shared by the 20th century Jew as well.[123] The situation was all but identical in that type of Gnosticism battled by the editor of the Colossians hymn.[124] And, if pressed, it would be preferable to regard Jesus' obedience unto death as entailing the fracture of his own conceptuality, his own hope for exaltation apart from death—he did, after all, pray, "Father, all things are possible to thee; remove this cup from me" (Mark 14:36)—than to fix the distance between him and traditional apocalyptic theology in an undefined experience at his baptism as does Wilckens in that vulnerable footnote of his essay.[125] The eschatologically new, renewed existence is one of promise, hence of ambiguity, of hiddenness, something not yet perceptible to the senses—"as if a man should scatter seed upon the ground, and should sleep and rise night and day, and the seed should sprout and grow, he knows not how" (Mark 4:26-27).

At the same time, the attempt to extract an ideology, whether in terms of a "supernatural existential" [126] or a metaphysical or "speculative Good Friday" [127] from the *sub contrario* aspect of Paul's or his successor's ecclesiology flies in the face of what is clearly the Colossian letter's theological *topos:* the mission of the believing community.[128] Christ, destined to be Cosmocrator, secretly, in hiddenness, enfleshes himself in the world by means of the missionary activity of his body. The cosmos is penetrated by Christ, not because his exaltation has rendered redemption and existing reality one and the same, but rather because his church, participant in the event of his cross and his instrument in its humiliation, its bodily dying, is extended and expanded over the earth. And it is that bodily dying that renders the church incapable of imperialism. The Christ in whose risen but earthly body his community is incorporated is thus captive to none and is therefore for all. He is Lord of the powers and head of his church, in process of becoming Pantocrator through the eschatological event of the church's mission—the "mystery" now made known to those who are his (Eph. 1.9)—though himself destined for subjection to him who will be "everything to every one."

NOTES

1. K. Rahner, *Schriften zur Theologie*, Zürich, 1967, vol. VIII, pp. 189, 190, 193, 195; cf. D. Sölle, *Atheistisch an Gott Glauben, Beiträge zur Theologie*, 2nd ed., Freiburg i.B., 1969, p. 74.

2. R. Bultmann, "Der Gottesgedanke und der moderne Mensch," in *Zeitschrift für Theologie und Kirche*, vol. 60, 1963, p. 337f.; cf. also R. G. Smith, "Christlicher Glaube und Säkularismus," in *Zeitschrift für Theologie und Kirche*, vol. 63, 1966, pp. 40, 42.

3. J. A. Sittler, "Called To Unity," in: *The Ecumenical Review*, Vol. XIV, January, 1962, No. 2, pp. 178, 180, 183.

4. H. Bürkle, "Die Frage nach dem 'kosmischen Christus' als Beispiel einer ökumenisch orientierten Theologie," in: *Kerygma und Dogma*, Göttingen, 1965, pp. 103, 110-113.

5. J. Ratzinger, "Der Christliche Glaube und die Weltreligionen," in: *Gott in Welt*, Festgabe für Karl Rahner, Basel, 1964, II, p. 290.

6. Bürkle, *op. cit.*, p. 112.

7. Rahner, *op. cit.*, p. 187.

8. *Ibid.*, p. 290.

9. *Ibid.*, pp. 198f., 201, 203.

10. Cf. H. Ott, "Existentiale Interpretation und anonyme Christlichkeit," in: *Zeit und Geschichte, Dankesgabe* an Rudolf Bultmann, Tübingen, 1964, p. 379.

11. Rahner, *op. cit.*, pp. 153, 159, 160, 188, 210; cf. Ott, *op. cit.*, pp. 372, 375.

12. Cf. Ott, *op. cit.*, pp. 377, 379.

13. *Ibid.*, p. 373.

14. *Ibid.*, pp. 374, 376 and O. Cullmann in H. J. Gabathuler, *Jesus Christus Haupt der Kirche—Haupt der Welt*, Abhandlungen zur Theologie des Alten und Neuen Testaments, No. 45, Zürich, 1965, p. 171.

15. Cf. e.g., Smith, *op. cit.*, pp. 45, 46, 48.

16. Cf. H. Braun's *Jesus*, Stuttgart, 1969, in which God is described as that "event" which "occurs" in the affirmation of one's own and the other's existence, p. 169, *et passim*.

17. Cf. Sittler, *op. cit.*, p. 178; Bürkle, *op. cit.*, p. 104; Gabathuler, *op. cit.*, p. 159. Cf. also the significance of the Colossians hymn for the "natural eschatology" of Pierre Teilhard de Chardin, C. F. Mooney, *Teilhard de Chardin and the Mystery of Christ*, Garden City, 1968, pp. 103ff., and H. Riedlinger, "The Universal Kingship of Christ," in: *Concilium*, Vol. 11: *Who is Jesus of Nazareth?*, New York, 1965, pp. 119ff.

18. The term *pleroma*, contrary to the RSV translation, appears without a qualifier in the Greek, and may conceivably be rendered "fulness of being". On the other hand, E. Percy, *Die Probleme der Kolosser- und Epheserbriefe*, Lund, 1946, p. 76f, interprets *pleroma* of the fulness of the deity dwelling in Christ. For a biblical-theological discussion, cf. J. H. Burtness, "All the Fulness," in: *Dialog*, A Journal of Theology, Vol. 3, Autumn 1964, pp. 257ff.

19. H. Schlier, *Der Brief and die Epheser*, Düsseldorf, 1958, pp. 62ff. and 300ff.

20. Rahner, *op. cit.*, p. 193.

21. Cf. the discussion in B. Rigaux, *Paulus und seine Briefe, Der Stand der Forschung*, München, 1964, pp. 142-150.

22. E. Norden, *Agnostos Theos*, Untersuchungen zur Formgeschichte religiöser Rede, 4th ed., Stuttgart, 1956, p. 253.

23. *Ibid.*, p. 254.

24. F. C. Porter, *The Mind of Christ in Paul*, New York, 1930, p. 197; cf. pp. 180ff.

25. Norden had stated that the writing used by the author of the hymn served as source for Philo and Theophilus as well and traced it to Hellenistic Judaism and Platonism, cf. Norden, *op. cit.*, p. 253f.

26. R. Bultmann, *Theologie des Neuen Testaments*, 5th ed., Tübingen, 1965, pp. 486, 503, 176f.; E. Käsemann, "Eine urchristliche Taufliturgie," in: *Exegetische Versuche und Besinnungen*, Göttingen, 1960, I, 40ff., 45; cf. E. Käsemann, *Paulinische Perspectiven*, Tübingen, 1969, p. 184; cf. H. Conzelmann, *Grundriss der Theologie des Neuen Testaments*, München, 1968, p. 366 and Riedlinger, *op. cit.*, p. 113.

27. Cf. J. Weiss, *Earliest Christianity*, trans. Frederick C. Grant, New York, 1959, II, 481ff.; O. Pfleiderer, *Der Paulinismus*, Ein Beitrag zur Geschichte der urchristlichen Theologie, Leipzig, 1890, pp. 377ff. On the non-Jewish character of the ideas expressed in the hymn cf. H. J. Schoeps, *Paulus*, Tübingen, 1959, pp. 155ff.

28. Cf. H. Conzelmann, *op. cit.*, p. 100.

29. R. Bultmann, *Theologie des Neuen Testaments*, p. 180; E. Käsemann, "Eine urchristliche Taufliturgie," p. 39; cf. H. Conzelmann, *op. cit.*, p. 345. Bultmann assumes a Christian editing prior to that of the final redactor—cf. *Theologie des Neuen Testaments*, p. 486.

30. R. Bultmann, *Theologie des Neuen Testaments,* p. 503; cf. Conzelmann, *op. cit.,* p. 345.

31. Cf. E. Kasemann, "Eine urchristliche Taufliturgie," p. 37 and *Paulinische Perspektiven,* p. 194.

32. E. Käsemann, "Eine urchristliche Taufliturgie," pp. 36f., 39.

33. E. Käsemann, "Eine urchristliche Taufliturgie," p. 46; cf. *Paulinische Perspektiven,* pp. 183, 193.

34. Cf. E. Käsemann, *Paulinische Perspektiven,* p. 203f.

35. E. Schweizer, "Die Kirche als Leib Christi in den paulinschen Antilegomena," in: *Theologische Literaturzeitung,* vol. 86, No. 4, April 1961, p. 242f.

36. Cf. L. Baeck, *Paulus, die Pharisäer und das Neue Testament,* Frankfurt a.M., 1901, p. 19; W. D. Davies, *Paul and Rabbinic Judaism,* London, 1948, pp. 150ff. A. Deissmann, *Paulus,* Tübingen, 1925, p. 150f.; B. Gärtner, *The Areopagus Speech and Natural Revelation,* Uppsala, 1955, pp., 155f., 186f., 201f., and A. D. Nock, *St. Paul,* New York, 1963, p. 227f.

37. Schweizer, *op. cit.,* pp. 244, 252f., 256; cf. also Gabathuler, *op cit.,* pp. 152, 167.

38. Reiterated by Gabathuler, *op. cit.,* p. 156.

39. E. Käsemann, "Das Interpretationsproblem des Epheserbriefes," in: *Theologische Literaturzeitung,* vol. 86, No. 1, January 1961, p. 5.

40. Schweizer, *op. cit.,* p. 243. Gabathuler makes special mention of the fact that in the verses following, every theme of the hymn is struck—the subordination of the powers; the question of the church and the mediatorship of Christ in the redemption—but not the reference to Christ's mediatorship in creation, *op. cit.,* p. 167.

41. Cf. Schweizer, *op. cit.,* pp. 245, 355f.; Conzelmann, *op. cit.,* p. 345; Gabathuler, *op. cit.,* pp. 160, 175, 179; E. Käsemann, *Paulinische Perspektiven,* p. 202.

42. Schweizer, *op. cit.,* p. 355f.; Conzelmann, *op. cit.,* p. 345; Gabathuler, *op. cit.,* p. 156, 164, 168f.

43. According to Käsemann, the earthly body of the risen and exalted one; cf. *Paulinische Perspektiven,* pp. 194, 202.

44. Gabathuler, *op. cit.,* p. 169.

45. Cf. Käsemann, "Eine urchristliche Taufliturgie," p. 37; Schweizer, *op. cit.,* p. 245f.; Conzelmann, *op. cit.,* p. 345; Gabathuler, *op. cit.,* pp. 165, 170, 174; cf. Percy who accents the reconciliation effected by Christ's death to such degree that what is reconciled, whether "all creation" or "all other existence," receives little attention, *op. cit.,* pp. 70, 72, 86f., 93f., 98, 424.

46. R. Bultmann refers to the notion of a cosmic church, *Theologie des Neuen Testaments,* p. 503.

47. E. Käsemann, *Paulinische Perspektiven,* p. 188f.

48. Schweizer, *op. cit.,* p. 254.

49. *Ibid.*

50. Cf. Gabathuler, *op. cit.*, p. 167.

51. E. Käsemann, "Das Interpretationsproblem des Epheserbriefes," p. 5; "Eine urchristliche Taufliturgie," p. 41; Schweizer, *op. cit.*, p. 246.

52. R. Bultmann, *Theologie des Neuen Testaments*, p. 505.

53. Conzelmann, *op. cit.*, p. 345.

54. Rahner, *op. cit.*, p. 125.

55. Cf. Conzelmann, *op. cit.*, p. 373.

56. Cf. Gabathuler's criticism of Sittler, pp. 165, 181.

57. E. Fuchs, for example, writes that "the word of faith . . . is not the servant of history;" that belief in Jesus is equivalent to acknowledging our space and time continuum as the sphere within which grace is possibility, E. Fuchs, "Muss man an Jesus glauben, wenn man an Gott glauben will?", in *Zeitschrift für Theologie und Kirche*, vol. 58, 1961, pp. 63, 67. Similarly, Smith describes faith as identical to space and time, the world, then, conceived as identical to the realization of faith, *op. cit.*, p. 35.

58. Rahner, *op. cit.*, pp. 200, 226.

59. *Ibid.*, pp. 223, 230, 235. Rahner, of course, adds that this presupposition in turn has its origin in God's saving will.

60. *Ibid.*, p. 231.

61. *Ibid.*, p. 223.

62. Sölle, *op. cit.*, p. 75. Bultmann's statements in "Der Gottesgedanke und der moderne Mensch," pp. 342, 346f., also deserve to be read in this context.

63. Cf. E. Käsemann, "Das Interpretationsproblem des Epheserbriefes," p. 6.

64. Cf. Schweizer, *op. cit.*, pp. 246, 254. Bürkle, *op. cit.*, p. 105, writes that Sittler's requirement, for all its cosmic breadth, falls easy prey to a static theology of nature and being which ignores the human element.

65. Cf. e.g., Sittler's statement: "Unless the reference and the power of the redemptive act includes the whole of man's experience and environment, straight out to its farthest horizon, then the redemption is incomplete," and Sittler's references to Irenaeus gleaned from A. Galloway's *The Cosmic Christ* on pp. 179-181.

66. Gabathuler, *op. cit.*, p. 158.

67. Cf. Ratzinger, *op. cit.*, pp. 302ff.

68. Ott, *op. cit.*, p. 279 *et passim*.

69. K. Frör, "Uberlegungen zur Rezeption der anthropologischen Theologie in der katholischen Katechetik der Gegenwart," in: *Der Glaube der Gemeinde und die mündige Welt*, Beiträge zur evangelischen Theologie, München, 1969, vol. 52, p. 110. On p. 114f., Frör attempts to explain current preoccupation with implicit Christianity in terms of a lingering distaste for objectifying language gleaned from the debate with positivism and historicism, a distaste which nonetheless reflects captivity to a one-hundred-year-old contest, and thus renders it twin to the theology of "saving facts."

70. E. Käsemann, "Das Interpretationsproblem des Epheserbriefes," p. 3.

71. Rahner, *op. cit.*, pp. 189, 192, 197, 208, 228, 233.

72. Cf. Sölle, *op. cit.*, pp. 80, 83, 86.

73. Frör, *op. cit.*, p. 113.

74. Fuchs, *op. cit.*, p. 57.

75. Smith, *op. cit.*, p. 46.

76. Cf. e.g., 2 Clement 14:1: "Thus, brethren, if we do the will of our Father, God, we shall belong to the first Church, the spiritual one which was created before the sun and moon . . . ," and the Vision of Hermas II, 4:1: " 'Who is she . . . ?' 'The Church,' he said. I said to him, 'Why then is she old?' 'Because,' he said, 'she was created the first of all things. For this reason is she old; and for her sake was the world established!' " On the other hand, cf. the Similitudes IX, 12:2, in which application is made to Christ's pre-existence. *The Apostolic Fathers, Loeb Classical Library*, Cambridge, 1959, I, 151; II, 25 and 249.

77. Cf. M. F. Wiles, *The Divine Apostle, The Interpretation of St. Paul's Epistles in the Early Church*, Cambridge, 1967, p. 79.

78. J. A. Cramer, *Catenae in Sancti Pauli epistolas ad Galatas, Ephesios, Philippenses, Colossenses, Thessalonicenses, Catenae Graecorum Patrum in Novum Testamentum*, Hildesheim, reprografischer Nachdruck der Ausgabe Oxford 1842, 1967, VI, 303f.

79. *Ibid.* This in contrast to Theodore of Mopsuestia who writes that "first born" is not only used in respect of time, but also in respect of preference, *ibid.*, p. 306.

80. *Ibid.*, p. 305.

81. *Ibid.*

82. On the Arian-orthodox interpretation of the hymn, cf. e.g., E. Haupt, *Die Gefangenschaftsbriefe*, Kritisch-exegetischer Kommentar über das Neue Testament ed. H. A. W. Meyer, Göttingen, 1897, p. 30; W. Lueken, *Die paulinischen Briefe und die Pastoralbriefe, Die Schriften des Neuen Testaments*, 3rd ed., Göttingen, 1916, p. 344; Wiles, *op. cit.*, pp. 75-80; Riedlinger, *op. cit.*, p. 114.

83. Cf. Cramer, *op. cit.*, p. 115.

84. W. Strabo, *Glossa Ordinaria*, J.-P. Migne, *Patrologiae, Series Latinae*, Paris, 1879, CXIV, 610.

85. *Ibid.*, p. 611.

86. Cf. the anonymous quotation in John Davenant: "The Arians . . . conclude from this passage that Christ is a creature, because he is the first-born of the creation, in such manner as the first-born of brothers, or of a herd, etc. are of the rank of brothers, sheep, etc." M. Pole, *Synopsis Criticorum Aliorumque Sacrae Scripturae*, London, 1686, V. 895.

87. J. Wettstein, *Novum Testamentum Graecum*, Graz, 1962, unveränderter Abdruck der 1752 bei Dommerian in Amsterdam erschienenen Ausgabe, vol. II, p. 282; similarly H. Grotius in Pole, *op. cit.*, p. 895f.

88. F. Gomarus, W. Estius, J. Daille, Davenant, Tirinus and J. Fischer in Pole, *op. cit.*, p. 895.

89. Cf. Gomarus, J. Cameron, Fischer, Davenant, Daille, J. Drusius, K. Vorstius and H. Hammony in *ibid.*, p. 895f.

90. Cf. *ibid.*, pp. 895-897.

91. Gomarus in Pole, *op. cit.*, p. 896.

92. Hammond in *ibid.*

93. Cameron and Hammond in *ibid.*

94. Gomarus in *ibid.*

95. Gomarus and Zanchi in *ibid.*

96. Vorstius, Zanchi, Estius, Gomarus and Cameron in *ibid.*

97. Gomarus in *ibid.*

98. Wettstein, *op. cit.*, p. 282f.

99. Current European histories of the exegesis of Col. 1:15ff. characteristically omit mention of Lightfoot, but cf. Percy, *op. cit.*, p. 97f. *et passim*, and the work of the Roman Catholic N. Kehl, *Der Christushymnus im Kolosserbrief*, Stuttgart, 1967, p. 128.

100. J. B. Lightfoot, *Saint Paul's Epistles to the Colossians and to Philemon*, New York, 1879, p. 144.

101. *Ibid.*, p. 151.

102. *Ibid.*, p. 150.

103. *Ibid.*, p. 156.

104. *Ibid.*, p. 155.

105. *Ibid.*, p. 159.

106. Cf. H. J. Holtzmann, *Lehrbuch der Neutestamentlichen Theologie*, Freiburg i.B., 1897, II, 250; Haupt, *op. cit.*, p. 33; Lueken, *op. cit.*, p. 345f.; A. S. Peake, *The Epistle to the Colossians, The Expositor's Greek Testament*, ed. W. Robertson Nicoll, Grand Rapids, n.d., III, 551.

107. Lightfoot, *op. cit.*, p. 157f.

108. Cf. the single reference to Lightfoot's interpretation of Colossians in A. D. Galloway, *The Cosmic Christ*, New York, 1951, p. 48.

109. In this connection cf. O. A. Piper's review of Galloway's volume in *Interpretation*, Vol. VI, No. 4, October 1952, p. 467.

110. A. Schlatter, *Paulus der Bote Jesu*, Eine Deutung seiner Briefe an die Korinther, 2nd ed., Stuttgart, 1956, pp. 255, 257.

111. V. Schlier, "Die Kirche als das Geheimnis Christi,—Nach dem Epheserbrief," in: *Die Zeit der Kirche*, Exegetische Aufsätze und Vorträge, 3rd ed., Freiburg, 1962, p. 303.

112. Cf. Riedlinger, *op. cit.*, on Mersch and Chardin, pp. 119-121.

113. Cf. Wiles, *op. cit.*, p. 38.

114. R. Bultmann, *History and Eschatology*, The Gifford Lectures 1955, Edinburgh, 1957, p. 151f.; Conzelmann, *op. cit.*, p. 347f.; cf, also Fuchs' discussion of the apocalyptic "formulation" as an expendable item to be distinguished from its occasion in the movement of faith, *op. cit.*, p. 61.

115. Cf. Sölle's comments on Bultmann's elimination of the eschatological due to a positivistic concern with the self, *op. cit.*, pp. 65f., 91; Frör, *op. cit.*, 114f.; Riedlinger, *op. cit.*, p. 115; cf. Käsemann's criticism of Conzelmann in *Paulinische Perspektiven*, p. 182.

116. Cf. E. Käsemann: "That the apostle hopes for the subjection of the All,

not as an ecclesiastical or cosmic process of ripening, but as an event of the Parousia, has long appeared certain to me," "Das Interpretationsproblem des Epheserbriefes," p. 7.

117. Sölle, *op. cit.*, p. 67.

118. Rahner, *op. cit.*, p. 194.

119. U. Wilckens, "Das Offenbarungsverständnis in der Geschichte des Urchristentums," in: *Offenbarung als Geschichte*, ed. Wolfhart Pannenberg, Göttingen, 1961, pp. 50ff.

120. C. K. Barrett, *Luke The Historian in Recent Study*, London, 1961, p. 59.

121. Cf. N. A. Dahl, "Der gekreuzigte Messias," in: *Der historische Jesus und der kerygmatische Christus*, tr. Helmut Ristow and Karl Matthiae, Berlin, 1961, p. 167f.

122. Cf. Wilckens, *op. cit.*, p. 67

123. Cf. E. Rosenstock-Huessy's correspondence with F. Rosenzweig in *Judaism despite Christianity*, University of Alabama, 1969, especially p. 126.

124. One author, at least, defines Gnosticism in general as little more than broken-hearted Jewish apocalyptic; cf. R. M. Grant, *Gnosticism and Early Christianity*, New York, 1959; on the other hand, cf. e.g., D. Georgi, "Der vorpaulinische Hymnus" Phil. 2, 6-11, in: *Zeit und Geschichte*, Dankesgabe an Rudolf Bultmann zum 80. Geburtstag, Tübingen, 1964, pp. 263ff.

125. Wilckens, *op. cit.*, p. 54, n. 31.

126. Rahner, *op. cit.*, *passim*.

127. Sölle, *op. cit.*, p. 73.

128. Cf. E. Käsemann, *Paulinische Perspektiven*, pp. 199, 204, 206; "Das Interpretationsproblem des Epheserbriefes," p. 7f.; Schweizer, *op. cit.*, pp. 247-250, 254; Gabathuler, *op. cit.*, pp. 176, 179f.

Chapter 3

The Cosmological and Anthropological Significance of Christ's Redeeming Work

INTRODUCTORY REMARKS

The theme of this chapter is indeed a vast one. I could not possibly treat it as it deserves to be treated. Only hints and indications can be given. But on the other hand, the very fact that at least part of the theme, the aspect of the cosmic Christ, has been seldom considered at any depth in modern theology may transform even fragmentary and quite insufficient hints into important mementos.

However, even formal limitations of the subject proved necessary in the outlining process. Although the main point in this chapter is that the cosmological and anthropological implications of the church's faith in Christ should be considered anew in the light of modern understanding of man and his universe, the bulk of these pages is devoted to a presentation of more or less forgotten aspects of the christological thinking of some of the fathers of the ancient church and of Luther, with the presumption that it is only in continuity with these ideas that we might discover the relevant implications for our own day. This chapter is mainly historical in character, but at least a few concluding questions will be indicated in the end, so as to allow for further and more creative thinking.

In addition, there are also some matters of definition to be shortly considered at the outset. It should be underlined that by "cosmological" and "anthropological" significance, I do not intend to refer

64

only to more or less abstract theological perspectives, but to facts, i.e. to the universe as it is and to man as he is. The question which I want to raise is thus none other than this: *To what extent and in what way does faith in Christ—even today—imply certain beliefs with regard to the nature and finality of man and the world?* In other words, have these latter both an ontological and teleological subsistence in Christ? Of course, I do not pretend to answer this question in any absolute sense, but my intention is to make it more believable that faith in Christ is bound to think out and live out implications on this level of understanding.

A second matter of definition is linked to the words "Christ's redeeming work." It is obvious that this expression can be understood in a narrow as well as in a broad sense. My basic assumption is that anything Christ is or does, according to Christian belief, is an integral part of his redeeming work. Since by definition redemption is primarily related to man as sinner, this means that the very presence of Christ the Savior is redeeming in all areas of the activity and competence of man the sinner. In biblical imagery there are many symbols and terms which denote this saving presence, but since Lutheranism for historical reasons is specifically connected with the symbol of justification, let us immediately add that these areas are, of course, also areas of justification by faith in Christ alone.

Yet these points of clarification are not enough as an introduction. Some general considerations ought to be added. For this chapter covers a field where the decisive basic perspectives may be very controversial. To those who cultivate inter-confessional polemics or hostilities of school theologies there are cases for real conflict here.

One possible point of conflict is that between a theology of history and a theology of creation. Traditionally, Reformed theologians have been inclined to prefer the former and Lutheran theologians the latter, but since the time of the Third Reich the classical Lutheran theology of creation has been in such a bad reputation, that even Lutherans have tried to avoid this aspect and adapt themselves to a theology of history. But creation and history are not mutually exclusive aspects of reality.

In the Faith and Order document on "God in Nature and History"—where the World Council of Churches' general study theme "The Finality of Christ in an Age of Universal History" was in the end integrated and provided the predominant aspect—it was stated, originally by a Reformed theologian,[1] that for many centuries non-human nature was considered an entirely earthbound static reality, which for modern man is no longer the case, and that the church is now bewildered by "this new experience and understanding," which should imply that it is only as the God of history that God is the God of nature.[2] But when this report was presented at the Bristol meeting of the Faith and Order Commission in 1967, an Anglican theologian asked for "some sort of natural theology or rather theology of the natural," and a Lutheran theologian argued that the documents reference to nature as a static reality was too simple and that a theology of creation was needed. Anglican and Lutheran theologians even presented a document of their own to meet this need and to provide a counter-balance in the form of a theology of the created order.[3] Their suggestions, however, were not adopted on an equal line with the original report.

This result shows that there is considerable hesitation today to accept a theological perspective where the aspect of createdness dominates over the aspect of dynamic history. And yet it seems important that the earlier stress on static creation (nature, essence, species and their qualities, etc.) should not simply be replaced by an equally exclusive stress on dynamic history *(Heilsgeschichte,* God's new acts, man's power to change, etc.), for however important and however enlightening this latter stress may be, it is nevertheless tempted to neglect the aspect of given forms of createdness, equally important to man in his concrete life.[4] As a matter of fact, this conflict between two theological trends is somewhat artificial: *Creation and history are two necessary dimensions of reality.* No "natural phenomenon" is entirely static (it is part of a process), and no historical event takes place regardless of "given" conditions of life in its various forms.

In addition, let me underline that in a series of studies dominated by the dimension of history, this chapter aims at re-establishing part of the balance at this point. There is a considerable need for a new ontology in the present situation.

Secondly, a conflict of equal amplitude may be discovered in the field of anthropology. Modern theological language about man is strongly marked by influences from existentialist philosophy. Seen in its wider anthropological aspect, however, existentialist terminology is primarily psychological in character, and covers only part of the reality of man, however important a part it may be. "Existential" analysis of life is an analysis of man's subjective experience of life. In whatever form it appears, it tends to underline the problematic nature of man's relationship to himself, the self-transcending and therefore bewildering character of his position, different from other created beings.[5] But this is a too one-sided or narrow basis for a full theological anthropology. Man is also a physical and biological being, sharing with the rest of creation some basic conditions of life. And if this is so, the universal claims of Christological faith cannot stop short of this fact. If it is characteristic of man that he is a part of biological creation, and at the same time a spiritual being who transcends this biological givenness,[6] Christological theology must take this double fact into serious consideration, and see what faith in the incarnation implies with regard to man as whole. It is precisely the man who is conceivable in biological terms who is also the *homo faber,* the co-creator, the changing dominator, the technocrat, and it is precisely this *homo faber,* with "spiritual" responsibility for whole areas of immense capacity, who is bound to act in relation to the rest of creation in such a way that he does not destroy or violate his proper conditions.

Finally, the cosmological and anthropological significance of Christ's redeeming work, when discussed today, cannot be isolated within a confessionally self-appreciative theology. It must be treated as an ecumenical theme, i.e. in a catholic perspective, if we use the term catholic in the sense in which it was used at the Uppsala general assembly of the World Council of Churches.[7] As a matter of fact, it already was so treated by Joseph Sittler at the New Delhi assembly in his admirable address entitled "Called to Unity." [8] There he reminded his listener not only of the "Christic vision of the eastern fathers" and the unfortunate split between grace and nature in western thought,[9] but underlined also that faith in the cosmic Christ precisely in our day provides a meaningful setting for a study of church unity.[10] As a matter of fact, this is not a question of inter-confessional understanding alone; it is a call to common responsibility in the world on the basis of an audacious faith. Unfortunately, Sittler's lines of thinking were not fulfilled by the ecumenical movement in the following years. His contribution stood isolated in its context, and it is perhaps not until now, after the Uppsala assembly, when we are faced with the tremendous task of understanding and putting into practice the *humanum*, that we are prepared to consider the importance of his concern.

This wider scope of my theme does, of course, not exclude the importance of its inter-confessional implications. Some of them have been indicated above. In a more systematic form they might be briefly enumerated like this: 1. Theologians of the Reformed tradition are inclined to accuse Lutherans of leaving creation to itself in their theology of creation (the danger of *Eigengesetzlichkeit*), while they themselves, at least on a Barthian basis, subsume creation under the particular revelation of Christ. A Lutheran cosmic Christology may restore the balance by showing the proper context of faith in a Christ, in whom all was created and consummated. 2. Roman Catholic, Anglican and specifically Orthodox theologians, explicitly, or at least implicitly, accuse the Lutheran estimation of man of neglecting some anthropological consequences of the doctrine of redemption through Christ. A Lutheran re-thinking of the redemptive work of Christ along the lines of an anthropology which considers not only the spiritual or psychological but also the biological and material aspects of man may again restore the balance by showing the full scope of justification by faith.

ASPECTS OF CLASSICAL CHRISTOLOGY
Some Fundamentals

That the New Testament witness about Christ contains a cosmological perspective need not be elaborated at any length here, nor that its messianic faith is closely linked to the common biblical belief that man was created in the image and likeness of God. From a strictly exegetical point of view, both the cosmological and the anthropological key texts will be analysed in another chapter. It is equally unnecessary to prove that these two New Testament aspects of faith in Christ were transferred to the ancient church and further developed in the *Logos* and *imago* Christology of the church fathers. In general terms these are well-known facts. What is important is to see whether there are some precise aspects of these Christological fundamentals which seem to be forgotten, or at least not to be used in modern theological reflection, and whether these were further developed in a way which opened the door for a more modern understanding.

Already in the biblical material there seem to be such precise aspects. Let us consider three of them: the aspect of *power*, the aspect of *subsistence* and the aspect of *mediation* or salvation, all of which have reference both to the cosmological and to the anthropological perspective. Only hints can be given.

The *power* aspect is obvious even in the most simple elements of the synoptic tradition. Emphasis on the power and authority of Jesus—as a power from God—is part and parcel of the messianic kerygma. In the cosmological perspective it is related to the acts of Jesus, particularly his healing miracles which claim to be performed by means of an authority over the natural forces in creation and by overcoming the evil forces of Satan.[11] In the anthropological perspective it is related to the words of Jesus which reveal the divine authority of the Son of Man.[12] A closer investigation of the concept of faith as power, e.g. in St. Mark, would probably also show that Christological assumptions of a cosmological and anthropological character lie behind these expressions of early Christian messianic conviction.[13]

The same aspect is also obvious in the more or less sophisticated theology of the Pauline and Johannine writings. In recording the story of the wedding miracle at Cana, John, using pagan and Jewish sources, affirms the creative and transforming power of Jesus as a sign of his position, not only as a fulfiller of Judaism but also as a bearer of supernatural power.[14] And in Pauline theology, especially as it is developed in Colossians and Ephesians, the cosmic function of Christ is depicted as one of dominion over the universe through powerful presence, made manifest through his ascension to the right hand of the Father.[15]

This has, of course, reference also to the *subsistence* aspect of

New Testament Christology. In St. John Christ is the Logos, through whom all things were made, and in Pauline Christology the universe is not autonomous or absolute but 'theonomous,' in the sense of 'christonomous.' Here originally Stoic ideas, mediated through an exegesis of Hellenistic Judaism, which referred the texts about divine epiphany to the figure of the Logos, were transformed into affirmations about the cosmic Christ.[16] This in its turn is intimately connected with the *mediation* or salvation aspect of Christ's cosmic function. Christ is described as a cosmic mediator of personal quality, e.g. in Colossians,[17] and—what is important for later development—it is on the basis of this Pauline understanding that later New Testament and early church tradition clarifies this faith to mean, not only that Christ acquired this mediating position in relation to the universe through his ascension (as was still the case in St. Paul's personal development of faith: through his belief in Christ's resurrection and ascension he came to his belief in his pre-existence and his cosmic function), but that the turning point in cosmic salvation is Christ's appearance, his epiphany as a whole, beginning with his incarnation and completed with his ascension.[18] Again these two aspects can equally well be integrated in an anthropological perspective. According to Pauline theology, for example, man as created in the image of God was created for Christ, who is the image of the Father, and thus man exists from the very beginning in a relationship to Christ.[19] Thus his salvation is one which is linked to Christ as the New Man, in communion with whom he is called to reach to the full estate of his manhood.[20]

On these fundamentals the Christology of the church fathers was further developed and reached its summit in profound speculations on Christ the Pantocrator, Christ the Logos and Christ the God-Man.[21]

The *Logoi* of Creation and Christ the Logos in Patristic Theology

When we now come to the fathers of the ancient church, the cosmological and particularly the anthropological material related to Christology is overwhelmingly rich. Thus we do well in concentrating even more on just a few precise aspects. As a matter of fact, I should suggest that we concentrate our attention on not more than two specific issues, which might also be of particular interest for a modern understanding of the implications of the Christian faith, and which at the same time seem to have been neglected in later thinking. The philosophical presuppositions of the fathers are certainly different from ours, but unless the aspects which they represent here are taken into consideration, in one way or another transferred to modern thought forms, something will be missing in the present day articulation of the content of a full Christian belief. It should be added that these two aspects are particularly relevant for the eastern branch of the ancient church tradition, but this fact just adds to the importance of them, since there was for a long time a tendency to forget the eastern heritage.

The first aspect is primarily of a cosmological character, and is intimately connected with the broad stream of Logos Christology, of which, however, it represents a particular dimension.

The fathers of the early church rapidly developed the embryonic Logos Christology of the Gospel of St. John. They did so in a more or less explicit coherence with the Jewish Hellenistic Logos speculation of Philo of Alexandria. This dependence on Philo is particularly apparent in the great Christian Alexandrian tradition represented by Clement and Origen, and indirectly by their inheritors. But on the other hand, at least some of them also departed from Philo at certain points, due to their particular Christian conviction that identification of Jesus Christ with the Logos implied a higher estimation of the Logos as God than was ever to be found in Philo. To the latter the Logos was identified with God at the first stage only as a thought in God but was created by him at a later stage.[22] To the Christian fathers this conception was not acceptable, which caused some difficulties with which they had to wrestle in their own development of a Logos Christology.

The majority of them used the Philonic understanding of the Logos as the place of the intelligible world, i.e. as the totality of ideas in a general Platonic sense, but differed from Philo in their understanding of the relationship between this Logos—who was to them a divine person—and God the father and creator, and consequently they differed also in their understanding of the relationship between the ideas contained in the Logos, and God.[23] Since they also generally agreed that this world of ideas, through the act of creation, was immanent in the world, this Christian application of the Philonic Logos speculation was of great importance to their appreciation of the world. Through Christ the Logos this world, not only the intelligible but also the sensible world, was related to God as a manifestation of his thoughts in Christ. Thus by this qualified adaption of the Philonic identification of the Logos with the Platonic world of ideas, the fathers of the church also arrived at an appreciation of the created order of things, which in Hellenistic terms combined the biblical understanding of creation with the New Testament vision of Christ as the mediator of the universe. The participation of the created world in the divine reality certainly became a philosophical problem, but the cosmological significance of Christ could not be denied without denial of Christ himself as a divine person. The theological qualification of the world was intimately linked to the development of the central doctrine of Christ.

It is also on this basis that our first particular aspect is to be discussed in its more sophisticated form. Since the presence of the ideas—what used to be called by the church fathers in Greek the *logoi* and in Latin the *rationes* of the world—in Christ the Logos was an established part of Christian theology, the cosmological implications of *all* dimensions of the Christological faith of the church had to be worked out in further detail. This was the starting point for a theology of creation characteristic of some of the later fathers and teachers of the church, particularly in the eastern tradition, which goes far beyond the simple affirmation that God created the world in Christ and redeemed it through Christ. It qualifies the world in its unity as well as its plurality, and in its development and motion towards a fuller consummation as well. In this process Christian theology advanced from a Christological idealism to a Christological teleology of the created order.

Here the different stages of this theological development can only be very briefly indicated. Origen seems to have been the first thinker of the church who presented a noticeable theology of the *logoi* of creation.[24] According to him they are identical with the ideas of the intelligible world and, as indicated above, form a model of the world of the senses and represent the original "good-

ness" of created things. (We leave aside here for a moment
Origen's particular understanding of the fall and his idea of a
double creation of man, which complicates the question of Origen's
estimation of matter.) The same line of thinking may be followed
in Athanasius, who affirms that God created the world in accordance with his own Logos, since he saw that a creation simply
differentiated according to individual *logoi* would be a divided
world, and is also reflected in Augustine who regards the *rationes*
as immutable and eternal principles contained in the Logos.

An important step further in this idea of the Logos and the *logoi*
of creation, however, is reached when it is combined with soteriological aspects of the same Christology. This is partly the case in
an Origenist writer like Evagrius Ponticus who speaks not only of
the *logoi* of creation in Origen's sense but also, in relation to this,
of *logoi* of providence and judgment, related to the *logoi* in the
first sense. This implies that there is a plan of salvation inherent
in the very *logos* structure of life, although Evagrius would interpret this in an Origenist sense, i.e. depreciating the present material creation. Important also is that Evagrius sets forth the idea
that in a final "spiritual contemplation" all the *logoi* may be seen
in mystical communion with God.[25] The soteriological aspect, in a
more positive sense, was further developed by Pseudo-Dionysius
the Areopagite, who completed and somewhat corrected the Alexandrian emphasis on the *logoi* of creation, in that he saw them
not only as the more or less static thoughts of God behind creation,[26] but in a dynamic sense as "divine and good wills," almost
identical with the worldly existence of things.[27] Another and very
important step further is later represented by Maximus the Confessor, who builds on both Evagrius and Pseudo-Dionysius but
whose conception is not identical with any of these. Since Maximus
is the exponent of a more complete theology of creation at this
point, and thus of patristic reflection on the cosmological significance of the work of Christ, we shall present his understanding
a little more in detail.

To Maximus, as to Pseudo-Dionysius, the *logoi* of creation are
divine wills or intentions, but this is directly related to an idea of
permanent and manifold incarnation. Maximus says: "Always and
in all God's Logos and God wills to effect the mystery of his em-

bodiment" (Ambiguorum liber 7), and he stresses that the *logoi* reveal a divine purpose. This purpose is also expressed in terms borrowed from Evagrius, when Maximus speaks of the relationship between the *logoi* of creation and the *logoi* of providence and judgment. In the Origenist conception of Evagrius these terms were closely linked to the myth of a prehistoric fall of rational beings and a subsequent second creation of the material world, judgment thus referring to this second-rate creation and providence to the divine restitution of the original spiritual unity. Maximus uses the terms in a quite different way. To him differentiated existence is not negatively evaluated but is seen as a good arrangement by God, serving a purpose indicated by the individual capacities for motion. Thus, judgment, with its *logos*, being the principle of purposeful differentiation, has a positive role to play within the context of divine providence, the *logos* of which is the principle of unification without violation of individual multiplicity.[28]

On this basis, three inter-connected ideas are developed by Maximus, which I only indicate here without going into a detailed analysis. The first idea is that the *logoi* of a differentiated creation reflect together the purpose of the Creator, in that they embody the Logos.[29] The second idea is the classical one that the *logoi*, pre-existent in God, are held together by the Logos.[30] This means that they can be contemplated and lead the mind to Christ the Logos. The third idea is that these *logoi* are intimately connected with the total economy of salvation and the purpose of Christ's incarnation in the flesh.[31] Thus creation to Maximus is an act of divine condescension, interpreted in terms of the embodiment of the Logos, which introduces a positive element of motion, inherent in created beings but imprisoned and misused because of the fall.[32]

Thus the fathers of the church from the third to the sixth century refined their understanding of the cosmological implication of Christ's redeeming work, so that it became capable of a coherent view of the world in its plurality and mobility as related to Christ as both creator and redeemer. In later times, the eastern part of Christendom developed the dynamic of its universalism in a somewhat different direction through the doctrine of the uncreated energies of God, actively present in the world, which in the long run may invite a more disputable sophiology,[33] but it can hardly be denied that the Christological cosmology of a Maximus represents a challenging invitation for a re-interpretation of the Christology of today, in a world where precisely the notes of plurality and mobility present a key problem for theology.

Implications of the Hypostatic Union of Divine and Human in Christ

The second aspect of a precise character within the Christological speculation of the ancient church is primarily anthropological, though it is of course also closely related to common cosmological presuppositions. It is intimately connected with the broad stream of the theology of incarnation, of which, however, it represents a particular dimension

The fathers of the early church developed their Christology of the incarnation on the basis of relatively clear New Testament indications about Jesus Christ as God (the son of the father, the divine Logos) on the one hand, and man (the son of man in its human aspect, the new adam etc.) on the other. The theological and philosophical difficulties, to which further speculation on these lines led the church, and how it tried to solve them in its Christological dogmas of the first four centuries, is too well known to be recapitulated here. Our point of interest in this chapter lies beyond the relatively definite settlement of these struggles at the Council of Chalcedon in 450.

For it is on the basis of Chalcedon—having specified the mystery of the incarnation as the hypostatic union of divine and human nature in Christ—that post-Chalcedonian and neo-Chalcedonian thinking developed its discussion on the idea of *the mystery of the theandric person* and *the mystery of mutual penetration,* on which we shall dwell for a while. There again Maximus the Confessor will be shown to represent a summit position in the patristic period.

When dealing with the question of the mutual penetration of natures within the same person—a concept that Maximus was the first Christian writer to give a central position within orthodox Christology—one should keep in mind that this concept is intimately connected with the more widespread and earlier idea of a communication of attributes *(communicatio idiomatum)*. The latter is found as early as in Irenaeus and not least in Origen, but it was particularly actualized in the fifth century, and acquired a more precise function after the Council of Chalcedon. However, the idea of *communicatio idiomatum* was also accepted, though with particular interpretations, by both monophysites and Nestorians.[34] The monophysites used it naturally in a one-sided way, and in Maximus' times monothelitism was equally inclined to interpret the term penetration or permeation *(perichoresis)* in the sense that there was a divine permeation into the human only and not a mutual penetration. What is characteristic of Maximus, however—and what is of special interest to us here—is that in the proper sense this term can be understood to mean mutual penetration within the hypostatic unity of the person of Christ. By preferring this term to that of *communicatio idiomatum,* Maximus gave to his Christological anthropology an interesting dynamic element.

Maximus once refers to a letter by Gregory Nazianzen, where the latter speaks of the inhabitation of Christ in the believer and about a certain "mixture" of the two natures and their attributes, finally stating that the two natures penetrate into each other on account of their mutual adhesion. In the context of this letter of Gregory the mutual application of attributes is seen more as a consequence of the permeation than as its cause, and this is precisely a line of thinking which attracted Maximus, in whom the idea of *perichoresis* predominates. Here is probably the very starting point of his own development of this idea.[35]

In Maximus' theory of penetration there are four elements which need to be stressed. First of all, there is a primary aspect of divine penetration into the human. In the person of Christ this is the very starting point. Hypostatic union means incarnation. But Maximus also underlines that for the believers, as being in Christ, this divine penetration continues as an incarnation of divine qualities in their own virtues in accordance with the amount of faith present in the individual believer. The second and equally important element, however, is the opposite aspect: there is also a human penetration into the divine. This is a fruit of the hypostatic union in Christ, and is again relevant also for the life of the believer. Thus, the third element is the aspect of reciprocity in the concept of penetration. Precisely because—according to the Christological formula of Chalcedon—the hypostatic union of the two natures is "without confusion," the aspect of reciprocity is an expression of the conviction that neither the divine nor the human nature ever becomes anything else than that which it is. Consequently, the fourth element in Maximus' understanding of *perichoresis* is the idea that interpenetration, in which—as it were—each nature reaches beyond what it acquires in isolation from the other nature, its counterpart, on the one hand means that the redemptive union of the natures is something entirely "new," but on the other hand also means only a true development of what is proper to each nature. As far as man is concerned, the hypostatic union in Christ thus reveals what man is called to be as man, capacities of his human nature which were hidden—by sin or non-development and non-perfection—until that process takes place which is modelled in Christ.[36]

What is apparent in Christ then is that God and man are exemplars *(paradeigmata)* one of another. They stand in a particular polarity, a relationship which finds its classical expression in the concept of the *imago Dei*. To Maximus this polarity is of a dynamic character. The incarnation of God and the deification of man condition each other mutually, and both are effected in a double process: once and for all in Christ and gradually and permanently in the life of human beings within the body of Christ. Consequently, Maximus can speak—in paradoxical terms—of a "blessed inversion," an active polarity, which makes God become man thanks to the deification of man, and makes man become god thanks to God's becoming man.[37] This aspect of activity serves to underline the element of motion and development, which is dear to Maximus, while emphasizing at the same time the inner coherence, the unified purpose of God and man, in itself capable of common qualifications.

This last fact forms the background of Maximus' attitude to the Neo-Chalcedonian position. For this reason it is of some interest here. So-called Neo-Chalcedonianism was an attempt at a compromise between a Chalcedonian position and some pre-Chalcedonian expressions, on the basis of which non-Chalcedonian positions were still held. Two expressions were important, both from Cyril of Alexandria: the so-called theopaschite formula and the expression "the one incarnate nature of the God Logos." Only the latter interests us here. Maximus' attitude to this expression also explains his understanding of what I called above "the theandric person."

In defending Cyril's formula Maximus says that the word "incarnate" simply denotes human nature in its fullness, and also that the formula thus contains a reference to both natures and should not be understood as denoting any "confused" status of the natures after their union. Maximus' position is consequently strictly Chalcedonian, and he uses Cyril's formula in such a way that it provides a rather perfect description of the relationship in Christ between two natures which remain intact.[38] In addition, one must ask: Why is Maximus so eager to preserve the formula, or at least to defend it? It is not only because he feels loyal to Cyril and wants to prove his orthodoxy. Cyril's expression also has a particular value to him: it underlines the unity aspect of the hypostatic union. It emphasizes a togetherness of the natures in Christ which is as equally important to the Chalcedonian vision as is the lack of confusion.

This again leads Maximus to speak of "identity" within the person of Christ, but also to use the term theandric about the result of the union. This latter term was probably borrowed from Pseudo-Dionysius, on whose expression "the new theandric energy" of Christ Maximus also commented. Again he accepted this formula, because it expressed the "newness" of the relationship between the natures in Christ, a newness which to man meant the possibility of living up to his natural capacities within the fully developed "paradigmatic" and dynamic reciprocity between human and divine. Thus in Maximus we have the basis of an idea of Christ as a theandric person, modelling man's life through his own to the point of transcending what is strictly known as human without violating human nature.[39]

Maximus illustrates here how a Christological discussion in the early church, in its more sophisticated stage, may lead to special insights about man, not only in that from Chalcedonian theology onwards the concept of person could no longer be strictly identified with what is only characteristic of the nature of a species, thus transcending the fixity of pure ontology, but also in the sense that the very idea of what is natural to man was extended to a realm of meta-man relationships in such a way that no simply "human" definition of man seemed sufficient any more. Like God, man himself could be seen as a mystery, open to "new" insights, having his point of unification, the model of his life in its entirety, outside of himself and yet indissolubly related to himself. This opens up the perspective of man as we see him today, bound by his conditions and yet free to use his capacities also to change what he has hitherto regarded as his destiny. And it shows that a patristic understanding of man is completely prepared to regard this development, not as contrary to man's destiny given by God or as separated from his relationship to Christ as his Savior, but as part of the perspective opened up by the fact that in Christ he is related to what is beyond himself.

In both their cosmological and their anthropological thinking the fathers of the ancient church thus came to implications of their faith which combined new Christological insights with a proper analysis of the created order, world and man as they are were seen as subsistent in Christ in relationship to God in both a historical and an ontological perspective.

ASPECTS OF LUTHERAN CHRISTOLOGY

With regard to the general context of this chapter it is only proper that attention should now be given to the Lutheran tradition, particularly to Luther himself. Consideration of this latter position seems to be a mediating link between what we have described as aspects of classical Christology and what we might wish for the future of a Christology able to cope with cosmological and anthropological problems of our time. However, it is evident that the Lutheran tradition puts the main stress on the soteriological perspective of its Christology, and is inclined to avoid general statements —whether of a cosmological or an anthropological character—without a clear connection with the doctrine of justification. This very fact confronts us with the problem how far a shift of emphasis is acceptable. But on the other hand, any soteriology, and not least the Lutheran, presupposes certain convictions about God, the world, life in general and the state of man, which might have once been self-evident but are hardly so any longer. And thus concentration on soteriology in a narrow sense today may cause a certain theological system to appear more closed in itself than it originally intended to be. For this reason, it may nevertheless be fair to this system to bring forth scarcely developed or neglected elements which can help to reestablish the scope of its convictions.

At least I will try here to discuss two such elements of Lutheran Christology which may fruitfully be related and compared to the elements of classical Christology analysed above. One of them belongs to the cosmological and one to the anthropological implications of Christology. As a matter of fact both of them are very central to the Lutheran understanding of the position and function of Christ. I refer to the idea of *the ubiquity of Christ* and to the general Lutheran interpretation of the doctrine of *communicatio idiomatum*. The former is built on the latter, but in order to make my analysis here parallel to that of the classical period, I start with ubiquity. Finally, it will also be underlined that the famous Lutheran *simul* formula might be most properly understood in the context of Chalcedonian Christology.

The Idea of the Ubiquity of Christ as a Contribution to Christian Cosmology

Luther's stress on the ubiquity of Christ, i.e. on the inherent omnipresence of Christ in the world, was sometimes regarded as alien to his theological system as a whole. Luther should have used it as polemical argument when he was struggling to defend his understanding of Christ's real presence in the elements of the Eucharist. But different studies in the theology of Luther have shown that this can hardly be the case. The idea of the ubiquity of Christ is part of Luther's stress on the doctrine of the *communicatio idiomatum,* and the latter is central to his soteriological Christology. On the other hand, it is quite natural that Luther does not actualize this aspect of Christology for its own sake, but only when a problem which concerns man's appropriation of the divine means of grace requires it

Luther distinguishes sharply between the two natures. There is no mixture. But he is equally eager to keep them together in his description of Christ. Here the doctrine of the *communicatio idiomatum* serves as his proper instrument. This double emphasis—

which is, of course, strictly Chalcedonian in character, to express his position in classical terms—implies that the question of Christ's presence in the world contains two different aspects. The cosmological significance of Christ is thus somewhat more complicated in Luther—who stood in dialog with a complex Medieval discussion—than we saw it to be in the texts of the fathers of the ancient church. For the latter the presence of the Logos in things was one problem, and the person of Christ with its anthropological implications another. In Luther's thinking they are connected. Thus he theologizes about two modes of the presence of Christ in the things of the world: He is present as the divine Word of God and he is present as man. The former aspect presents in fact no real problem. It is characteristic, however, that Luther also sees the divine presence, which is a consequence of the simple fact that Christ is the Son of God, as a kind of incarnation. The Word of God is God in his omnipresence in the world.[40] We recognize here the classical idea of the presence of the Logos, though not via the concept of *logoi,* or ideas.

The second form of Christ's presence, as man—the ubiquity of Christ properly speaking—is of course less self-evident. Here Luther puts the weight of his argument. The basis is the idea of *communicatio.* Through the hypostatic union of divine and human, Christ's humanity shares in that which is proper to God. This happens thanks to a process of communication which is obviously conceived in factual terms—the *communicatio idiomatum* is real and not only nominal, it is not simply a linguistic exercise or a doxological application of attributes.[41] Four important elements are characteristic of Luther's thinking at this point.

First, the omnipresence of Christ is not regarded as a consequence only of his ascension. It is thanks to the incarnation that the humanity of Christ is in God and thus present in all places.[42] As a matter of fact, Luther bases his teaching about the ubiquity of Christ on two fundaments: the hypostatic union of the two natures in the incarnation and the ascension of the whole of Christ to the right side of the father.[43] Thus, the Chalcedonian formula lies behind Luther's argument, and precisely as in the ancient church, the form of the presence of the Logos is consequently that of the incarnation.

Secondly, this presence of Christ in all places is unique. Luther speaks of three kinds of presence: bodily or material presence in one particular place, spiritual presence in a number of places without bodily presence, and finally "divine or heavenly" presence in all places. Christ's presence is unique in that it is a complete presence of the last type.[44] This is, of course, possible only because of the mystery of the hypostatic union which allows for a divine mode of human presence. Characteristic here is that Christ's presence is "in all places" and thus universal, and it is of such a nature that the world does not contain him but is rather transcended in him.[45]

Thirdly, it is always the whole of Christ which is present: God and man. Where he is present in the one capacity, he is also present in the other.[46] For it is the person of Christ who is present. This aspect has, of course, a clear soteriological motivation.

Fourthly, from what we know of Luther's thinking about the ubiquity of Christ we see that on the basis of the hypostatic union he affirms about Christ as God that he is there in a human mode of presence, and about Christ as man that he is there in a divine mode of presence. In both cases for soteriological reasons. If his divine presence were in a divine mode, it would be an aim in itself and not communicate the mercy and love of God to human beings, and if his human presence was in a merely human mode, it would not be a redeeming presence.[47] Thus, Luther's ontological fundament is clear, but his soteriological interest predominates.

The doctrine of Christ's omnipresence thus is no aim in itself to Luther. It is subordinated to his soteriological Christology. This implies also that any pantheism is avoided. Luther distinguishes between presence in general and presence "for you," [48] and the doctrine of Christ's volipresence is in Luther's theology of the Eucharist a complement to his doctrine of his omnipresence. Luther is not of the opinion that in the Eucharist as sacrament Christ becomes present where he was not present before—this was the opinion of Biel—but he becomes present to the salvation of a concrete human being in a concrete amount of bread and wine because he wants to.[49] Luther's ontological presuppositions are oriented towards the soteriological consequences. This, however, does not make them less relevant as ontological presuppositions.

It should be added here, of course, that my interpretation of Luther is rather on the line of Johannes Brenz than on that of Melanchton. The dispute on the doctrine of the Eucharist around 1550 showed as a matter of fact that when having to choose, as it were, between the ontological presuppositions and the soteriological consequences—in itself a paradoxical choice—Lutheranism, in full harmony with Luther's intentions, preferred the latter. The result of the dispute was that the Lutheran doctrine became a doctrine of the person of Christ rather than a doctrine of the two natures in Christ.[50] This, however, does not necessarily imply a satisfactory answer to the problems of today. The time may be ripe to ask again for ontological presuppositions, though not necessarily expressed in the same thought forms.

Communicatio Idiomatum as a Key to Luther's Understanding of the Life of the Christian

We have already seen how important to Luther the doctrine of *communicatio idiomatum* is as a consequence of the Chalcedonian formula, applicable to the saving activity of Christ. As a matter of fact—as was convincingly shown by K. O. Nilsson in his Luther study of 1966—this doctrine is a key to his whole theological system. It can be argued that the famous *"simul* formula"—righteous and sinner *at the same time*—is only one expression of this fact. It seems as if Luther was always inspired by this Christological key concept, and worked it out in various aspects of his theology.

It is important here, of course, to underline again that for Luther the *communicatio idiomatum* was not nominal, but real. He accuses the enthusiasts of his time of having a wrong conception of the relationship between the two natures in Christ. They regard them in isolation from each other, but by doing so they handle them in the abstract and not, as one should, in the concrete. This however, does not mean that the communication is possible only in exclusive relation to the person of Christ—who represents, as it were, the concrete. In this person there is a real communication between the natures as such, but it is in him—the concrete person—that the communication actually takes place. It makes no sense—soteriologically—to speak of communication outside of him.[51]

We notice here that in denying a *communication* in the abstract, Luther also shows his lack of interest in what the incarnation might mean for the human nature as such. His theology is Christocentric, and it is for the soteriological consequences that the idea of *communicatio* is so important to him. Further distinctions within this concept do not interest him.[52] An yet these soteriological consequences are drawn with regard not only to Christology properly speaking, or to his theology of the Eucharist through the idea of the ubiquity of Christ, but also in relation to the created world of human beings, the church and the ethical situation of Christians. Of a special interest to us here is the last aspect. On the one hand, the Christian is seen as dead with Christ in his solidarity with the world which is under sin, and on the other risen with Christ to a status of justification and freedom. Faith in Christ conveys to man freedom from the law, from sin and death, and places him in the world of God (in the divine sphere of justification). But in his works as man he is still bound to serve other human beings under the same conditions of law, sin and death. And as a Christian he can be both, using his freedom as well as his vocation to serve until death, only thanks to the communication between divine and human in Christ.[53] Man remains man, and yet he lives in freedom.

We can quite clearly see that the doctrine of *communicatio* is to Luther an instrument by which he can demonstrate the newness of man's life in Christ without denying his full humanity. But on the other hand, Luther's understanding contains certain problems, which may be seen even more clearly against the background of classical theology, as I have sketched it above.

First of all, the fact that Luther teaches a real *communicatio* indicates that something new and transcending happens to man in Christ. But this transcending quality could hardly be expressed, as in the case of Maximus, by the term *perichoresis,* penetration.

Secondly, Luther does not identify anything that belongs to man's "natural" capacities even after the fall with the image of God in man, nor does he distinguish between image and likeness. At this point his theology differs from that of the fathers.[54] On the other hand, by tending to interpret the image and likeness spoken of in the Genesis story as referring to Christ, he follows the classical tradition.[55] The combination of these two positions leads to the consequence that Luther does not very clearly distinguish between Christ as man and Christ as sinner for man's sake. Sin belongs to the human conditions, and thus redemption from the state of sin through Christ is almost identified with an elevation to the sphere of the divine. This in its turn, results in a very sharp distinction between the two sides of the life of a Christian: his status as justi-fied and his continuing status as sinner.[56] Thus, there is in Luther's theology no proper place for a perfection of the humanness of man on the human level—in virtue of man's created purpose as carrying the image of God. In other words, there is no place for Maximus' idea of God and man as exemplars one of another, at least not before death. Only the divine sphere stands under the sign of life, while the sign of death remains over the sphere of the human.

This leads in the third place, easily—as has often been the case in later Lutheranism—to a kind of identification between certain outward forms of life—so-called orders of creation—and humanness, an identification which threatens to become outdated when these outward forms demonstrate that they can be changed. And it does not lead to those unprecedented possibilities of man which were indicated by a father like Maximus the Confessor when he allowed for a perichoresis in Christ of the human nature into the divine, understood as a new incarnation of God in human form.

CONCLUDING QUESTIONS FOR
FURTHER CONSIDERATION

From what I have here analyzed—choosing my examples, one may argue, in a very haphazard and subjective way—we have seen that both the classical theological tradition of the ancient church and the Lutheran tradition as represented by Luther himself, put a considerable stress on the cosmological and anthropological as-pects of the redeeming work of Christ. But we have also become aware of problems of today which need to be analyzed in the light of these traditions, treated in a critical way. At the end I will just shortly indicate more precisely a few of these possible fields of study.

a. God's and man's relationship to the physical universe is of utmost interest for a theology of the space age and an age of unlimited technological inventions. Does faith in Christ imply an evaluation of the data of this age which may help to establish a purposeful relationship to them?

b. If Christians still believe in Christ as in any sense being the Logos, this faith should imply a relationship between the scientific understanding of the *"logoi* of things" and the mystery of redemption in Christ. But how can this relationship be expressed in such a way that man is no longer alienated from his world but present with faith in it? And how can the "ubiquity" of Christ be confessed with respect to scientific formulas about what we use to call matter?

c. The implications of the Christian faith in the manhood of Christ for biological life and biological evolution should be seriously considered. Is the incarnation only related to man as sinner or also to his biological context, shared with non-human beings, and if so, what does this imply?

d. Man has become aware of his power to change not only his "natural" and social surroundings but eventually the very conditions of his own life. If Christian faith in a *communicatio idiomatum* in Christ implies that divine and human attributes are inter-penetrable, what does this mean for the understanding of man's use of this power?

e. If Christians can still believe in the subsistence of "things" in Christ, what indications may this faith give as to the permanence and/or mutability of that which is under the stewardship of man?

f. The presence of Christ in the Eucharist is usually seen in isolation from God's presence in the world. Nevertheless, it is through material elements, refined through human production, that this presence becomes a presence with us as composite beings. What consequences does this fact have for the relationship between the Eucharist as Christ's real presence and the human society of production and consumption?

—Translated by Paul-Gerhard Nohl

NOTES

1. H. Berkhof, God in Nature and History, in *Study Encounter*, Vol. 1, No. 3 (1965), pp. 142-160.

2. See L. Vischer (ed.), *New Directions in Faith and Order*. *Bristol 1967*, Geneva 1968, p. 7ff. Cf. Berkhof, *art.cit.*, p. 142.

3. L. Vischer (ed.), *op. cit.*, pp. 90 and 133-140.

4. This has been most convincingly pointed out by K. E. Løgstrup in his writings. Løgstrup's concern also marked the first part of the Anglican-Lutheran document "Creation, New Creation and the Unity of the Church" (jointly signed by D. E. Jenkins, G. W. H. Lampe, K. E. Løgstrup and G. Wingren), see *ibid.*, especially p. 133ff. There reference is given to "the structure of life itself" and "a 'givenness' which we are constrained to interpret theologically in terms of creation." These are further called "spontaneous possibilities of life" and "created 'spontaneities'."

5. A succinct summary of existentialist anthropology is given in R. Wisser, "Der zu sich kommende Mensch und das Sein," R. Schwarz, *Menschliche Existenz und moderne Welt* I, Berlin 1967, pp. 245-295, where Sartre, Jaspers and Heidegger are considered.

6. For an excellent presentation of this double aspect, see Th. Dobzhansky, "The Pattern of Human Evolution," *Lutheran World* XVI (1969), pp. 107-123. For a more existentialist interpretation of man in his distinctiveness from animals, cf. P. Christian, "Aspekte der Medizinischen Anthropologie," in R. Schwarz (ed.), *op. cit.*, pp. 689-699.

7. See the report from Section I on "The Holy Spirit and the Catholicity of the Church" in N. Goodall (ed.), *The Uppsala 68 Report*, pp. 7-19.

8. J. A. Sittler, "Called to Unity," *The Ecumenical Review*, Vol. XIV (1962), pp. 177-187

9. J. A. Sittler, *op. cit.*, pp. 179ff. and 184ff.

10. See the article by R. Harrisville in this volume.

11. For an early exegetical appreciation of this Messianic context of the synoptic material, see W. Manson, *Jesus the Messiah*, London (1943) 1952, pp. 33-50. On the miracles as symbolic acts, see also H. Riesenfeld, *Att tolka Bibeln*, Stockholm 1967, pp. 159f. and 163-174.

12. Mark 13:31. Cf. the discussion of the primitive Christian idea of Jesus as the Prophet in O. Cullmann, *Die Christologie des Neuen Testaments*, 2 ed., Tübingen 1958, pp. 42-49.

13. Mark 9:23, 11:23.

14. Cf. C. K. Barrett, *The Gospel according to St. John*, London, p. 156ff. and 159 (comm. to John 2:11).

15. See M. A. Wagenfuehrer, *Die Bedeutung Christi für Welt und Kirche*, Leipzig 1941, p. 79f. and p. 60, and H. Hegermann, *Die Vorstellung vom Schöpfungsmittler im hellenistischen Judentum und Urchristentum*, Berlin 1961, p. 200.

16. See Wagenfuehrer, *op. cit.*, p. 81f.

17. See Hegermann, *op. cit.*, p. 200f.

18. *Ibid.*

19. See E. Larsson, *Christus als Vorbild*, Uppsala 1962, pp. 188ff., 207 and 277ff.

20. See the discussion in Larsson, *op. cit.*, pp. 197-210.

21. The speculation on Christ the Pantocrator must be left out in this short study, but the importance of this aspect of ancient christology as a development of what I have called the power aspect should be underlined. Cf. P. Beskow, *Rex gloriae*, Uppsala 1962, pp. 295-307.

22. See H. A. Wolfson, *The Philosophy of the Church Fathers* I, Cambridge, Mass., 1956, p. 177.

23. See the clarifying presentation of this theme in Wolfson, *op. cit.*, pp. 256-286 and especially his conclusions p. 285f.

24. Origen obviously based himself both on Stoic and Platonic ideas as well as on Philo, though the latter according to his general understanding, regarded the *logoi* as a kind of angels, see Wolfson, *op. cit.*, pp. 270-280 and J. Danielou, *Philon d'Alexandrie*, Paris 1958, pp. 163-167.

25. For references, see further L. Thunberg, *Microcosm and Mediator*, Lund 1965, p. 77f., n. 1.

26. Cf. Wolfson, *op. cit.*, pp. 258 and 286.

27. For references, see Thunberg, *op. cit.*, pp. 68 and 78, n. from p. 77.

28. For further details, see *ibid.*, pp. 67-76.

29. For details, see *ibid.*, p. 77ff.

30. *Ibid.*, p. 80f.

31. *Ibid.*, p. 81ff.

32. *Ibid.*, p. 85ff.

33. V. Lossky, *The Mystical Theology of the Eastern Church*, London 1957 suggests that Maximus' theology of the intentional *logoi* is directly related to the idea of uncreated energies, as it was developed by Gregory Palamas, but this is not entirely certain. It is true that Gregory bases himself on Maximus and interprets the *logoi* as identical with the divine energies (see J. Meyendorff, *Introduction à l'étude de Grégoire Palamas*, Paris 1959, p. 305), but his speculation is less Christological in general than that of Maximus. In *Du Verbe Incarné*, Paris 1943, S. Boulgakof, p. 45ff., develops his well-known sophiology in relation to creation.

34. See further Thunberg, *op. cit.*, p. 22f.

35. *Ibid.*, p. 26f.

36. For further references, see *ibid.*, pp. 27-32.

37. *Ibid.*, p. 32f.

38. *Ibid.*, p. 43f

39. See further, *ibid.*, p. 35ff.

40. See K. O. Nilsson, *Simul. Das Miteinander von Göttlichem und Menschlichem in Luthers Theologie*, Göttingen-Lund 1966, p. 92f.

41. Cf. *ibid.*, p. 253-257. See further below.

42. See A. Peters, *Realpräsenz. Luthers Zeugnis von Christi Gegenwart im Abendmahl*, Berlin 1960, p. 78.

43. See further H. Grass, *Die Abendmahlslehre bei Luther und Calvin*, Gütersloh 1940, pp. 61ff. and 69.

44. Peters, *op. cit.*, p. 81.
45. Cf. *ibid.*, p. 82f.
46. Nilsson, *op. cit.*, p. 252.
47. *Ibid.*, p. 263f.
48. See Grass, *op. cit.*, p. 63.
49. See F. Cleve, *Luthers nattvardslära*, Turku 1968, p. 307f.
50. On the Eucharist dispute, see Th. Mahlmann, *Das neue Dogma der lutherischen Christologie*, Gütersloh 1969, for the conclusion on this point particularly p. 245.
51. See Nilsson, *op. cit.*, pp. 253-260.
52. *Ibid.*, p. 260.
53. See Nilsson, *op. cit.*, p. 431 with ref.
54. See B. Haegglund, *De homine. Människouppfattningen i äldre luthersk tradition*, Lund 1959, p. 78f.
55. *Ibid.*, p. 82.
56. This is part of Luther's general tendency towards dualism, i.e. the concept of antagonism between God and Satan. A pioneer study of this problem is R. Bring, *Dualismen hos Luther*, Lund 1929.

Chapter 4

The Presence and Acts of the Triune God in Creation and History

INTRODUCTION

Because the working-situation out of which I write is incessantly pressing the question of the very possibility of "doing" theology in our time, a word of introduction is clearly called for, lest the manner and the matter of what is said be read in abstraction from the actual circumstances.

In a time when theology as a realm of discourse is literally fighting for its life as an intelligible and thereby legitimate field of human activity one must try to go beyond the venerable tradition of theological work as that tradition understood its task as preservation, clarification, transmission. For so powerful have been the reassessing necessities laid upon us by historical and critical studies in all areas, and so disintegrative and reconstructive have been the shifts in center and in effective force of the components of modern culture, that the theologian is forced to regard the past, not as a place to stand, but rather as a place from which to work toward shaping-the-possible in Christian theology.

It is for such reasons that this essay cannot be an essay in systematic theology in the usual mode, nor claim to more than responsible probing toward possible fresh and larger ways to speak of grace—which is to be the central term of this effort in contemporary reflection upon the acts of the triune God in creation and history.

The phrase "The Triune God" in the topic assigned to me will be understood in a specific way—a way alone consistent with the preceding paragraphs' description of the fiercely critical theological situation in which I live. I am forced by that situation to "bracket the previous question" as it were; to lay aside my own debt of mind and confession to old ways of speaking of the doctrine of the trinity, to regard these as not now useful to the clarification of the doctrines of God or of grace. One may the more boldly do this when he is aware that the New Testament witness to Jesus in the unfolding circumstances of the life of the community of faith moved toward a manner of articulating the relation of God, Jesus and the Spirit in terms not indeed separable from, nor intelligible except within, an ontological schema which is no longer congruent with most men's perception of reality or language about it.

A triadic-organic way of speaking about what Psalms called "the energies of God" would seem to offer a presently promising way to honor the richness and operational adequacy of the traditional confessions of the trinity, make the affirmation about the interior relations of Father, Son, and Spirit in a manner that preserves faith's intention but escapes the no longer sufficiently intelligible categories that were believed necessary in the period between Nicea and Chalcedon.

For what the doctrine of the trinity affirms, and labors to protect against misunderstanding and diminishment, is that creation, redemption, and sanctification have their source in God, that this God is not identical with but is present in what he creates, is present in the redemption of what he creates, and is present in all restoration, uniting, and upholding of his redeemed creation.

If this indeed be the reality to which the doctrine points, then the terms of ascription and the language of confession must be appropriate to a time that understands creation as continuous, and understands anthropology as not extractable from the story of *man* in an evolving world-process. One therefore cannot separate the doctrine of redemption from the doctrine of creation, and cannot speak of the Spirit's presidency to "call, gather, enlighten and sanctify" except from within the nexus of actualities whereby man has the self he indeed does have, and apart from which the term Spirit is an abstraction.

If, however, in thus speaking about the reformation of theological language and concepts, I have been understood to assume that such efforts could if carried through accomplish all that is necessary—I should have been misunderstood. For the context of fact and reflection within which such a reformulation must occur is by no means acknowledged if we think we can do what needs doing by an ever so radical rearrangement of the furniture within the unopened and venerable theological house. There is much "modern" theology, and much modern repristination effort within confessional theology, which makes that assumption. In the several paragraphs to follow I shall cite a few sentences from a contemporary physical anthropologist—and use it to make concrete the affirmation that a vastly enlarged context for reflection is the primary and troubling necessity if theology is again to become a credible form of discourse. And I am aware that in such an exercise of creative imagination one is certain to be accused of theologizing beyond the generally accredited rules.

This anticipation of an objection is stated only in order to repudiate its legitimacy! How strange indeed that theological practice in the tradition of Luther should have become suspicious of creative theological imagination! Imagination among modern men is commonly regarded as a quality of mind expected of poets, artists, and all who out of what is given "create" something that, until the moment of their accomplishing, literally was not. But what other term is adequate to denote that perception, clarification, bringing-into-existence of an insight, a relation, a fresh focus upon the all-generating core-reality in virtue of which an entire way of regarding God and history and human life is powerfully released? Was it not precisely a mark of theological imagination which once put together in fresh, dynamic, living, and organic ways such ancient terms as faith, law, Word of God, grace, repentance? When Luther did that he did not "discover" anything; he did not introduce into Catholic tradition a single new idea, force, term, concept. All the clay which under his hands was shaped to morphologically novel contours had been lying within the fields of catholic faith and life for centuries. The dynamism inherent in biblical language which, perhaps during his many years as a teacher of Scripture penetrated his entire way of regarding all things, emerged in him as a huge power of creative imagination. And catholic christianity is today acknowledging that it was this freshly amazed way of seeing and hearing that lies with primal force underneath the exegetical perceptiveness and responsibility. Luther's affection for the term "Tat-wort" is the leading clue to his entire theological accomplishment; and if one tries to account for him only by accumulations piled up by history of doctrine, or in terms of environing circumstances of 16th century church history, he is guilty of a lack of precisely that creative imagination before whose accomplishments one stands astonished.

By context, then, reference is made to that scope and substance of contemporary data within which the life of reflection as such occurs. When one reflects about anything, what is the ambience of everything within which such reflection has its life?

Most descriptions of cultural history of western reflection since the Enlightenment obscure the truth in efforts to disclose it. For they assume that the world-as-nature, following the work and thought of Galileo and Copernicus, has been the focal point of man's attention. In a secondary sense that is so; in a primary sense that is not so. For it is precisely the investigating, systematizing, describing, and ultimately the practical utilizing for man's purposes of the energies and processes of nature which permit, indeed invite, this misunderstanding. The central, operating factor in world-reflection since the Enlightenment has not been the world-as-nature; it has been, rather, the world-as-history as this world, with man its primary agent, has been instrumentally anthropocentrized in fact. That vast intellectual and investigative energies of post-Enlightenment man have gone into investigations of natural fact must not seduce us into the assumption that nature as such retains its actuality, force, fundamental life as the determining reality of modern reflection. Nature as the field of intellectual and instrumental operations is, indeed the focus, both as material for reflection and as productive of a methodology for reflection. But in this process nature as a primal reality is subsumed under *nature as resource for historical transformation.*

Modern anthropocentrism has arisen as a function of this vast accomplishment of man-as-history operating upon nature; the life of nature has been drawn up into the volitional and fatefully decisional life of man-as-history. It is within the whorls of man's fiercely expanding managerial activity as historical actor that nature presents itself to man for reflection.

But that man, in such a reflective life inclusive of rationalized, ordered, and used nature is really admitting the creation as such into his reflections—is a delusion. It is a fallacy to suppose that because we know about and think about atoms, genes, astrophysical space and organization we are thereby thinking about the creation. That fallacy arose out of the ironical fact that human exuberance about knowledge and control of aspects of nature has really nothing to do with nature-as-creation. And until we get this through our heads, and admit nature as the *creation* into our reflective nexus, and permit nature there to retain its intransigent reality, we shall neither theologize soberly or be theologically guided to act constructively. This theme will be reintroduced in a later section; at this moment some concrete illustration of the foregoing must be introduced.

> There is something wrong with our world view. It is still Ptolemaic, though the sun is no longer believed to revolve around the earth.
> We teach the past, we see further backward into time than any race before us, but we stop at the present, or at best, we project far into the future idealized versions of ourselves. All that long way behind us we see, perhaps inevitably, through human eyes alone. We see ourselves as the culmination and the end, and if we do indeed consider our passing, we think that sunlight will go with us and the earth be dark. We are the end. For us continents rose and fell, for us the waters and the air were mastered, for us the great living web has pulsated and grown more intricate.[1]

Is it not indeed true that the spacious realism of that paragraph has been muted almost into silence by the drama of man's historical accomplishments upon nature? And have not humanistic studies—which one might suppose capable of exposing this humorous and ironical diminishment of the nexus of human reflection—actually participated in the shrinkage? For these studies, too, anthropocentric and sometimes excruciatingly acute in their exposition of awareness, sensation and introspection, have invited the mind of modernity to fold itself inward upon its own and its fellows

cerebral and emotional past and present, and by the very virtuosity
of that accomplishment diminished the reality of unregarding and
ever persistent nature. The questions men ask (and in theology
the questions God puts!) are thus dealt with by a reflective capacity shrivelled by the very attentions which constitute its pride.

Let us suppose—as an exercise in creative imagination—that one
curiously unshrunk in primal humanity falls into reflection while
standing in the midst of a great, proud modern city. Its very form,
structure, vigorous systematic of production, communication, destruction is a microcosm of a triumphant technology fashioned
upon scientific knowledge as its base. And then let one suppose
that by catastrophe or plague all human life were in a moment
annihilated. Within decades all the piled up accomplishments of
man would fall into dissolution—rotted, fallen into debris, dissolved, their slowly disappearing remnants covered over by the
creeping greenness of a fecund and luxurious nature. Chartres
would become a squat mound with vines entwined about broken
fragments of interesting shapes, the Rembrandt canvasses soggy
strips of fungus-splotched fiber. And the waters of the man-defiled
Rhine, Hudson, Thames would run to the sea again sparkling and
clean, and their banks resound to the calls of the returning birds.

If, then, older ways of speaking of the trinity must be set aside
and new ways attempted in which an effort is made to relate
contemporary questions and the trinitarian affirmation, this effort
(as the topic correctly suggests) will require a fresh address of
trinitarian doctrine to the contemporary problems acknowledged
under the terms *creation* and *history*. Indeed, the very statement
of the topic whereby the discussion of the triune God is proposed
within the context of Presence and Acts indicates that what the
writer of this essay affirms as a necessity has not been unanticipated
as a theological possibility by those who have suggested it.

What follows is not a systematic theological effort in the traditional sense; for that we are not ready. The most that can be done,
given the convulsive character of contemporary changes, is to set
forth the problem by a description of what esem to be the principal components of it, to make an effort to discern how these
relate to and impact upon each other, and in ways that push
beyond accepted ways of thinking, reach speculatively for a deeper

relation between nature and grace and a broader frame of reference for those venerable terms.

The sections to follow do not add up to a conclusive argument; it is hoped that their cumulative force serves to specify what facts must be admitted to a properly complex statement of the issue: i.e., how may a gracious God be proposed as present and active for man?

THE SIGNIFICANCE OF THE TERM PRESENCE

The clock of actuality cannot be turned back: the vitalities that informed a culture of a previous time cannot be in their once-living form recovered, and sheer will cannot raise the dead. For that reason it is quite futile to speak in our time of the presence of God and Christ and the Spirit in theological or liturgical modes that, in another day, pointed to, conceptualized or symbolized the meaning of presence, and, to a degree, mediated it to men.

For it is a capital cultural fact of western life in our time that what the term presence has meant it no longer means, and the personal self-force it once specified and transmitted has been radically diminished in the entire complex of forces that constitute man's modernity.

Christian theology dare not declare that the power of God to be present to men is annihilated by men's difficulty in achieving "presence" among themselves! But neither can theology answer that proclamations of that possibility need not attend to the fundamental changes required in its concepts and language if the phrase "God Himself is Present" is again to be heard.

For the reality of personal presence has indeed undergone grave erosion. The specification of personal *meaning* in terms of personal *role*, the deepening absorption of individual, integral personal particularity in the work one does, the position he holds, the institutional relation his life is webbed in, the sheer thickness of the covering that buries his actual identity within his official identity —these are some of the elements that have created modern man's crisis of presence.

Out of this stifling personal diminishment and aloneness men long to emerge, and find themselves as persons-in-the-presence-of-persons. In fact, the very notion of personhood is not a possibility save in the presence of the other in whom and by whom a person is postulated into reality. One has only to relate a body of current cultural fact with another body of theological fact to secure the force of this judgment and gain insight into its meaning.

The cultural fact is illustrated by a leading motif of the lives of those who, since the close of World War II have come to maturity. In film, novel, dance, drama, verse, folksong and, in the churches, fresh forms of life-celebrative impromptu "liturgies," the ground-motif comes strongly and singly through. It is a powerful proclamation of the survival-necessity for life of personal presence, a lamentation of the hurt to life when this be not achieved and a celebration of the fulfilment glimpsed as distinctly possible if presence can be realized. Any effort to account for the startling breaking loose of sexual mores from traditional patterns which is content only to moralize about the phenomena is superficial. For in these relationships—and dramatically in the failures of them, which are creating an entire literature of pathos—as in the fresh realizations of "care and tenderness for persons" is clear evidence of a powerful reconstruction of lost presence which must be assessed as significant regardless of one's judgments about adequacy. What has been called "experimental transcendence"—whether by way of sex, rock-music-ecstasy, drugs, or exotic meditational techniques—is not an equivalent to the theological idea of the transcendent; but the data of the need is not unrelated to the theological issues which inform these essays.

The theological fact germane to reflection upon the contemporary crisis of presence can be gleaned from the extensive literature, Roman Catholic, Evangelical, Orthodox, which is being produced by the ecumenical discussion of inter-communion. Two foci characterize these essays and discussions. The first is a clearly felt necessity to ethicize the doctrine of the Eucharist in order that the social meaning, promise, bestowal, hope of the supper of the Lord may intersect in a direct way with the demonic personal and societal powers that distort and diminish human life. Those who direct their thought in this direction are neither naive about the tradition or merely romantic in their hope. They know the finite and limited character of all that pertains to man's historical exis-

tence, but insist that communion is an act that, while centered
in the community of faith, has its larger orbit of reference in the
worldly, the material, the social. It is an act of world and life
affirmation combined with an often sardonic clarity about the
meaninglessness that pervades, the recalcitrancies that resist, the
stupidities, evils, prides, structures of secure and affluent content-
ment that stand over against such a world re-ordering that might
engender hopeful sense amidst the terrors of human need as these
are made mockingly absurd by the wealth that is available to
ameliorate them.

The second focus of this discussion of intercommunion is the
effort to speak of the "presence" in the sacrament in such terms as
might intersect with and clearly address for faith's confession the
reality of Christ's presence amidst the broken or frustrated "false-
presence" that characterizes so much of human interaction—or the
absence of it. What is surprising, particularly among the young,
is the persistence of biblical and church-traditional fullness in their
expectations of the promise of Christ's presence. Neither biblical-
critical reformulation, nor demythologization, nor questions raised
for Christian knowledge of God by the historizing of epistemology,
nor the seduction whereby many sectors of the Christian community have been identified with economic ideologies and with
the "embourgeoisment" of society, nor anachronistic and largely
non-intelligible forms of worship—all of these have not in their
cumulative force been able to dim the haunting allure of the receding historical figure of Jesus on the night of Holy Thursday,
nor empty him of the force, judgment, and grace that he embodies.

The one who is the focus of the Christian reality stands today
not so much within piety as a presence "closer than hands and
feet" but as a strange presence made more a "real presence" by the
human diminishment and debacle of an "absence." This negative-
presence has a power of its own, for it destroys illusion about what
kind of presence will ultimately suffice for redemptive human communion. We are experiencing, to put the matter in another way,
the coming together of two realities (and in their collision and
interpenetration we gain insight into the first term of our title):
the power, allure, prophetic passion, whole-manhood of that immolated "outsider" Christ—and an "outsider" self-awareness of man

within an increasingly impersonal culture. The intersection of these realities is so many-dimensional, so rich in symbolical potential, so capable of the recovery of liturgical force in a language-disenchanted time, so deeply rooted in and engendering of hope, so transparent to the redemptive not-self, so serenely itself over against the homogenized or diluted identity of modern man, that presence, even as that term defies analysis, is nevertheless the term upon which must turn all speech about God in creation and in history.

The preceding paragraphs about presence places us properly before the next term—grace. The content of that presence, even when negatively envisioned, is certainly identical with the meaning of grace, the most comprehensive term the scripture uses for the reality of the presence and acts of the triune God. If presence and grace belong together, and if this presence and grace are to be confessed by men who have their existence within the realms of nature and of history—and if men of the 20th century experience their life in these realms in ways that are markedly and specifiably discontinuous with all previous human life—then nothing short of a restudy of the doctrine of grace can suffice to illuminate the relation of God to nature and history. It is to that effort that the following several sections will be addressed.

GRACE IN THE SCRIPTURES

It sometimes happens that a confessional viewpoint, or a conventional focus, or an habitual starting-point for theology, weighs so heavily upon thought that data which might open the familiar to the impact of the fresh is acknowledged in particular studies but ignored in more general reflections. Something like this seems to be the case with regard to the career of the concept of grace in evangelical theology. The familiar benediction phrase "The grace of the Lord Jesus Christ and the love of God . . ." is an epigram disclosive of a profound theological tendency: to understand the biblical speech about grace virtually exclusively under the rubric of the second article of the creed, and in so doing insulate the mind against the dimensions of the term which in Scripture permit no such restriction.

There are no exact Old Testament equivalents for the New Testament *charis*, but the fundamental meaning of the term as applied to Israel's God is absolutely clear. That clarity is only obscured when the Old Testament is read exclusively in the light of the New. For trinitarian formulations have begot a triadic sequence of creation, redemption, sanctification. Appropriate and useful as this triad may be in Christian theology, the application of it to the experience of Israel—and the more unconscious the more obscuring—pulls into wrong proportions the Old Testament way of understanding God, the place and scope of the goodness and power of God, and the implications of faith in him for the formal ethics of Israel and for her mode of life in its various cultic manifestations. For the magnetic and dominating central term, redemption, tends to draw about itself the meaning, presence and promise of God to Israel, which, in her own understanding, were disclosed to her in creation, in historical covenant, and in that interpretation of historical events whereby the fidelity of God to his people was known and celebrated.

The fundamental meaning of grace is the goodness of God and the activity of this goodness in and toward his creation. Israel knew God in that way, to be sure; but this knowledge is never specified in the sense of being identified with a term, or a concept, or a single action having an absolute primacy. The uncovenanted, pre-covenanted, will and disposition that does what it does from within itself (and then "covenants" to secure the reality of the doing)—the most common names for this are *Chen* and *Hesed*. The content of these terms shines through such passages as Exodus 33:17-19 and 34:6-7.

A feeling for the form and function of such statements, integral as they are to Israel's understanding of God, of how he manifests, rules, blesses and intends for his people, indicates that later large categories under which life was divided into life-as-nature and life-as-history are useless for grasping the structure of Israel's faith. Rather it must be seen that God is "the Holy One," that all that is, is given, and all that happens as event and process is to be related to his faithfulness in mercy and in judgment. This fidelity and presence is manifested in "the glory"; and nothing that is or happens is intrinsically incapable of refracting this glory. The "glory of thy people Israel" is the lens in the eye of faith through which all things—natural, personal, social, historical—were beheld. Nebuchadnezzar can be the strange agent of this glory; and the glory which "thou hast set above the heavens" is also declared *by* the heavens. Nature is not an entity or a process set along side of God and having its own autonomy, its own "insides," its "laws." It is rather continuous with the reality of God as Creator. This is not to say that for the man of the Old Testament God is knowable by *Naturwissenschaft*, just as God is not knowable by *Geisteswissenschaft!* God is made known to man in the matrix of space, time, matter—which are the substance of that mortal theatre in which God deals with his people in their historical actuality.

These comments about Israel are intended as a kind of background whereby what shall presently be said about the movement of New Testament testimony to Christ and the scope of his grace may be understood both in its Christ-concentration, and in its extent. For if the doctrine of the divine redemption there centered upon Christ is not assessed as moving toward the same spacial largeness as characterized the Old Testament celebration of the "space of the glory," such a movement will continue to be ignored or rejected in Christian theology, or regarded as marginal and esoteric.

If grace, as witnessed to in the New Testament, is to be proposed in fresh ways of address as actually the will and power of God in Jesus Christ for the redemption of men, and if the actuality of contemporary man's formation-as-man in virtue of his life-conditions and transactions with nature is to be taken seriously—then Christian theology must explicate a doctrine of grace in continuity with the Scriptures and in such bold and new reformulations as the reality of grace in its salvatory power demands.

To undertake that task of obedience is a large order placed upon the desk of the theologian; and the task falls with both particular inquiry and promise upon all who stand within the Lutheran tradition. The urgency does not require much amplification; when a tradition announces that its peculiar contribution to catholic Christendom is its clear and permeating witness to the freedom of God in his grace, and organizes its theological systematic around that proclamation, the urgency is in the tradition itself; and the promise lies in the evangelical insight that made it central there.

But even so tentative an essay as this one in that direction must specify some practical embarrassments as the task is undertaken. The chief one is this: the same confessional tradition which has been relentlessly acute and productive in biblical studies hesitates (particularly in such theological statements as emanate from its self-conscious Confessional Assemblies) to introduce the results of such studies into its theological schematizations and formulations. The same church whose scholars have contributed so richly to the clarification of the conditions within which the New Testament was written, the variety of its focus and terms of witness, the startling fecundity of its faith-responding speech and the vast reach of its vision and reference—has permitted highly stylized accents and motifs in the scripture to control its present as, in quite a different era in biblical scholarship, they controlled its past.

With no diminishment in gratitude for the past, and in the conviction that Lutheran centeredness upon grace is indeed proper and obedient, we must re-acknowledge with our fathers that formulations must follow the energies of realities, and that theology has a trans-biblical obligation to be exercised in that creative reflection to which reference has been made. And if such reflection is to be creative some responsible risks have got to be taken, some realities and meanings have got to be proposed for faith within, but not derived from, the ever changing formation of man within the convulsions and creativities of culture.

There is within the New Testament no single, or simple way of speaking of God and man and grace and history and the natural world. Indeed the New Testament witness to God and to Christ discloses a process, with the scriptures of Israel back of it and a variety of world situations in front of it, which can be characterized as a process of fusion, transformation, clarification.

Fusion means that elements disclosed in separated episodes are put together in fresh combination. Transformation means that the resultant motif is more and different from the sum of the components. Clarification means that what was partial, opalescent, potential in components thus fused becomes more full, transparent, and concentrated. That such a thing characterizes the New Testament is here argued; it is not the point at the moment to evaluate that happening.

The community that produced the New Testament did not undertake its task of witness to Christ with a full heart and an empty head—or fashion its statements with minds that were innocent of the substance, texture, referential opulence, or historical solidity of the terms, images, symbols of the people of the old covenant. They bore witness to Christ as the center and intention of all these; but the Christ to whom they bore witness was in continuity with the God of Abraham, Isaac and Jacob; and that this witnessing Christocentrism was intended as a modification of the theocentrism of the faith of Israel was a notion that would have been regarded as both incredible and blasphemous. When the community spoke of Christ's doing they were speaking of God's doing; when they cherished and transmitted his speaking they were reporting what they believed to be an address to them and through them of the reality of God. This faith, this continuity and this intention was, indeed, generative of a community that knew itself to be constituted by an event that was nothing less than a new form of the God-relationship; but the articulation of that new form at the same time testifies to the old in the very substance of its reportorial and testimonial language.[2]

Generations of scholarship have noted and specified the huge variety of the New Testament witness to Christ. And dogmatic response to that variety has very often been an imposition upon it of an order dictated by concerns foreign to the data—but creative of an hierarchy of importance by which the wilderness of the data could be given the neatness and sequence so satisfying to system. But the vitality of the variety continues to trouble the seeming solidity of the system. One tradition begins with the prophetic announcement in dramatic terms that the time of the kingly rule of God is imminent; another tradition sets the incomparable evaluation of the event of Christ within the birth stories; another sets the events it employs for the construction of its pattern within the vast matrix "In the beginning was the Word"—and thus *completes* the redemptive grace which is the burden of its message with the uncovenanted and covenanted grace of God in creation and in Israel's history.

Nor is this variety, or the conceptual magnificence of the Fourth Gospel, an aspect of the testimony to Christ that comes to us only in those literary forms that we know as the Gospels. In the Pauline and other voices of the first century there is a language of testimony, an articulation of vitalities and relations into concatenated forms that reach back historically into Israel's past, grope forward into the future, and impart an eschatological cruciality to the present eon.

Is it possible to speak of this variety in such a way as, on the one hand, to honor the warning against dogmatic "arrangement," and on the other, acknowledge that there is movement in this witness, that the referential amplitude is vastly wider in some voices than in others, that the vision of the meaning sweeps in some an arc whose circumference enfolds things near and clear and in others an arc whose axis is "before the foundation of the world" and whose out-riding reaches are ". . . the mystery of his will—a plan for the fulness of time, to unite all things in him, things in heaven and things on earth."

It is possible not only to remark these differences but to behold them as differences-in-motion. That motion is clearly not chronological; and efforts to make "high Christology" late and "low Christology" early in the community's recorded experience are clearly illegitimate. If then that "motion" was not chronological how may its nature and direction be designated? It is here proposed that christological momentum may be the most accurate term for what the literature of the New Testament discloses. Differences in the size of the circles of range and reference is clearly in the material, and the types of the rhetoric of celebration which these employ can be noted.[3]

As biblical and theological scholarship moves toward a more inclusive and precise formulation of the hermeneutical problem, more serious attention is being given to what theological implications inhere in style of speech, forms of rhetoric, as these come to us from the earliest Christian communities. The phrase "style of life," common among contemporary ethicists, is a reminder that there is an organic and integral *Gestalt* which is back of, down under, and formative of lived-experience and response, and is a force that escapes overly systematic efforts to specify and contain it.

The New Testament rhetoric about the epiphany and bestowal of the grace of God in Jesus is a way of speaking that displays a richness, a momentum, a blooming into expanding referents, a pushing outward of the dimensions of its fields of force. And while this essay cannot expand the point in any detail, the entire argument for a reassessment of the presence and acts of the triune God in creation and history demands that it be noted for further reflection. A tentative typology would certainly include the following.

1. There is a rhetoric of recollection. The witness to the incomparable grace of God known in Christ was not fashioned into ascription to Christ as if Israel had not existed. The rich and various vocabulary of Israel's hope in the promises of God is fused with, transformed and clarified into new and bold claims for Christ. And not only in the Gospels which remember in order to give force and continuity to what the community expressed—but also in the letters of Paul, and in other documents. This way of testifying—forward by remembering—backward is a rhetorical device of great power; the miracle story, parable, startling logion, passion-account, crucifixion-account—these are fused within and kerygmatically uncoiled from the historically attested realities of faith in God. And when the process is resisted the resisters are warned "you know neither the Scriptures nor the power of God."

2. There is a rhetoric of participation and reenactment. This type of speech invites christological reflection of a specifiable form. The sequence—obedience, suffering, death, resurrection and ascension of Jesus Christ—is modular *both* of the reality of alienation and its conquest by the grace of God. The morphology of this divine-human action is a "model" of redemption; and the reality of the Christian life is nothing short of a reenactment of the tensions and resolutions of it. God as the all-engendering Father, God as the absolutely obedient Son, God as the illuminating and empowering Spirit constitute one action—and redemption is reenactment. The vine and the branches, having a mind formed by the mind of the son, life in history as a recapitulation in human actuality of suffering, dying, rising—these are characteristic images of the process-working of the grace of God.

This "uncreated" grace from above, as love and forgiveness and empowerment begets responding life-as-grace; and how it forms man's residency among and evolution of all things within and around is illustrated in the final chapter of the Philippian letter. The grace of God whereby "Christ Jesus has made me his own" has its center in the will of God. But the center is not the circumference. The circumference of that grace is no smaller than the entire theatre of life and awareness and reflection—that is, the whole creation. The grace of God which ". . . came in Jesus Christ" is a "mighty working" of grace of the triune God who is also creator, sustainer, law-giver. But from the pinnacle of this grace manifested, as Luther loved to put it "in contrary sense and sight"—in the desolation and victory of Christ's immolated life, all things are to be seen, regarded as of God, evaluated, used, enjoyed, understood and received as fields of grace. And therefore, says the Apostle, ". . . all that is true, all that is usable, all that is just and pure, all that is lovable and gracious, whatever is excellent and admirable—fill your thoughts with these things."

3. There is a rhetoric of cosmic extension. Prefatory to a description of this type a general consideration must be introduced. As systematic theological reflection moves through historical time it must not only discard biblical literalism (and that battle is far behind us); it must also discard a subtle form of literalistic thinking which persists in what might be called "quantitative literalism." By that I mean a higher or lower regard for the power and implications of a theme according to the frequency of its presentation in the Scripture. The Christian reality is not separable from the Scripture, and it is not identical with nor limited to the Scripture. Theological reflection is in continuity with themes, records, episodes, teachings, etc. as these meet us in Scripture, and has in these its engendering and controlling norm. But hearing the Word and doing theology is an exercise in faithful reflection which, if it is to be intelligible, must partake of the dynamism of all historical, cultural, experiential life. In the evolution of man's biological form and capabilities across the millennia of time, nature probed in an infinite virtuosity of effort the possibility for higher forms—some abortive, some rich with phyla that did lead to higher forms. And

as from one strand among the very many, and that one not in its earlier stages notably different from others, fashioned the progenitors of man, so the christologies that emerged in the first several centuries, while certainly not "wrong," do not in their number or structure actualize all the potentialities that lie resident within the magnificent doxological witness of the community to Christ.

Theology always, to transform a statement of Goethe, in the need of the moment, seizes that which shall serve and bless it. Such a strand of early witness to Christ is here alluded to under the phrase of cosmic extension. That this theme is in the New Testament a tentative, probing theme, that, in some expressions, it seems to have been evoked by the gnostic, or another, heresy, that the theme has not been worked out with the systematic fulness that characterizes clearer and more amply attested christological images and ascriptions—all of this must be acknowledged. But it must also be insisted that the theme is a legitimate accent in the rhetoric of the earliest community, that its referential roots in the Scripture are deep, that confessional or other solid continuities dare not impose impediments to its scrutiny. The contours of need and interest in the long life of the people of God have time after time found contours of disclosure in the Scripture. St. Augustine's treatise on the Holy Trinity is no less admirable because we know the cultural crises that evoked it and gave to it the particular analogical form it has.

Ready at hand for the thought and language of the Christian community was the testimony of the people of the Old Covenant to the power and the scope of the reign of God. That it was both possible and necessary to gather up such affirmation into Christological reflection is not disputable; the ascription of Jesus as Lord demanded that. In Israel God-understanding and nature-understanding are not separable.

In his *Inspiration and Revelation in the Old Testament*, H. W. Robinson has the following paragraph:

> The Hebrew vocabulary includes no word equivalent to the word "nature." This is not surprising if by "nature" we mean "the creative and regulative physical world and as the immediate cause of all its phenomena." The only way to render this idea into Hebrew would be to say simply "God." We would

have to describe a particular physical activity through anthro-
pomorphic phrases such as the "voice" of God, heard in the
thunder; the "hand" of God felt in the pestilence; the "breath"
of God animating the body of man; the "wisdom" of God ultimately conceived as his instrument in Creation.[4]

Our modern view of nature as by definition not having anything
to do with the divine is in complete hiatus with the Old Testament
view. There nature comes from God, cannot be apart from God, is
capable of bearing the "glory" of God. And that is why the redemption of God is celebrated in prophetic visions of a restored nature.
For the realm of redemption cannot be dynamically conceived as
having a lesser magnitude than the realm of creation. The creation
as "fallen" is never permitted to exempt its form and creatures
and destinies from the great salvation.

As we turn to the Epistles for a type of Christological momentum which swings out to cosmic dimensions we are aware that we
are dealing with statements which, in Western Christology at least,
have remained marginal, if admitted at all, to the most influential
christological treatises. In the section to follow this one we shall
indicate the eccentric character of this development and propose
some speculations to account for it. But a preliminary task is to
face and put into proper perspective two common objections to
such attention as shall be given to sections of the letters to the
Colossians and to the Ephesians, where the type receives fullest
statement.

The first objection is the still unsettled problem of authorship
of both Epistles, and in the instance of the Colossians, the literary
integrity. This objection is legitimate but not crucial. It has the
greatest weight for those scholars whose purely textual work has
alienated them, or kept them from even having been interested in,
that entire process whereby documents achieve status in a tradition, or in the theological and historical importance of the fact that
such status has never been withheld from these letters. The theologian cannot, to be sure, formulate serious statements by scooping
up fragments from whatever he finds interesting in the milieu of
the early church. But he is also forbidden to permit open questions
of a technical nature to dash from his hand sources which have
indubitable standing in the tradition, have from the earliest times

been accepted as having apostolic authority, and whose substance is not severable from very powerful strands of patristic teaching, preaching and catechesis.

The second objection arises most commonly from those scholars who are aware of the gnostic influence against which the "cosmical" passages from the Colossians are likely addressed, and who, while admitting the scanty state of accurate knowledge of gnosticism, feel that these verses should be regarded as marginal to any theological employment of Paul's (or the church's) thought. And while the hesitation of such a position must be attended to, other facts have balancing weight. There is, first of all, the fact that the Christological scope of these verses is not esoteric within the body of the Epistles. The organic nature of the language and of the concepts is continuous with, although bold extensions of, central and repeated celebrations of the role and rule and scope of Christ's presence and power. And, secondly, the occasion for the statements —and this regardless of how clear or how problematical the gnostic incitement of them may be assessed—has really little to do with the substance of the argument. Occasions may explain why something is said as it is said to those to whom it is said. But clarity about occasions does not validate or invalidate substance.

If then it is granted that the gnostic heresy was the occasion for raising the issue of the scope of Christ's redemptive reign, and if our knowledge about the peculiar vocabulary of gnosticism provides the clue to the language of some parts of the epistles to the Colossians and to the Ephesians, some kind of systematic reply was required and these epistles supply it. The reply is clear, unambiguous and has a magnitude that matches the size of the issue. Galloway has a summary of the reply.[5]

> The implication of this teaching (gnosticism) places a limit on the work of Christ. It says in effect: Christ has redeemed us from Satan and from the spirits of the lower air. But are we still subject to the elemental powers beyond that? In other words, some doubt has arisen whether Christ's work really was cosmic in scope. (Note the implication of this heresy: That if it was thus limited, then something further was required for our complete redemption. . . .) The essence of the answer is the assertion that the work of Christ is universally effective for all creation. The demonic powers in all parts of the universe have

been 'disarmed' by Him (Colossians 2:15). . . . The argument
runs as follows: Christ is eternally pre-existent. (Col. 1:17),
therefore he has power over eternal spheres. He is the image
of the Father (Col. 1:15), and this ensures his supremacy over
all created things. He was actually the divine agent in the
creation of all these things (Col. 1:15-16). Therefore, His
redeeming work which has been declared ἐν πάσῃ κτίσει τῇ ὑπὸ
τὸν οὐρανόν is unlimited in its efficacy. Through him God chose
to reconcile all things, whether on earth or in heaven, through
him alone.

To appreciate what has been called a type of Christological
teaching that employs a "rhetoric of cosmic extension" we should
have the entire pericope before us.

> He rescued us from the domain of darkness and brought us
> away into the kingdom of his dear Son, in whom our release is
> secured and our sins forgiven. He is the image of the invisible
> God; his is the primacy over all created things. In him every-
> thing in heaven and on earth was created, not only things vis-
> ible but also the invisible orders of thrones, sovereignties,
> authorities, and powers: the whole universe has been created
> through him and for him. And he exists before everything, and
> all things are held together in him. He is, moreover, the head
> of the body, the church. He is its origin, the first to return from
> the dead, to be in all things alone supreme. For in him the com-
> plete being of God, by God's own choice, came to dwell.
> Through him God chose to reconcile the whole universe to him-
> self, making peace through the shedding of his blood upon the
> cross—to reconcile all things, whether on earth or in heaven,
> through him alone. (Colossians 1:13-20)[6]

How the scope of this claim, and its language of absolute inclu-
siveness, bear upon the issues of grace and nature, grace and
history, grace and the problematic of the modern self is to be the
matter for later discussion. What is required here is that we permit
this Christological affirmation to question, profoundly modify, open
to fresh dimensions of interpretation types of Christological thought
which have a less broad reference. For the range and interior reso-
nance of this doxological theology is astounding. Nothing less than
the vast orbits of natural structure and of historical process and
mystery constitute the far-circling of it. Even in these times, when
events have tightened human thought around the tormented center
of the meaning of personal existence—and when, consequently,

the church's Christology has focused about a radically existentialist interpretation of Christ the redeemer—this polyphonic hymn to the scope and energy of the divine redemption sounds to haunt the church's mind.

When in the doxology that marks the long and tortuous argument in the letter to the Romans, St. Paul gathers up the elements that enter into his reflections about the destiny of Israel under the fresh manifestation of God in the Gospel of Christ, the apostle does not really solve the problem—and the continuing history of this argument in the career of the church attests that. He thrusts the insoluble into the indisputable!—the recalcitrant historical fact that ". . . God has consigned all men to disobedience, that he may have mercy upon all." And the doxology that follows is the language of startled praise, a rhetoric of wonder before God's mercy and the puzzle of history that has the same magnificence as characterizes the Colossian rhetoric about grace and nature.

> O depth of wealth, wisdom, and knowledge in God! How unsearchable his judgments, how untraceable his ways! Who knows the mind of the Lord? Who has been his counsellor? Who has ever made a gift to him, to receive a gift in return? Source, Guide, and Goal of all that is—to him be glory for ever! Amen.

The eighth chapter of Romans is another occasion in which we see the conceptually insoluble gathered into a doxological affirmation in which elements that are resistant to logical penetration are fused together. The statement in verses 27f. that the spirit ". . . pleads for God's own people in God's own way,"—and cooperates for good with those who love God, is not a logical outcome of the mighty themes of the chapter; it is rather a remembering at the end of the insoluble only the unmerited fact that he who "did not spare his own Son" is one who in that action is to be trusted to "lavish upon us all he has to give." Then follows, not a fresh attack upon the issue, but a doxological celebration of the God who having done the central act will not ultimately have his love either frustrated or bounded by whatever meaninglessness persists in natural structures or historical mysteries.

> . . . and yet, in spite of all, overwhelming victory is ours through him who loved us. For I am convinced that there is

nothing in death or life, in the realm of spirits or superhuman powers, in the world as it is or the world as it shall be, in the forces of the universe, in heights or depths—nothing in all creation that can separate us from the love of God in Christ Jesus our Lord.

These instances from the Pauline manner and speech are not proposed as supportive of the substance of the Colossians hymn in 1:15-20, but as evidences that the scope of that passage shall not be thought marginal either to the Apostle's thought and range or to the imperial Christological momentum of which he is in other contexts capable. The entire axis from the "invisible God" to the repeated "all things" is unbroken. And the reality of that Godly-action, Christ, is declared present in, the agent of, the goal and meaning of literally all that is. The relational prepositions *in* him, *through* him, *for* him are here constitutive of a Christological claim that stretches out endlessly in time, space, effectual force. The reality of Christ as the focal-point for world and life meaning is sunk back into the "invisible God," is that energy whereby "all things hold together," and is proposed forward into the yet uncut pages of historical life as God's purpose and power "to reconcile to himself all things."

The "systematic" of this energy as it may be proposed as conceptually apposite to our time, with its radically new understanding of nature and its excruciatingly acute historical consciousness, is a task that must be taken up in the following sections of this essay. But in order that the clarity of the claim shall not rest upon too narrow a formulation in the New Testament witness the language of another document must be heard.

The salutation to the letter to the Ephesians, as in every Pauline or probably Pauline epistle, fuses into a unity what older dogmatic treatises differentiated by the terms "created" and "uncreated" grace. But grace is single. Its source is "God the Father," its historical agent and embodiment is "the Lord Jesus Christ," and its gift and work is "Grace to you and peace." (In 2 Timothy, "Grace, mercy, and peace").

To relate style of speech to the task of understanding is an often neglected component of exegesis. Chapter 1:2-14 in the Ephesian epistle is a passage whose very structure demands that this component be considered as somewhat more than the idiosyncracy of interpretation by those peculiar persons who attend to rhetoric as an art. For the sheer fecundity of the reality of grace in these verses creates a syntax and a diction to serve its abundance, and a rhetoric to resonate to its richness in unity. The concatenation of phrases, as each within the ordering mind of the writer begets clauses to amplify its reference, is astounding even for one accustomed to and sometimes impatient with the Pauline style. The English translations commonly break up the rushing momentum of the Greek text; but such a convenience does little to check the felt-unfolding of the single massive fact of grace as it multiplies celebrative clauses to adore and proclaim the mystery.

> Grace to you and peace from God our Father and the Lord Jesus Christ. Praise be to the God and Father of our Lord Jesus Christ, who has bestowed on us in Christ every spiritual blessing in the heavenly realms. In Christ he chose us before the world was founded, to be dedicated, to be without blemish in his sight, to be full of love; and he destined us such was his will and pleasure—to be accepted as his sons through Jesus Christ, that the glory of his gracious gift, so graciously bestowed on us in his Beloved, might rebound to his praise. For in Christ our release is secured and our sins are forgiven through the shedding of his blood. Therein lies the richness of God's free grace lavished upon us, imparting full wisdom and insight. He has made known to us his hidden purpose—such was his will and pleasure determined beforehand in Christ—to be put into effect when the time was ripe: namely, that the universe, all in heaven and on earth, might be brought into a unity in Christ. . . . In Christ indeed we have been given our share in the heritage, as was decreed in his design whose purpose is everywhere at work. For it was his will that we, who were the first to set our hope on Christ, should cause his glory to be praised. And you too, when you had heard the message of the truth, the good news of your salvation, and had believed it, became incorporate in Christ, and received the seal of the promised Holy Spirit; and that Spirit is the pledge that we shall enter upon our heritage, when God has redeemed what is his own, to his praise and glory.

The subject of the pericope is God. The substance of the affirmations is the work of Christ. The intention of that work is to the "purpose" and "counsel" of God's "will" and "pleasure." The theatre of the action is "when the time was ripe." The *telos* ". . . that the universe, all in heaven and on earth, might be brought into a unity in Christ." And the leit-motif of the passage, which twice gathers all together upon a plateau of *praise,* breaks again loose to magnify and clarify the action in fresh ascription, and comes to its target and summation in the third repetition—"to the praise of his glory."

The manner and the matter are one. The graciousness of the structured strophes seem to form their sonorous rhythms from the awesome grace they declare. And if the bordering phrase "praise of his glory" seems to modern ears too vaporous to control the great song, that fault lies in us and not in the phrase. For if the clear, powerful, absolute meaning of "the glory" strikes no comprehending fire there may be some relation between that failure and the apostle's later word in chapter four where we read

> This then is my word to you, and I urge it upon you in the Lord's name. Give up living like pagans with their good-for-nothing notions. Their wits are beclouded, they are strangers to the life that is in God, because ignorance prevails among them and their minds have grown hard as stone. (Ephesians 4:17-19)

The implicit Christology of this hymn to grace goes in unbroken sequence from the purpose of God "who has bestowed on us in Christ every spiritual blessing in the heavenly realms" to those communities in concrete historical places where men by the Holy Spirit have "heard the word of truth" and by faith live on acknowledging life "in all insight and mystery." This acknowledging community is the body of Christ who is its head. And when, later, a conceptualization of the scope of grace was compelled to give dogmatic precision to these organic images of the energy of grace operating in so wide a range, nothing short of the dogma of the Holy Trinity was adequate to set it forth.

We began this section with the assertion that there are within the New Testament types of rhetoric which can be specified, and that such a specification is useful for correction in view of a dogmatic tradition that has not always attended with equal gravity to each of them. It is now necessary to look at but one moment in the development of the doctrine of grace and see something of the persistence and proportion of these types in that long career.

In the following section of this essay the intention is to describe and emphasize a particular strand of the developing doctrine of grace. The intention is to restore a proportion, not to establish a dominance. Such reflection upon the rich and various elements, movements, leading motifs and receding interests is a constant task of historians of dogma. It may, indeed, be the greatest contribution of this discipline to constructive theology that it engages in such reflection, over and over again, pondering the long story from the perspective of each moment in the church's life. For such reflection discloses how intimately related are the thoughts in men's minds and the circumstances of their bodies! Out of this plentitude of possibility a time draws forward now this, now that—thrusts one aspect of a manifold theme aggressively forward and permits other aspects, equally venerable and well attested, to fall into the background.

Every historian of doctrine has observed that the development of Christian thought is not of equal force and creativity along an entire front. Thought does not move like a wave at full crest. Its movement is rather like that of a slow incoming tide that reaches forward along an uneven beach—pushing forward into low places with long probing fingers. And these low lying or mounded contours are what they are by the working of historical forces which it is the task of research to isolate and describe. The political involvements of a particular people at a particular time in a particular place, the emergence of a single strong person to a position of leadership, a theological position stressed into dominance by the chance congruity of that doctrine with a regnant political position— these and a hundred other influences have a part in the shaping of the undulating life of doctrinal development.

And while, to be sure, there are those who resist the admission of such fortuitous forces as an embarrassing modification of the presidency of the Holy Spirit over the thoughts and practice of the church, such resistance must finally give way before the facts. Nor is this acknowledgment of historical force an abandonment of the integrity of Christian doctrine in its development, or a dismissal of the working of the Spirit. It is rather the coming to effective maturity in historical consciousness of what it really means that God discloses his will in history, that the Word really becomes flesh, that the Word of God and the word, and works, and always mixed intentions and protestations of men, exist in a mortal relationship.

If then in the pages that follow we shall be selectively attentive to a few figures in the history of doctrine, stress a single theme as it sounds in concert or even dissonance with others, the intention of the essay must be the defense of the practice. For if, quietly present but available within the story of Christian thought there is a christological pattern that has very special power for the life of both faith and culture in this moment, it is both right and good to draw it forth and propose it for reflection.

CHRISTOLOGY, GRACE, AND A PATRISTIC MODEL

Between the material to which we have thus far been attending and a constructive section to follow, the present section has a clear and urgent task: to recognize that the traditional scope of christological understanding is under pressure to achieve vaster amplitude in virtue of contemporary man's apprehension of the world-as-nature, and further, to enquire if the doctrine of grace does not also require a way of proclamation which shall be correlative with self and world understanding. In order to give sequence and concreteness to my reflections on these matters I shall recapitulate the theological course whereby I came to ask the question.

For many in this generation of theologians the Faith and Order movement has been a kind of ambulatory post-graduate school! For in the conferences, committees, reformulating tasks of that group all regional, parochial, even world-confessional traditions are subjected to two forces: a) a vigorous and incessant criticism from the broad spectrum of traditions there ably represented and b) the steady necessity to state, in such terms as might transcend the interior structure and vocabulary of each tradition, the substance and forms of one's own. After some years of participation in dialog of such vigor and unity-seeking intention one's mind becomes aware of a triple-process at work: confidence in the comprehensiveness of all theological formulations is relativized; motivation

toward fresh forms of theological discourse in recognition of powerful cultural changes is energized; and conviction about the endur-
ing and incomparable realities of the Christian faith is solidified.

In such a situation one learns to be wary of sentences which
begin "There is only one way . . .", or ". . . the central and persisting teaching of the Church (on this or that topic) is clear . . ." or
". . . from the earliest times Jesus has been regarded as," etc. The
Christological ascriptions in both New Testament and theological
reflection resist report under any general statement that can claim
ecumenical plenitude or common authority.

It was the heightened participation of Orthodoxy in the conver-
sations of Faith and Order which first turned my attention to
aspects of New Testament words about the grace and the lordship
of Christ which, muted or ignored in entire ranges of western
Christology, have been enormously formative of both theological
position and piety in the churches of the East.

If one were to analyze to its roots the theological embarrassment
that has occurred within ecumenical encounters because of Orthodox participation, one must be careful not to stop at surface factors.
Almost a thousand years of theological, ecclesiastical, even personal alienations have begotten a strangeness that proclaims itself
in personal bearing, liturgical forms, ceremonial mores, exegetical
style, etc. But underneath, and absolutely pervasive of the two
styles—Eastern and Western—is a different way of speaking about
the work of Christ. In the West that work is centered upon redemption from sin; in the East it is centered upon the divinization of
man. In the West the doctrine central to that work is atonement;
in the East the central doctrine is participation, illumination, reenactment, transformation. In the West the work of Christ is spoken
of chiefly as restoration, in the East the work is reunification. The
Western *Savior* is the Eastern *Pantocrator*. The Western corpus is
the Eastern *Christus Rex*. The Western representation of Christ is
Dürer, Grunewald, Rembrandt, Roualt and a thousand others who
center upon the oblation in the passion of Christ. These are
matched in the East by the iconography in mosaic, in fresco, in
panel-icon by the known and unknown artists, Byzantian, Russian,
and others in which the serene and cosmos-ruling Christ is acknowledged in the heroism of the figures of the saints. The reality

of this heroism is not different in the two—but the style and visage and mien of the figures is almost totally different. In the West these figures speak of a rescue from sin, mortality, aberration. In the East this rescue is ontologically total; the realization of restored being bestowed by the transformation of grace is manifest in the strong docility, the passionless visage of absolute serenity. Since Harnack, who understood this "stillness" as death, this docility as debility, and this serenity as a defect in personal identity, the West has not known how to understand energy in any form or attitude save motion and activity.

Two paragraphs, the first elaborating the Johannine life-mingling participation in Christ, the second elaborating the theme of cosmic harmony in virtue of the whole creation as brought within the effectual compass of redemption, are here selected. Both are from St. Gregory of Nyssa—and both illuminate the differences in East and West to which we have alluded.

> Let no one accuse us of seeing two Christs or two Lords in the one Saviour. But God the Son, who is God by nature, Lord of the universe, King of all creation, the Maker of all that exists and the Restorer of what has fallen, has not only deprived our fallen nature of communion with Him, but in His great bounty He has deigned even to receive it again into life. But He is Life. Therefore, at the end of centuries, when our wickedness had reached its height, then in order that the remedy might be applied to all that was diseased, He united (lit., 'mingled') Himself with our lowly human nature, He assumed man in Himself and Himself became man. He explains this to His disciples: "Ye in Me, and I in you" (John 14:20). By this union He made man what He Himself was. He was the Most High; lowly man was now elevated. For He who was the Most High had no need of being elevated. The Word was already Christ the Lord. But that which is assumed becomes Christ and Lord.[7]
>
> Since He is in all, He takes into Himself all who are united with Him by the participation of His body; He makes them all members of His body, in such wise that the many members are but one body. Having thus united us with Himself and Himself with us, and having become one with us in all things, He makes His own all that is ours. But the greatest of all our goods is submission to God, which brings all creation into harmony. Then every knee shall bend in heaven, on earth, and under the earth, and every tongue shall confess that Jesus

Christ is Lord (Phil. 2:10). Thus all creation becomes one body, all are grafted one upon the other, and Christ speaks of the submission of His body to the Father as His own submission.[8]

What is remarkable in that paragraph, so characteristic of Orthodoxy, is the way in which the confession that *Jesus Christ is the Lord* gathers about itself images of the divine energy. This gathering, incohering divine energy is testified in the strongly active verbs—he *takes into himself*, he *makes them members*, he *makes his own all that is ours*. The starting-point of this theology, as has been remarked and carefully worked out by Professor Charles Moeller, is the efficacious and divinizing presence of Christ in the world and in the church. The classic aphorism in Greek Patristic asserts:

> Whoever is not assumed is not saved. . . . This doctrine, absolutely common to the whole Christian Church has taken a particular form in the theology of Gregory Palamas, who has had great prominence in the Orthodox tradition since the XV Century. His distinction between the essence and the divine uncreated energies is probably unfamiliar to us. . . . What interests us here is the meaning this construction takes on in the theology of grace. The choice of terms "uncreated energies" stresses that God reveals himself by acting, which excludes all "passion" from God; but as the energies are "uncreated" there can be no question of making them the fruit of man's merit in any way at all.[9]

A citation from Palamas will now be better understood.

> Since the Son of God, through his inconceivable love for men has not only united his divine hypostasis to our nature, and taking a living body and a soul endowed with intelligence, appeared upon earth and lived among men, but even, O wondrous miracle!, unites himself to human hypostases, and fusing himself with each believer by communion of his sacred Body, becomes concorporeal with us and makes us a temple of the whole divinity, for the plentitude of the divinity dwells corporeally in Him (Col. 2:9), how does He not enlighten, by surrounding them with light those who participate in it worthily, as He enlightened even the body of the disciples on Thabor? Then, indeed, this Body possessing the source of the light of grace was not yet fused with our bodies; He enlightened from without those who approached worthily and sent

light into their souls through their bodily eyes. But today He is fused with us, He lives within us, and naturally, enlightens our soul from within. . . . Only one can see God . . . Christ. We must be united to Christ—and with what an intimate union!—in order to see God.[10]

It has not, however, been only by the instigation of Orthodox participants that Faith and Order has come to attend to what, in Section 3, pp. 106-107 above was called a Christology of cosmic extension. Against powerful theological forces upon a Christocentrism that would confine the reality of grace to the rubric of redemption alone, Gustaf Wingren has been a leading advocate of a broader understanding. His work on Irenaeus has been influential; and the focus of that influence can be specified at two points.

The first is Irenaeus' way of interpreting the meaning of Adam and as Christ the second Adam. This interpretation has had a strangely alluring impact upon many modern theologies for a reason that is quite clear: it opens a centuries old and doctrinally solidified anthropology to the impact of modern evolutionary and developmental fact and thought.

Adam, Irenaeus says, was created by God in God's *Imago* and *Simultudo,* and was put into God's creation by the same God who sent Christ into the world. Like Paul he plays out the strong contrast between Adam and Christ. But whereas in the prevailing western theology after Irenaeus the fall of Adam was stressed almost exclusively, Irenaeus fastens attention upon what Adam was created *for!*—to live, body and soul, in accordance with God's will. By virtue of this accent upon the possible divine intention for man, what is stressed between Adam and Christ was not their separation but their connection.

Christ was the pattern upon which God created man. Christ is the man about to be—the *homo futurus.* While all things were being formed Christ was in the mind of God, and all things have within themselves this intention: "For this reason the Son also appeared in the fullness of time to show how the copy resembles him."[11]

Adam as the child is the dramatic figure Irenaeus uses to give concreteness to his interpretation. For man to be unsaved means to remain undeveloped; salvation is maturation and fulfilment.

Christ is called and is man's Savior because in him man is shown what maturation is, called to be nurtured into it—to grow up into the form of the Son. The healthy, newborn child, says Irenaeus, while unable to talk possesses every likelihood of being able to do so. An injury may, to be sure, prevent the development. And this is the situation of Adam in the world. He is a child, created in the image of God. That he lacks something is not due to sin. No injury has yet happened to the child. Uninjured he is yet a child; he does not realize what he is yet to be. All the while, however, there is already in creation one who is the full image of God, the Son.

In such a teaching, apparently naive and simple as it is, we find a pattern that is capable of relating Christology and evolutionary- and history-drenched anthropology. And the teaching is not idiosyncratic; it has profoundly shaped the fundamental operational concepts of a huge community of Christian believers.

A second influential focus in the teaching of Irenaeus is the large place he gives to the New Testament notion of *anakephaliosis,* and the quite systematic extension it receives in his hands. In this treatment the parallel, contrast, and connection of the two Adams is central; but a "way of thinking" about the relation of God, the grace of God, and man's condition as a part of the natural world does not remain confined within the terms of the image. What begins as a "process-soteriology" originated by grace and fulfilled in recapitulation, participation, and reenactment unfolds into something approaching a Christian ontology.

Fr. E. Mersch describes Irenaeus' use of the term as follows:

. . . By the word recapitulation as applied to Christ Irenaeus means a sort of recommencement in the opposite direction by which God, reversing, as it were, the process whereby sin infected the earth, gathers together and reunites all creation, including matter, but especially man, in a new economy of salvation. He gathers up His entire work from the very beginning, to purify and sanctify it in His Incarnate Son, who in turn becomes for us a second stock and a second Adam. In Him, the first Adam and all his posterity are healed; the evil effects of disobedience are destroyed and as it were reversed by their contraries. Man recovers the holiness which was his at the beginning and he is divinized by union with the God from whom he came. As we see, the term presents many meanings: a résumé, a taking up of all since the beginning, a recommence-

ment, a return to the source, restoration, reorganization and
incorporation under one Head. But these meanings are all related; in spite of their diversity they fit into one another, and
even when expressed singly, each one suggests all the others.[12]

It is, I think, significant that the more deeply the contemporary
church searches tradition as well as exercises her current mind
toward a Christological understanding having a formal and sub-
stantial largeness appropriate to man's rootedness biologically and
culturally in the natural world, and, as a correlative effort ponders
grace as a Godly power whereby to assess and sanely deal with
science-born technology—the more lively is the church's attention
to the figure of Irenaeus.

The studies of Faith and Order disclose a deepening and expanding effort precisely in the direction of the nascent images of Irenaeus. In the decade 1930-1940 concentration was on the nature of
the church. A notable address by Bishop A. Nygren at Lund in 1951
turned those investigations toward *Christ and the Church* as a fresh
study that continued for an entire decade. And since New Delhi in
1961 the central topic, now significantly enlarged, has been *Christ,
Church and World.*[13]

An examination of the studies that preceded and attended the
Vatican II council of the Roman Catholic church discloses a re-
awakened attention, not only to Irenaeus, but to the possibilities
inherent in a theological method operating less with faith-proposi-
tion and more with such energies of faith as are specified by the
congruity and mutual energizing of organic images.

A CONSTRUCTIVE EFFORT

The preceding sections of this essay do not, as they stand, add
up to a constructive direction for such fresh theological formulations as the first paragraphs affirmed to be necessary. All that has
been accomplished is, one hopes, a breaking open of the possibility
for such an effort, and an indication of data in biblical images,
and in one patristic figure, of neglected but recoverable lives of
reflection. It is now necessary to suggest, with space-imposed
brevity, what some of such directions might be. This will be done
under four topics:

Modernity: Its Demand upon Theological Formulations

By modernity one means many facts and forces. But no catalog of these could exclude the following: life as dynamic, in-motion, developmental. Progress is a moot question; change is not. From astrophysics to gene-mutation the evidence is conclusive: there is no such thing as a steady-state. For all realms of knowledge, all exercise of projection and hope, all conceptions of a "usable past" are presently penetrated by this mind and feeling.

Man gains power by knowledge of the structure and processes of the world as nature. It is inevitable that that kind of knowledge, and refinement of the methods of its increase, should grant prestige, even domination to reflective and operational modes of the human. And precisely that in its permeative influence is at the heart of modernity's spirit and practice. My late colleague, Professor Joseph Haroutunian, put the point crisply—and pointed out its intersection with the traditional doctrines of grace.[14]

> The traditional paradox of grace and freedom has become academic. When a man sets out to achieve a given good, he looks for suitable means to do it, and "grace," the favor and agency of God, is not one of them. What a man needs is a certain combination of knowledge, skill, opportunity, power, and the freedom to make use of them. No man will trust his good to grace, and no man will question his freedom provided he has ability and is not prevented from using it. . . . When we are able to do what we will, we know ourselves as free, and when we are free, we need no grace. When we are unable to achieve our ends, we do not turn to a supernatural power but try to devise some new means that will give us success. Failure is a call, not to prayer, but to renewed calculation and effort. If success appears beyond our reach, we prefer to "accept the facts" rather than resort to "faith" which savors of superstition. If a miracle were to give us the success we seek, we should be greatly surprised and even discomfited. Hence, grace as supernatural or divine power is not what we live by, and freedom, the opportunity to act, has nothing to do with it. . . . Our way of life is not conducive to faith in God's power. It is no longer natural or rational for the human mind to meditate upon nature as a scene of good and evil emanating from a power or powers beyond man's knowledge and control. Given our physical and biological sciences, our experimental methods and mathematical explanations, together with our miraculous and extensive suc-

cesses in manipulating nature and creating a second world of artifacts that dominate our effective environment—given all this, there is something incongrous about talking of power of God. . . .

If, then, man has his hand upon sources of enormous strength whereby to understand, analyze, manipulate, transform, all traditional language about sin, guilt, pride, grace, redemption must be addressed to the peculiar predicament of that man in his perilous strength. This does not imply that his predicaments are not as profound and as destructive as ever, or that his sin is less; it does imply that the word of judgment and of grace must be spoken to his actuality in that perplexed strength, which is rich in both disaster and promise.

Operational Man: His Demand upon the Location and the Scope of Grace

The largeness and depth of man's operational and effective sphere of knowledge and working is not a one-way traffic whereby man's mind transforms nature: the operating-self has redefined itself in the process. To the several generalities our fathers have proposed as designative of man's uniqueness—*Homo faber, Homo politicus, Homo sapiens, Homo ludens*—must now be added another. Millions of contemporary men, as empirical evidence attests, think of themselves as *Homo Operator!* Theological certainty that this is a banal error as an ultimate judgment must not blind the theologian to the requirement the error imposes upon proposals of the truth. The philosophical and spiritual superficiality of the assumption in the error is a negative way of pointing to a positive requirement.

When man knows as a good the sphere of his life-operations, the range of the work of his hands, the satisfactions he feels in discovery, accomplishment, disclosure, fresh and exciting constructions, and when he knows that realities of his nature are drawn toward joy, creativity and fulfillment in these ways of thought and life, he has come upon an important element in his constitution as a man. And the theological requirement of this anthropological fact is clear: the grace of joy and creativity, the realm of goodness and life enchantment there experienced, the sense of a self-transcending engagement with the mystery and allure and power of the world-as-creation refuses to be negated in its relation to the realm of redemption. In this is disclosed the necessity to speak of the Triune God and his grace in a way that breaks out of a Protestant disposition to confine the reality of grace to the second article. Grace came by Jesus Christ, has in him its absolute embodiment, incandescence, historical presence and agency—but grace was not created by Jesus Christ. Men beheld him—and said, *Immanu-el!*

Both nature and history are neutral and mute as regards God and meaning. But life and experience and prehensions within nature and history can become occasions where the absolute grace of the divine redemption is postulated as the truth and meaning of the divine creation. Israel's faith produced Deuteronomy before it produced Genesis; and that sequence is not without importance: that which is salvatory for men cannot be adequately acknowledged as other or less than the Creator of the world. The scope of lordship dare not be specified as less than the scope of creation. The divine redemption by grace cannot assess the realm of grace to be discontinuous with the world as creation.

Precisely in the ambiguity of the gracious presence of God in nature and history is the generative power of it. For love that promises but does not suffice is a negative testimony to a possibility; glimpses that lure but do not focus into clarity and final satisfaction constitute a witness by the pathos of their partiality; meanings that slip and slide with mercurial elusiveness amidst the patterns of history form a mind and a sensibility that can neither dismiss them as of no worth nor combine and accumulate them into the solidity of certainty. Is it not perhaps the strange symbolic power of the Ingmar Bergman films that they explore this theme in a contemporary medium? That God is the transcendent mystery behind the world; that his grace is not redemptively given in the love and laughter of men; that he is given only as we receive his sovereign love through the shattering of the human world, including the love and laughter of men—this holy presence cannot be articulated under the rubric of law but only under such a term as the premonitory prehension of grace.

Not only is it true that a dynamic interpretation of the doctrine of the Trinity moves toward such a specification of the forms and occasions and realms and works of grace as these are proper to the persons and the functions of the Trinity *as such*, but this effort, although not evident in the Lutheran theological work, is an important item for many contemporary theologians.

Among contemporary theologians who have reformed the issue of grace, Karl Rahner has brought to the task the most impressive strength and the most varied approaches. His stance within the Roman Catholic tradition makes him heir to the richness of patristic and scholastic thought. He is aware of the changing formation of awareness in modern selfhood. And his effort to read according to their intentions the teachings about grace of the Reformation and post-Reformation Protestant theologians is open and sympathetic.[15]

Theological criticism, with Rahner, is always but an aspect of a constructive and fresh argument. And often the new substance lies so meekly under the ponderous prose that seems on the surface to be but a restatement of one or another item of traditional positions, that the explosive new direction, or freshly perceived relations, can remain unnoticed. Caution may devise a manner to mask its fresh advances!

The full argument of Rahner is impossible even to summarize in brief compass; the point at which his accent sets him off from most of his "standard" Roman Catholic colleagues is, however, quite clear and can be briefly stated. Speaking of the "standard view of the subject" he writes:

> Super-natural grace is a reality which we know about from the teaching of the Faith, but which is completely outside our experience and can never make its presence felt in our conscious personal life. We must strive for it, knowing as we do through faith that it exists, take care (through good moral acts and reception of the sacraments) that we possess it, and treasure it as our share in the divine life and the pledge and necessary for life in heaven. But the conscious sphere in which we experience ourselves is not itself filled by this grace.[16]

Grace, then, is commonly thought of as ". . . a superstructure above man's conscious spiritual and moral life," and the relationship between nature and grace is envisioned as two layers laid one on top of the other. And for this reason it is not difficult to understand why, within a growing understanding of the organic and totality-understanding of man ". . . this grace is not present where man is present to himself, in his immediate self-awareness." [17]

In other essays Rahner has pointed out that all truth cannot be less than the truth that specifies one's being. There is therefore not only a requirement placed upon the proclamation of grace from within self-awareness, but also a recognition that grace, proclaimed and received, alters the structure of human consciousness. The spiritual horizon or light in which one experiences individual objects and *Gestalts* is illuminated by God's self-communication. This is what is meant by revelation even if no new conceptual object is presented to the mind.

Speaking of the issue from another angle, and in a way congruent with the suggestion above concerning grace as a proper divine energy of the Trinity as such, Rahner writes,

> If grace and glory are two states of the one process of divinization, and, as classical theology has always held, in glory God communicates himself to the supernaturally elevated created spirit in a communication which is not the *efficient* causal creation of a creaturely quality or entity distance from God, but the quasi-formal causal communication of God himself, then this can also be applied to *grace* much more explicitly than it commonly has been in theology up till now. "Uncreated grace" will then no longer be regarded as merely the consequence of the creation of "infused" grace, constituting the state of grace, as a "physical accident"; but rather as the very essence of grace (which also explains much better how grace can strictly be a mystery, for a purely created entity as such can never be an absolute mystery). God communicates himself to man in his own reality. That is the mystery and the fullness of grace. From this the bridge to the mystery of the Incarnation and the Trinity is easier to find.[18]

Although in the essay cited Professor Rahner does not enlarge upon the implications of the statement that "grace and glory are two states of one process" such enlargement is quite possible. Indeed, it is likely that theology may be unable intelligibly and effectually to propose a doctrine of grace that shall be useful to practical human understanding and obedience short of a radically fresh conceptualization of the doctrine of the Trinity. For that doctrine, while formally affirming that the life and energy of each person of the Trinity is the function of all, it is in fact commonly understood so as to enclose the giftedness and power of grace within the second person. The realm of redemption is so dominantly the realm of grace that the presence grace of God the creator in and through his creation as also a realm of grace is muted.

And the Spirit? Here, too, the ministrations of the Spirit are commonly given content by primary reference to his work as transmission and illumination of the grace of the second person. And certainly Rahner's statement about "a bridge to the mystery of the Trinity" invites one to ask if the Spirit's illumination of man's spirituality is not so common, immediate and evident a theatre of grace as to suggest that a phenomenological way of elaborating the church's intention in the ancient doctrine might be a necessity for our time.

The following citation is even more fascinating with reference to such a fresh formulation.

> . . . The order of grace and the Incarnation both depend on a free gift of God. But does it follow that these two objects of his free gift, in both of which he communicates his very self to man (although of course in different ways) are *two* acts of his loving freedom? Isn't it possible (on Catholic principles) to hold with the Scotists that the original act of God (which settles everything else) is his emptying of himself, Love giving up himself, in the Incarnation, so that with the Incarnation the order of grace is already *there* and without this decision of God to give up himself it would be quite inconceivable? And who can produce fully convincing arguments to refute the man who holds that the *possibility* of the Creation depends on the *possibility* of the Incarnation, which is not to say that the reality of the Creation (as nature) necessarily involves that the Incarnation should happen. If this is accepted (its very simplicity recommends it even apart from other more positive indications, e.g., pre-Nicene and pre-Augustinian Logos-theology), then grace takes on a much more radically christological character; the incarnate word come into the world is not only the actual mediator of grace through his merit (which is only necessary because Adam lost this grace), but by his free coming into the world he makes the world's order of nature his nature, which presupposes him, and the world's order of grace his grace and his milieu.[19]

A final consideration (which does not strictly belong under this section unless one includes under "operational" forces the more revolutionary biblical criticism) arises out of the hermeneutically sharpened problem of extruding "confessional statements" from the Scripture. The event of Jesus Christ is the clarification of God, and as such the proclamation of grace. That event is given its rootedness and content in Israel's faith and hope, in the life, words, deeds, and the death and resurrection of Jesus Christ "by the glory of the Father."

But the entire context from out of which and by means of which this content emerges into history is riddled with questions: there is the stubborn fact (although only stubborn from a Christian point of view) that the faith of the people of the ancient covenant remains a living and authentic faith while repudiating the Christian claim that fulfillment of God as grace is given only in Christ. There is the further probability of no historical or other road to the clear and certain knowledge of the "intention" of Jesus. What seems most clearly established is that that intention is most authentically displayed in the eschatological act for and message about the kingdom of God. But even that relative clarity but exacerbates the problem. For "the eschatological" expressed in an earlier period of thought in terms of temporal and historical relations of the world to God, is simply not translatable into the mind of an era that lives ever more consciously out of notions of beginnings, developments and transformations, ascribes primal agency to nature, and understands destiny as a secret folded within the coils of human history.

There follows inevitably a process of demythologization of the "event" into the various lines of subjectivity—and this is followed (and this process is already well advanced) by such a remythologization of the event as shall move in dimensions of inquiry which are also cosmic in scope. Because men's minds follow the fortunes of their bodies with absolute seriousness, the moon-explorations have a premonitory symbolic significance for Christian theology. Men seek answers that are correlative in scope to the magnitude of their questions. Theologians may reject this expansion of the scope of men's questions, but such rejections are counter-productive for my children who cannot but ask them so! A generation that has its hands (for better or for worse) upon the very large, in astrophysical investigation, and upon the very small, in sub-atomic and gene-investigation, will not turn aside from asking the Christological and the grace-question in dimensions of an equivalent magnitude.

Ethicality, Grace, Truth

In this section it will be proposed that when all accredited ways of knowing have been disclosed as inadequate as guides for the issues of practical life, new possibilities arise out of the very absurdity and threat of the impasse. Is it not possible, indeed necessary, that from such a presupposition the church reopen the old problem of the relation of the Triune God to the realms of creation and of history? And is it not legitimate, further, that such an inquiry center upon the doctrine of grace in such a way as to ask after the sufficiency of older elaborations of grace? In such an inquiry the truth of Jesus Christ as the focus and indicator of grace is not questioned; what is envisioned is the theological advance that might be made if the realm of creation—as men presently probe it, use it, abuse it, relate themselves to it—were postulated as a realm of God's grace with a presence and an order-of-grace proper to its nature.

The moment one raises this possibility, however, he must consider the present state of scientific reflection upon ultimate questions of world and life origin, process, direction, etc. Such consideration discloses a learned and sober agnosticism, quite different from the olympian claims of 19th century statements about the total explanatory adequacy of indefinitely elaborated scientific method. And this difference is not merely a revised and more modest time-schedule for the progress of such a method. The difference is a qualitative one in which the problem is stated in a radically different way.

Characteristic is the postion of Sir Hubert Dingle of the British Academy of Science.[20] He contrasts the Victorian notion of science as accumulative with the contemporary view of science as modular. The natural scientist no longer says the world is like this or the world is like that. He only proposes that this or that model best represents what seems to be the case. And another generation of scientists will surely have other models. The late Percy Bridgeman, a Harvard University philosopher of science, affirms that there is no necessary connection between the thoughts in the scientific mind and the way things are. And Professor Robert Oppenheimer, in an essay on style in thought, in conceptualization, and in expression, sums up the matter in the fascinating epigram, "style is the deference that action pays to uncertainty."

It is precisely the intersection of this "open" situation in the scientific world and the trans-scientific facts and problems that the world now confronts in its dealings with the world-as-nature (the ecological crisis) that is back of the proposal that begins this section.

Man's actual operations with the world of nature constitute a steady occupation of his mind, his hands, and evokes the excitement of his spirit. This engagement with nature, now for the first time and in a large and public way, is also malleable to the decisions of his will. Nature is pathetically open to what he decides for good or for immeasurable woe to do with her. Man stands with an unparalleled potentiality in his hands; he can decide for such evaluation and use as shall create a new human environment or he may incinerate this theatre in which he has come to be, to know, to love, constantly to refashion, and to dream.

These considerations suggest that Christian theology move toward a more precise and descriptive, full "sociology of redemption." The social nexus within which redemption is actualized has long been recognized as regards man's human companions in the world. Man becomes a self, and is aware of the particuarity of his selfhood only in communion with the fellowman. One is postulated into selfhood and identity by the acknowledgment of the other. When this acknowledgment is withheld, or repudiated, there results a bitterness that has the absoluteness of death for all.

But a second and less obvious step must be taken. The world of nature within which men actualize their personhood both in solitude and in society is also a self-constituting datum. Just as a man is unable to envision eternal blessedness with God apart from communion with his fellowmen, so he is unable even to know an eternal blessedness with God without a conservation and renewal, in that consummation, of that theatre of nature which is the immemorial placenta of his personal being. Any thinkable consummation (cf. the social and national images of beatitude in the Scriptures) must be in some sense (perhaps unutterable) in continuity with the things that are. Residency in the world, under the sky, in silent or articulated creature-conversation with the given, nonhuman, world is a fact of life that belongs to redemption.

The enigmatic but undismissable vision of the relation of redemptive grace to man and nature in their created togetherness in the eighth chapter of Romans lives in restless imprisonment within traditional dogmatics.

It might also be suggested that the typically Lutheran refusal to dematerialize the "presence" of Christ in the Eucharist makes difficult any theological effort to transmit Christological meaning in terms of purely intellectual or spiritual relations. Advent is a festival of God's radical invasion of the realm of creation in an act of personalized, gracious presence ("The Word became flesh and dwelt among us"). The radicality of the invasion is matched by the desolation of immolation ("Why hast thou forsaken me?"). The Eucharist is thus a celebration of the continuing radicality of the presence of the triune God—and the materiality essential to the celebration is but a sacramental acknowledgement, in the factic bluntness of real bread and wine, that incarnation and cross and resurrection demand.

When, then, by this declaration we assert, via the materiality of the sacrament, the world-residency of Christological meaning and the orbit of his Lordship, we dare not exclude as a theatre of grace that same order of creation within whose form and substance God willed in Christ to make the place of his gracious presence. A Christian theology cannot go from nature to grace; the incarnation demands that it so relate grace to nature that the presence of God as grace in nature is not in principle excluded.

There is, that is to say, no Christology or grace in the sheer neutral, mute phenomenology of nature as such. But when grace as a redemptive reality, originating in the determinate will of the Father, is beheld as the meaning of the Son, the Spirit bears witness with our spirit that we are, indeed, children of God; and the reality of grace known *there* names the Son as the life-principle and mystery of meaning in all that is. If such a position be entertained in the mind, along what lines might a warrant for its truth be proposed? Two propositions might be valuable for the ordering of reflection.

1. Ethicality sensitizes cognition. By that statement it is suggested that problems, requirements, possibilities experienced in ethical reflection draw the mind forward into fresh expansions of cognitive life. Cognition is sensitized by re-cognition and urged into the perception of hitherto unregarded relations. The incessant pressure of the question *What ought I to do* modifies decisively the question *What can I know.* As old as Augustine is the notion that "there is no entrance into truth save by love."

2. Ecological fact must be ethicized; and an adequate Christian ethicizing of man's care for the earth dare not stop short of the affirmation of faith that reality is an order of grace, and Christ, "in whom all things cohere" is both the principle of God's agency in creation as well as in redemption, and that the evaluation of nature a place-of-grace is faith's investiture of the creation with holy meaning and holy demand. And is it not possible that a kind of Christological logic of natural reality might be both Christianly possible and ethically necessary? Now that man's scientific knowledge of nature, even if modular, has been translated into a technology that can render the world unfit for human habitation, the probing of the possibility here presented dare not be assessed as but the product of superheated theological imagination. For nature herself "groaning in travail, waiting . . ." suggests that at long last we consider a principle which, emerging from fact, intersects with a neglected strand of the church's Christology, to wit: What is necessary for the existence of things, and essential to prevent the perversion of things, may be logically postulated as indicative of the truth of things!

When the terms truth and meaning become absolutely engaged practically as well as theoretically with a fateful ecological disclosure of man in cosmic context, and when man's survival is clearly to be sustained or ended by knowledge and intelligent action, the older and prestigious ways of specifying truth and locating meaning are radically altered. When one takes the measure of this anthropology-in-context one is forced to ask the question about truth in this way: if man's existence is absolutely dependent upon his operations with the world-as-nature, must not truth as reality be integral to and in part knowable by assessments of nature, care for the creation, and an ethics supportive of these? Indeed, one might venture for reflection a proposition: what is necessary for the continuation of the life of both man and the earth must be resident within their interrelation. To evaluate the gift of the world at a sufficient elevation to deal with it sustainingly requires nothing less than a trans-pragmatic evaluation and use. Christianly this fact invites a sober rethinking of the scope of grace.

NOTES

1. L. Eiseley, *The Immense Journey,* New York, 1957, p. 57.
2. Form critical methods in New Testament study have in our time so powerfully intersected with the evaporation of transcendent categories as to produce the current hermeneutical impasse. For the purposes of this discussion it is not necessary to come down with a decision for or against any of the many parties and positions of that effort to forge an ample and correct method of interpretation. I have in another place (*The Anguish of Preaching,* Philadelphia, 1966, Chapter II) stated my conviction that the radical either-or's of the academicians are excessively rigid, and achieve their apparent total demolition of opponents by a strange humorlessness about the richness of the modalities of historical life. Kerygma without narrative leaves unaccounted for the very substance which made kerygma effective; and narrative without kerygmatic proclamation leaves unaccounted for the very evaluation that preserved and cherished the narratives. And there is happy evidence that the more doctrinaire proponents of various positions in this debate are beginning to be embarrassed by their departure from sober attention to the multi-phasic force and form of the Gospel proposal as this proposal was made to both Jew and Gentile.
3. The phrase "rhetoric of celebration" is calculatedly chosen to break this discussion loose from the grip of such language-analysis as would bestow intelligibility and "truth-claim-possibility" upon only such statements as can be shorn of their force-constituting images and reduced to verifiable components. For when theological discourse consents to divest itself of speech appropriate to the modalities appropriate to the historical, and acquiesces in the lust for clarity, intent, purport and meaning as these take their model from a-historical operations of the mind—Christian theological discussion will have bowed itself out of the company of significant disciplines.
4. H. W. Robinson in: *Record and Revelation* (ed. by H. W. Robinson), Oxford, 1938, p. 333f.

5. A. Galloway, *The Cosmic Christ*, London, 1951, p. 48.

6. The translation here, and following, are those of the *New English Bible*.

7. E. Mersch, *The Whole Christ*, London, 1962, p. 315f.

8. *Ibid.*

9. C. Moeller, *Lumen Vitae*, Vol. XIX, (1964), No. 4, Brussels 5, Belgium, p. 721f.

10. Originally from a lecture by J. Meyendorff. It is reproduced in C. Moeller and G. Phillips, *Grâce et oecuménisme*, coll. Irénikon, Chevetogne 1957, p. 57.

11. Epideixis, 22.

12. E. Mersch, *op. cit.*, p. 230.

13. Cf. the essays by G. Lampe, W. Dantine, P. Evdokimov in *Midstream*, Indianapolis, Vol. 4, No. 2. All explore in detail the relation between the triune God and *Ktisis*.

14. J. Haroutunian, *God With Us*, Philadelphia, 1965, p. 136f.

15. K. Rahner, *Nature and Grace*, London and New York, 1963. Discussions of nature and grace occur in many places throughout Professor Rahner's enormously rich production of books and monogaphs. All citations here are from this monograph.

16. *Ibid.*, p. 4f.

17. *Ibid.*, p. 8f.

18. *Ibid.*, p. 20ff.

19. *Ibid.*

20. Cf. W. Gibson, *The Limits of Language*, New York, 1962. Essays by biologists, philosophers of science, mathematicians, analysts, of the meaning of changing uses of language.

Part Two

The Acts of Man in Creation and History

Chapter 5

The Dialogical Character
of Human Existence

In the second half of this volume, in correspondence to the first half in which the acts of God in creation and history were discussed, we now have to present and think about the acts of man in the same time and space. It need not be shown again that this division does not jeopardize the unity of the God-man relation, but that it is only methodological considerations which lead us to present successively what can only be thought simultaneously, if the central concept of revelation is not to be lost. For in it, as is most clearly reflected in the concept of the incarnation, one can only think of God and man in relation to one another, never in an abstract juxtaposition. That must be emphasized, for it lies at the basis of how this book has been put together and above all shows why this section on the "dialogical character of human existence" forms the beginning of the second half-volume. The claim is thus made that the dialogical aspect forms a basic element of an anthropology conceived in the light of revelation, which however also does justice to reality insofar as dialog evidently corresponds to a basic structure of anthropology. The dialogical aspect in the gospel only sheds light on an elemental determination of human nature, thus drawing it into the realm of knowledge and conscious reflection.

With this insight we are given the task of bringing important basic anthropological problems into a theological discussion, which from the start must be oriented towards the problem of human action in order to remain true to our goal. That means for our particular case, that the problem of action as an ethical question must go hand in hand with an inquiry into the basic anthropological facts; this gives the question of ethics priority over the question of truth, to the possible consternation of some. But in fact, this order provides the necessary preparation for the discussion of how "truth" can express itself in "dialog" so that the apparent subordination of dogmatic to ethical interests only serves to clarify the dogmatic question and to give "truth" the honor it deserves.[1] Then this leads on quite naturally to a more precise definition of dialog, which is appropriate to the faith and characterizes its "conversation" with other partners, so that with these last considerations we are given an outline of this paper as well as its divisions.

THE DIALOGICAL ASPECT OF ANTHROPOLOGY AS A BASIC DESTINY OF HUMAN ACTION

As we said, the problem of human action stands in the foreground of our thought because this volume deals with the gospel and the "destiny of man." This of course implies a certain definition of the concept "destiny," namely one which excludes any deterministic-fatalistic understanding. "Destiny" is understood as human action in creation and history, in closest analogy with the action of God. A whole series of insights are clarified if one understands human "action" in the same sense as modern philosophical reflection; that is, as an historically responsible, interpersonal deed of man—including, but not limited to just "work" and "making"— through which man becomes a "person" and gains his true humanity. Even the "fatum" is made historical, understood as a task to be done, and drawn into a total responsibility for the world which knows no times or spaces in which man could be thought of as exempted from his "dominium" (cf. Gen. 1:28). The destiny of man is thus related to action in history, to the acceptance of responsibility for himself, his fellow-beings and so for the whole world. And this is true regardless of how he accepts his freedom; whether he presumes to find its source within himself, or as something to be fatalistically endured ("condemned to freedom"), or whether he sees it as something to which he is called in faith.

The Creation-Salvation Dimension of the Theme

The last half of our title, ". . . in Creation and History," brings to mind the second possibility: that of accepting freedom. "History" is of course a concept which can be understood and used both profanely and theologically, while "creation" clearly possesses a theological quality, and leads to misunderstanding when used without relation to divine action. The title of the second part of our volume in relation to the titles of the first part shows clearly what is meant by the ending common to both: Divine and human action belong together, but in a relationship characterized by a basic tension. That in turn casts further light on the concepts "Creation and History," and as they are of such importance for all that follows, they must be more precisely defined.

First of all it is important that creation and history are named in one breath, i.e., although different from one another, they are not separated and can in no case set over against one another; they belong for Christian thought very close together. It must further be seen that "creation" always also includes what we generally designate with the concept "nature"; consequently, it is of crucial importance theologically that creation and nature are not identified with one another. The concept of creation means that faith views nature as willed and founded by God. Understood in this way, God's rule in nature is included in his historical acts. It is also of great importance that one speaks here of divine and human action "in" creation and history, in order to show that the function of action characterizes the relationship between God and man. In as much as both are thought of as acting, they relate to one another as partners bound together in freedom in spite of, or better, because of their qualitative difference and the absolute dependence of man upon God's grace. Men act as "co-workers" [3] of God in creation and history, so that both appear associated in a certain togetherness. [4] The theological task arising at this point, which we can only mention, is to prevent the intrusion of pelagian or semi-pelagian errors based on a proportional relationship between divine and human responsibility.[5] To speak of human action in creation and history, one has to do of course with the whole breadth of theological knowledge. The short reference here can only remind us that from a theological point of view, all of the anthropology to which we now turn is set, and must be thought of, within these dimensions. As our special interest is in the dialogical aspect of anthropology, a short excursus is necessary to clarify the present meaning of "dialog."

Excursus on the Present Role of the Concept "Dialog"

It can be said today that dialog has become fashionable. While many view it as a passing fad, others are so fascinated that they expect from it the beginning of a new epoch of thought and human behaviour. In any case, the word has become a slogan suitable for use as motto and periodical title,[6] because everyone can more or less understand its intention even without an exact formal or material definition. Especially in church literature, which generally cannot be accused of a careless use of concepts, one presently meets this word without being offered a closer definition.[7]

In general, this means that the fascination which this word possesses is sure of a broad, although unreflective, agreement which must be taken seriously, since this slogan evidently points to man's longing for a new self-understanding. In any event, serious thinkers can call for a "necessary intellectual decision" in the name of dialog and set monolog and dialog over against each other as contrary thought forms.[8] As in most such cases, the roots of dialogical experience lie further in the past; it is generally agreed that the basic ideas were formulated by Martin Buber and Ferdinand Ebner[9] and transmitted to a wide circle of followers. Already at that time it had a strong influence on philosophy and especially theology, and had an ecumenical scope including Judaism. In the meantime the literature in this field has grown immensely, and it can be mentioned that even traditional philosophy, which long resisted this development, is now seeking to come to terms with it.[10] At the present we are evidently in a phase of critical reassessment of the basic idea of the dialog, which will last some time: new, far-reaching problems arise with it. Thus we cannot yet deal with clear definitions, or with final results but rather with the impetus of new thought processes which point into the future.

It is important to understand that "dialog" is not a new "doctrine" or "system," but a basic method of thought which exists only as structure or model. Therefore it cannot be limited to a certain content, but rather casts a new light upon all problems. To this end the defensive, negative effect of this thought-form is just as important as the positive. The brusque No to monolog as a thought structure which develops everything from a single point and so is capable only of soliloquy will prevent the formation of monolithic world views and ideologies whether religious or profane; but even deeper than that defensive reaction, this No is grounded in the recognition that every monological interpretation of self and the world leads to a disfiguration of the essence of human existence. Human existence is open to the world in the sense of responsible partnership with it, and can only achieve self-realization in communication with fellow-beings. At the same time this No is a tremendously productive Yes to the dialogical structure of man as such, and hence has far-reaching consequences for the way in which man understands himself in relation to society—consequences also for dealing with the sociological and political problems with which men are confronted.

Such far-reaching consequences of "dialog" are seldom expected since, as we said above, it is viewed by many as a mere fad at the periphery of things. There are several reasons for that, two of which must be mentioned: on the one hand it must be repeated that the proponents of dialog [11] in their enthusiasm often failed to reflect upon the full scope of their own insights, while on the other hand the attempt to do so was overshadowed by distrust, resulting from the failure of previous attempts in this direction. Here we have to do with the fact that previous theories viewed the individual as a part of his social context and derived from that his interpersonal relations. These theories were for the most part unable to hold fast to the individual as individual, and that means to man as a person. Leaving aside various pseudo-socialistic phenomena such as National-socialism, this is true of the historical forms of Marxist socialism as well as of the older and newer concepts of a univeralistic holistic philosophy. Othmar Spann [12] understood man as determined by *"Gezweiung"* (split-in-two). Based on this concept, he developed a philosophy of society which was appropriated almost without resistance, although against the author's intention, by a fascistic world-view of the monological type. Anticipating later proofs, it can be said that these two streams of social philosophy, despite their opposition, belong together insofar as they do not attempt to ground man's social character in dialog, i.e. in "conversation," in word or language, but in his nature itself. This then corresponds to the nature of their theologies, or better, their non-theologies.[13] That means that the failure of those social philosophies to move from their starting point, properly taken with the "fellow-being," the "other," to a genuine inter-humanity in the sense of the openness of the individual for the other and for society, is in their lack of the category of "word-liness"[14] *(Wortlichkeit)*. They thus forced man into the frame of a "closed society" so that even in his individuality, man is degraded to a manipulated participant of society.

The wide-spread mistrust we mentioned is thus understandable; it should not die out, as it is necessary to stimulate the critical question. Such a critical attitude is needed if the "dialog" truly holds what it promises, namely the real opening of man for the other, whether individual or representative of society or society itself.

The Anthropological Dimension in the Light of Dialog

The catchword "anthropology" is in the same boat with the term "dialog." It, too, is in vogue, the difference being that it was already in fashion in the last century with Ludwig Feuerbach. But otherwise it is the object of similar reservations and misunderstandings. One simply needs to call to mind that until recently one could only study anthropology at the university as a member of the natural science faculty. This subject was and is a branch of zoology, is closely related to theology, and the name "human biology" can be seen as a meaningful synonym for it. It was acknowledged of course, even during the rule of a positivistic naturalism, that other sciences have a contribution to make to this question, and it can be said that this insight has grown with time—at the present we are witnessing a remarkable collective view of anthropology to which a whole series of sciences contribute. It is evident that not only philosophical, but also theological anthropology again take part in this, making their contributions and receiving impulses from the others.[15] The main point here is not what the different sciences contribute, but the insight that "anthropology" is evidently not a "discipline" in itself at all, but a whole dimension which can never be fathomed from one viewpoint alone. A good example of this is theology, which not only speaks of man from different viewpoints as creature, as sinner, as reborn and in his eschatolog ical destiny, but also as the recipient of Word and revelation, or as the partner of God in conflict with him or related by faith to him. In a final sense there is no "theology" which is not also "anthropology" and vice versa—and this insight alone forbids making anthropology a separate discipline. It is rather a conglomerate of many disciplines which seems to pervade everything, as man himself is totally involved in all his thinking, speaking, and feeling.

It is not mere accident that at the same time that theology has come to see the necessity of always interpreting itself in terms of anthropology, a remarkable integration of numerous disciplines around the anthropological focus has taken place. Not only can one point to a series of processes within the history of human thought, and more particularly within the development of the sciences, which lead directly to the present concentration on the anthropological problem, but this phenomenon is evidently related to the process of secularization. This process has reached the point at which we are confronted by the alternative either to view this process in terms of disintegration, and so as a purely negative phenomenon, or to understand it as a change in which the traditional belief in providence is reshaped into the personal responsibility of historical consciousness.[16] Knowledge and experience of the historical nature of man, and his cosmic role in view of his ability to create his own future, make it even more necessary than ever that man should become the object of his own thinking. This must be carried out in a far more self-critical manner than did, for example, the Enlightenment, which first discovered the anthropological dimension, but whose optimism we can no longer share. It is also important to realize that a rediscovery of the central function of the anthropological dimension of all truth takes place in connection with a growing awareness of the historical character of human existence. One could also say: the discovery of his responsibility in and for history forces man to seek a basis for his humanity—a basis capable of bearing the terrible burden of this responsibility. The affirmation of the contemporary relevance of this knowledge is only a first, but unavoidable step in this direction.

Historicity and Sociality

There are important reasons for underscoring the elemental meaning of "history" for the role we ascribe to anthropology. For historical experience itself necessitates a certain insight into the social immersion of man. This we must now speak about more clearly. It is not difficult to show that monologically-structured anthropological schemes are characterized by an absence of history. This is true, for example, of abstract individualism in all its forms. But history also teaches us that the struggle of individual persons to free themselves from the domination of earlier forms of society is also a part of the development of society. Thus, such struggle exhibits its own process of self-determination, inasmuch as society not only consists of individuals but is also personally represented in the individual. The emancipation of the individual from society runs parallel to the emancipation of society from powers ruling it. Seen in this way, history is full of indications of the reciprocal relationship between individuals and society. Yet individualism views man as a final, indivisible reality and understands society only as an arbitrary postulation by individuals united together out of practical considerations. This leads to a dangerous underestimation of historical institutions, compensated for from the other side by an unhistorical idealization of institution which suppresses the realities of historical life. In reverse manner, every idealized collectivism ends up with unhistorical utopias and tyrannical dreams, either because it fails to acknowledge the historical reality and basic rights of the personality of the individual, or because it judges the possibilities of man exclusively according to the needs of the collective. Both ideologies, the individual and the collective, falsify the reality of man's historical existence in attempting to determine it with the help of abstract postulates. The phenomena of these two conceptions are so interesting because both represent elemental truths of human existence and promise to bring them to realization. And yet they fail precisely in this realization because they seek to ground the one truth in the other ideologically, i.e. to set the one truth absolute above the other. Man's historical existence, however, is determined by both—the social connection as well as the consciousness of freedom from it—and whenever the one is neglected, the balance must be restored by a swing to the other. The whole history of mankind can be presented in the light of this tension.

This means, however, that one can only seriously speak of the historical nature of human existence by accepting sociality as one of its basic elements. In the same manner one can only meaningfully speak of the social character of human nature when its historicity is given full due. Now neither of these are self evident; not only is the concept of "historicity" controversial and open to many interpretations,[17] but this concept has only recently gained wide acceptance in connection with existential philosophy, in which it now plays a role itself. This use of the concept "historicity" does not necessarily imply its openness to the immersion of existence in sociality. The existentialist concentration on the decision in *hic et nunc* easily causes the dimension of human history, with its sociological components, to be neglected, or onesidedly draws attention to the personal confrontation of the individual with the Thou.[18] Despite the burden of this misleading terminology (which is especially evident in the theological realm),[19] the insight that there is a reciprocal correspondence between historicity and sociality is of great importance. A rational clarification of this relationship must show historicity as personal responsibility exercised by an existential decision within and for the sake of society. Such a clarification avoids the possibility that the reciprocal relationship of the two elements takes the form of a fatalistic, unhistorical speechlessness. This leads us to a problem which cannot be taken seriously enough: sometimes the personal responsibility of human being and acting, as well as the awareness of the sociality of human existence, are present in equal measure, and yet appear to exist, in two realms, side by side, without any means of contact. Thus they seem more or less sentenced to a kind of schizophrenia of the personal-ethical and the social-political consciousness.[20] It is evidently not enough to acknowledge both historicity and sociality and reflect upon each in turn; they must not only be considered together but drawn into reciprocal relation and conversation with each other. Here evidently lies the chance of the so-called dialog.

Language and History

The criticism is often leveled at dialog that like all "conversation," it remains in a noncommittal realm. It is not claimed of course that all speaking from person to person is of lasting import; indeed it is not. Language like other means of human expression can remain at a superficial level, and as such adds to the color of life. The wordplay, the frivolous use of words to disguise and veil, undoubtedly also belongs to the total dimension of language and is not to be shamefully overlooked. All this, however, is but the reverse side of human mobility without which man could fully express neither his creaturehood nor his historicity. The question then is not the frequent superficiality of "conversation," which is obvious, but whether it represents a basic expression of man's being, so that its absence would necessarily mean a diminution of his humanity, or even further, whether his speaking is able to change his existential situation. Both are to be decisively affirmed. How and in what sense—this must now be spelled out more exactly without attempting to deal with all the complex questions involved.

That "language" belongs somehow to the ontological make-up of *homo sapiens* need not be discussed further. It is more important for us to underscore the fact that with the capacity of language, man is given a possibility of entering into contact with his fellow-beings and the world about him. In this capacity speaking has a mediating function, forming so to speak the bridge between thinking and acting. This entering into contact with the world about him is, however, not an incidental or arbitrary matter for man, but conditions and grounds his existence. In so far as this is so, the function of language is a basis for mastery and change of man's world without which he cannot live, as human biology now teaches us,[21] and which in a theological framework the Old Testament already knew.[22] The capacity to speak and communicate is in part the means, in part already the presupposition of man's total relating to the world and its realization through him. This stands as a fundamental insight even before knowledge leads us to differentiate between the means with which man relates himself on the one hand to his fellow-beings, and on the other to mere nature, its exploration and technical use. The importance of this difference, as well as the fruitfulness which the clear distinction between history and nature must have for all cultural action, should not overshadow the unity of human relating, as expressed precisely in his capacity for language. We have already seen that speaking and acting are directly connected—we call to mind here the presentation of Hannah Arendt[23]—but on the other hand speaking and thinking belong so closely together that the latter could be understood as silent speaking. Setting these relationships in a formula, we can say that in understanding and acting man actualizes his existence in the world, therein finding his inner unity and glorifying himself in his historical uniqueness. If man's mode of relating to the world differs according to the object (immediate contact with nature or confrontation with the fellow-being), so he gains his special, personal unity which is represented above all in his capacity for language as the mediating function between understanding and acting. It is obvious that insight into the deepest anthropological relationships can be interpreted, presented, and reflected in quite different ways; the variety of anthropological schemes is correspondingly large and is related with other philosophical and theological presuppositions. This variety, however, means an enrichment which only confirms the basic fact under different aspects. Further, it is not necessary for our purposes to go into the rich history and literature of this thought. Nevertheless, a word about the present situation is perhaps appropriate, since from the viewpoint of cybernetics man is again seen as constituted in his capacity for language even though this is understood differently than heretofore. The struggle in that field to define the decisive concept of "information" should be seen as an important contribution to man's self-understanding today, and clearly shows the scope of the problem of language.[24] In view of what we said above about historicity and sociality it is no longer necessary to show in detail how language must be of greatest importance for man's historical confrontation with the human-social world about him.

After this excursus on language as an essential function of human nature as such, we can now answer the other related question: is his speaking able to change man with regard to his situation? It is not only a question of whether man speaks out of his situation and to the other in his situation, thus taking the other seriously as a conversing partner—something which is doubtlessly to be reckoned to the essence of dialog—but further, of whether the situation both of the speaker and of the one addressed can itself be changed by language. We affirmed this question above with the reasoning that only in this way can the historical relevancy of man's capacity for language be shown. For history means that change takes place; it means the dynamic of moving and being moved. We speak seriously of historical relevancy only when we apply it to events in which a change in situation takes place, new accents of existential nature are set, a new level of historical existence is introduced. The doubt that language has such relevancy is as old as it is new and has its tradition in the history of thought—"the Word I cannot set supremely high: a new translation I will try." [25] But we also know another tradition: one that begins in the Old Testament,[26] is taken up essentially in the New Testament, and comes to full flower in reformation theology,[27] from where its influence continues into the present.[28] Here we can merely call attention to these traditions in the history of theology, which are themselves closely connected with philosophical conceptions. We note in particular only that still rather mysterious branch of this tradition, leading from the "Magus of the North," Johann Georg Hamann, through Johann Gottfried Herder, to romanticism's philosophy of language as well as that of the present.[29] Although we cannot deal with this whole complex here, it is of greatest importance for our considerations to be aware of these lines of thought. They point out that the question of whether the word has the power to become relevant for history in a final sense is, at least in its origin, closely connected with the biblical tradition. This tradition received its special expression, but also its fatal uncertainties,[30] in the Word-theology of the Reformation.

The circle of "Word" and "faith" which appears again and again in the Christian-Jewish stream of tradition is not only historically but concretely constitutive for the connection of language and history. This can be shown by the fact that "history," in the specific sense that—in spite of all variations—it is generally understood again today,[31] stands in closest connection with the function of the "Word" in the realm of "faith." On the other hand it could be shown that whenever in the Jewish-Christian tradition this circle of faith and Word is ontologically loosened so that one begins to think in terms of "substance" and its transformation, a fatalistic bent appears which passively endures "history" rather than takes responsibility for it. The fatalism in regard to history which arose again in Protestant Orthodoxy—at the very moment when the ontologizing of theology was completed [32]—can be shown most clearly in the development of the concept of "providence" [33] and in the piety based on it. It was precisely in this conceptual realm where history finds its "place" in dogmatics that the circle of Word and faith, of language and historical deed, failed to maintain itself. Because pious faith in providence transformed "history" into fatalism once again, the whole doctrine of providence was made untenable for modern historical consciousness. Consequently, interest in "language" and "history" is in the process of emigrating out of the realm of the church and Christianity. The surprising phenomenon in the course of this secularization process, however, is that language and history in some cases have preserved that meaningful relationship which appears to be grounded in the circle of Word-faith-history. The preservation of this dynamic relationship of Word and history involves more than the mere confirmation of a remarkable theory. It concerns the principle manner in which the world is interpreted, when this relationship is understood as the unity of responsibility for and understanding of the world. Such an understanding is of world-wide importance precisely for the epoch of technology now beginning and in connection with questions of the world's future.[34]

Dialog as the Language of Sociality with the Fellow-Being

It is now not difficult to draw the conclusions from the preceding considerations in light of our special theme. From our insight into the connection between historicity and sociality on the one hand and language and history on the other, there arises a relationship between language and sociality that is of elemental importance for all anthropological knowledge. If we further consider that language is the bridge between the individual's understanding and acting as well as the bridge from the individual I to the Thou, and also between the individual and society (and vice versa), then it becomes immediately clear what the dialogical structure of human speech is, as opposed to the monological. Monolog, in the principle sense of the introverted conversation or soliloquy of an individual or a monolothic social group, now appears as an anthropological curtailment despite its mighty claims. A monological structure of thought and speech will only force the other into submission, and so confront him only with proclamations and appeals or resorts to the dumb dictate; consequently, although it is often able to impose its will, still it remains closed in itself, autarchic, isolated, and powerless to confront the other in a real sense. The monolog can thus introduce and uphold social dictatorships; however, it is precisely in such that real sociality is not verified but made into an abstract ideology and concretely changed into its opposite. Dialog, however, is the act of language in which the historical sociality of man is not only proclaimed, but is realized in a concrete way.

Such a claim naturally raises basic epistemological questions which will be discussed further in the second part of the essay. But first of all our task must be to take up the postulate that the form of word-liness is a basic anthropological element of historical sociality. To be specific, if human existence takes place basically in the realm of interhumanity through the personal I-Thou relationship on the one hand, and as an individual-social relationship on the other, then it is only through a dialogical structure that human language can become a genuine bridge, an instrument of mutual meeting and confrontation. But having seen that human existence *per se* cannot be realized at all without language, it must be concluded that the social-interhuman act of existence can only be realized by way of dialog. Hence, dialog is no longer simply optional, no longer merely an additional plus to the fundamental make-up of the humanum—the humanum itself should be seen as dialogically structured in its fundamental elements, and in view of its existential self-realization. One could also say that the dialogic is to be understood as an anthropological existentalia.

The Ethical Relevance of the Dialog

Consequences must also be drawn from our previous insights, and especially from the knowledge just gained, for the question of human action. We were able to show the central mediating role played by language in the circle of understanding and action. If now this capacity for language is defined as dialogical because of the interhuman sociality in which man finds himself, then the dialogical existentalia must necessarily apply also to the action of man himself. That then has further basic consequences, for it means that all action—personal-interhuman, as well as social—needs the dialogical element for its genuine realization. Ethics must then call attention to the dialogical problem in its anthropological dimension and in its functional importance for the context of understanding and acting. That of course would presuppose that this problem be taken up, studied, and discussed more exactly than heretofore. We thus stand before an important task that is becoming more and more evident but as yet has not been treated with sufficient depth and breadth.

A theological ethics is doubtlessly responsible for the inclusion of the social and political sciences because they can be seen as sciences of human action.[35] It is beyond the range of this paper to present a concrete discussion of our own, but it must be pointed out that relatively little has been done in this field of research, which then has implications for the dialogic itself since it will not be taken seriously until convincing work is performed in this regard.[36] We can here do no more than raise the call for more intensive work on the dialogic in relation to the social and political sciences. It is to be expected that these sciences will in turn make inquiries of ethics.[37] The relevance of the dialog for the basic ethical problem could thus be increased, while at the same time raising the possibility of a deepened differentiation of this relevance. This differentiation could then clarify the important connections between language and action.

The relationship between anthropology and ethics from the perspective of dialog has now been sufficiently clarified, in as much as the fundamental problems have been made visible and the alternatives with which we are concerned have been enunciated. At the same time, however, the question of authenticity of the dialog, untouched until now, awaits an answer: does the dialogical structure possess the nature of truth? Could it be that the dialog offers help in the practical life with neighbor and society, but at the same time is strictly limited to anthropological-ethical problems? Does dogma, truth itself—that of revelation as well as of knowledge in general—remain untouched by it? Is then dialog a handy instrument for solving problems between men, but unsuitable for the knowledge of truth itself?

THE DIALOGICAL CHARACTER OF TRUTH
IN THE CONTEXT OF HUMAN HISTORY

The urgent question at the conclusion of the preceding discussion must be addressed principally because, if affirmed, a menacing schizophrenia of thought as well as action will result. For, we have seen thus far that it would lead to a break in the starting point as well as in the fact of thinking, i.e. that it would bring understanding and action into hopeless contradiction. When in spite of this the problem is seriously raised, the inherited tradition of monological thinking is so strong that the temptation to escape into it is evidently difficult to resist. If one asks about the motives of such frequent and relatively quick surrender to this temptation —one which must draw social ethics into a hopeless contradiction with dogmatics—then one finds that it is the concern, indeed the fear, that truth itself would be abandoned were it to be grasped and thought dialogically. That which convinces in anthropology and ethics is refused in dogmatics for fear that otherwise the identity of truth with itself might be lost. Seen theologically, one fears not only the dissolution of dogma or the undercutting of its authority, but the very loss of the unity and singularity of God.

Behind this fear and the resultant resistance to the dialogic stands the long tradition of viewing the final truth as a "thing in itself" and the impression of the consequences when philosophy abandons this fortress,[38] or threatens to dissolve it in philosophical speculations on the holy Trinity.[39] The return to a supranaturalistic theology in the post-idealistic epoch of the 19th century, in conjunction with the Enlightenment concept of religion and the related idea of "monotheism," produced a concept of God as an otherworldly, metaphysical final reality adorned with the features of a fatherly personality. This idea still remains today.[40] Such a concept of God, associated with the idea of a monolithic truth, logically formed a concept of revelation as "self-revelation" and thus, often against its own intentions, also understood the mediating function of revelation as its own monopoly.[41] Add to this an ontological system of thought working in neoplatonistic-mythical categories of the "self-sufficiency" or "autarchy" of God, and it is not surprising that in the wake of an anti-trinitarian tendency which began with the Sozinians and found allies in the modern representatives of an economical doctrine of the trinity, i.e. Friedrich Schleiermacher and Albert Ritschel,[42] an idea of God rules the scene, which, concerned with defending transcendency and aseity, in fact teaches something like a "God" closed up in himself, who in his self-communication could again only set "himself" as the absolute object of worship and faith. How problematical it is to objectivize God, always thinking of him as identical with a "final" truth, can be seen especially in the doctrine of the divine "attributes." Here in an especially conspicuous way God is viewed as an objectivized "thing" in itself,[43] which remains eternally identical with itself. Finally, if one considers the effects of the change of metaphysical ideas and the claims of ideological values upheld for social reasons, then one can understand the factual speechlessness of an idea of God and truth which can no longer communicate itself and thus seals its loneliness in monolog. The widespread claim that dialog has a dissolving effect and threatens God and truth arises out of such a mentality. Can such claims be verified in view of the biblical witness and dogmatic criteria?

Biblical and Dogmatic Considerations

Theunissen at the end of his social-ontological study speaks of "the kingdom of God" as the decisive dimension. It is "between the men who are called to it as present future," and on the other hand: "The kingdom of God however is not God himself. In it thought imagines—and in this already surpasses itself—merely the brilliance of God or the Holy, which reveals itself in the Thou. . . ." [44] This distinction between God himself and his kingdom is not to be understood as a separation but witnesses to unity in distinction, as the author's interpretation of Luke 17:21 confirms. Thus the "philosophy of dialog" is to be shown as its "theology." Ferdinand Ebner is called as witness: "The kingdom of love is also the kingdom of God. . . . For the kingdom of God is not in man in the inner loneliness of his existence, in the loneliness of his I; rather, as that the I opens itself in word and in love, and in word and in deed of love, to the Thou—then it is also 'in the midst of you' as the fellowship of our spiritual lives." [45] The "'theology' of betweenness," as the dialogic of Martin Buber, is similarly characterized. [46] A quotation shows in a flash what is meant: "God cannot be derived from something—for example from nature as its origin, or from history as its governor, or even from the subject as the self that thinks itself in Him. No something other is 'given' and God then derived from it, but God is immediately and first of all and finally reality over against one: this reality can only properly be addressed and not expressed." [47] This radical rejection of western metaphysics for which God is essentially *causa*, that which lies at the ground of things, becomes necessary for Buber because he wants to bring into play the immediate presence of the "Eternal Thou" [48] who confronts us as the other. Thus is developed a wholly changed understanding of the revealing Word. For as God can "only be addressed and not expressed," so his speaking is address, call, and speech directed at man. The self-communication always begins as communication with man, is already oriented and directed at man as "partner," and despite the sovereignty of the divine speaker, also aims at "answer." [49] The question is whether these Judeo-Christian insights are to be seen as fundamental and authoritative for theological thinking or not.

The traditional western metaphysics and ontology have so strongly infected Jewish, Christian, and even Islamic thought with the idea of the objectification of God and truth, that a direct reference to the theological tradition is of no help in answering this question. If, however, one considers the biblical origins of the Word-concept,[50] and the specific Christian implications in the history of theology, then there can be no doubt about the answer: the dialogical structure presents the really basic line and the monological a superposition on the original way of thought. Only consider how the concept of "truth" in the Old Testament is connected with "faithfulness," how on the other hand "faith" can also be identical with "faithfulness."[51] Further, this concept of faithfulness has to do with biblical covenant theology, which has been rediscovered and thought through by Ernst Käsemann and his school[52] in its relation to the expectation of the kingdom of God on the one hand, and to the doctrine of justification on the other. The insight "that righteousness in the Old Testament is not primarily a personal-ethical quality, but means a relation, originally the faithfulness to the community and in a legal case the reestablished "esteem" of an acquitted member of the community,"[53] snatches a decayed doctrine of justification away from an egoistic individualism, and grounds it anew as the event of God's relationship with mankind, with the people of God. It is thus put in a field in which God's action and man's action become clear both in their distinction and in their corresponding relation. In terms of traditional concepts this could be expressed in the following formula: the *iustitia coram deo* and the *iustitia coram hominibus*, or the "kingdom of the right hand" and the "kingdom of the left hand," become visible both in their difference and in their reciprocal relation. Thus, at the same time, the responsibility of man for the latter is grounded in the former. The wide-reaching field of problems touched on here, including general human questions,[54] is really first opened up through the knowledge of the dialogic through which God reveals himself as a Thou and lifts man to this Thou, mediating to him the self-knowledge of being an I. This brief list of references could be further expanded, especially in the field of Christology, and above all in the doctrine of reconciliation. This would demonstrate that the soteriological-christological element of faith in all possible respects expresses how God's act of salvation in Christ is unthinkable as monolog, but rather opens up a genuine dialog. It is not accidental but of final necessity that Christ is presented under the cipher of the "Word."

The same can be seen in regard to the pneumatological dimension. It is necessary to emphasize this because the spiritual sphere of the "Spirit" is often usurped by mystical or enthusiastical or philosophical-idealistic thought patterns. The trinitarian barrier in the "Filioque" doctrine has not proven effective in preventing this invasion of the spiritual sphere by monological thinking. Even a witness who stands above suspicion in this matter, such as Martin Luther,[55] is not infrequently misunderstood as teaching that faith and God melt together in such a way that the dialog between them becomes a monolog, although the famous prooftext for this view—"For the two belong together, faith and God"[56]—expressly speaks of the connection of two entities. But the monologistic tendency always to proceed from a dominating subject and to objectivize the vis-à-vis is so strong that one of two extremes generally result: Either faith is made a submissive, pre-programmed and speechless consumer of political speech or, vice versa, appears as the real master of this divine speaking. Luther already—three centuries before Feuerbach—grimly complained that here man becomes a "fabricator dei." We must be content here only to point to the many problems without entering into detail. The biblical and Reformation view in any case holds that faith comes from hearing the Word,[57] and therefore without the function of language can achieve neither its own existence nor its own function. The relation of "Spirit and Word" belongs in a real sense to the fundamental basis of pneumatology. It forms one of the foundations of ecclesiology[58] on the one hand, and of the special order of salvation[59] on the other, and is traditionally handled under the concept of the means of grace.[60] The reminder of these traditional doctrinal contexts is sufficient here to show the problem in the realm of the spiritual dimension.

These short references to certain aspects of christology and pneumatology lead us naturally to the trinitarian dimension of Christian thinking about God. Whether or not one views the traditional doctrine of the Trinity as a help in thinking about the problem of God, it cannot be denied that in it certain indispensable elements of Christian faith are expressed. Among these it is central to this doctrine that God does not appear as a one-dimensional fixed point, but is conceived of as in movement in himself and in conversation with himself, and therefore also outside himself. In that God's unity is grounded precisely in his three-in-oneness and, vice versa, that three-in-oneness presents the unity, a monological singleness of an autarchic God is made impossible. With their doctrine of the intercommunion of the divine persons—with their "moving into one another" as Karl Barth has genially described it—on the one hand, and their so-called "doctrine of the relations" [61] going back to Augustine on the other, the church fathers made provision for Christian faith to remain open for an understanding that could dare to put God himself in relation to himself.[62] The reciprocal relation of the *opera trinitatis ad intra* and the *opera trinitatis ad extra* along with the distinction between the economical and the immanent trinity did indeed open the door to a multitude of problematical speculations. At the same time, however, a means and criteria were provided for thinking of God in juxtaposition to himself and in conversation with himself, and for believing that he could never be reached through man's self-interpretation, but that man may participate in his dialog. If God's truth is thus discernible only "through Jesus Christ in the Holy Spirit"—so the classical closing phrase of liturgical prayers—should it not also hold that the truth is not one-dimensionally but dialogically revealed?

Although one cannot speak of a formal doctrine of the Trinity in the New Testament, there are already signs of a trinitarian structure in that a clear distinction is made between Christ and the Spirit. Both, however, are identified with the truth, which is a predicate of God. It must be kept in mind that this is a peculiarity of Johannine theology [63] and thus we have no right to see in its elements of a fixed dogma. On the other hand, despite closest, interchangeable identification of the Son and the Spirit, a difference is maintained throughout,[64] and is not lost in the historical development of dogma. Consequently, the essence and function of the Spirit almost always follows in analogy with the state of the christological discussion.[65] One can speak directly of a law in the history of dogma which is traceable in the relationship between Word of God and sermon, proclamation and faith, truth and action. Such a law is also visible in the double aspect of *fides* as *quae-creditur* and *qua-creditur*, in which, moreover, the difference and unity of the whole of soteriology is reflected. While truth as such is indivisible and inexchangeable, as God himself, it comes to its own importance in a functional process in which the Father, Son and Spirit participate. If one considers by the cipher "Son," the incarnation, i.e. the unique history of the *deus pro nobis*, and by the cipher "Spirit," the inspiration, i.e. the ever new history of the *deus in nobis*, then it becomes convincingly clear that, seen theologically, the concept of truth allows no onesided objectification either in terms of the object or the subject. The truth of God is always a "for" man and an "in" man and therefore never only an "above" or "outside" him;[66] it arises in the historical confrontation of speaking and hearing which is the reason why it is always formulated anew in confession and actualized anew in the deed of obedience. This, however, is precisely what the theological aspect of the philosophy of dialog means.

The Historicity of Truth *(Geschichtlichkeit)*

If "truth" is never to be abstracted from the knowing subject and if man as this knowing subject is characterized by the history we spoke of above, then it follows that all truth bears historical character. In the light of our previous results it must be stated that truth then can only possess historical relevance when it is seen as historical and reflected upon accordingly. Christian theology has eloquent witness in the writings of the Old and New Testament of how easily historical change in language, thought forms, and literary forms can be accepted without fear that this means a loss of truth. However, reference must be made here to the phenomenon of the formation of a concept of dogma and orthodoxy for which the flexibility of historical thinking was unknown, without going into the rise and spread of the ontologism responsible for it. A new understanding of the historical nature of dogma gained ground in

Protestantism and is visible even in the Formula of Concord,[67] although it itself marks the beginning of a renewed ahistorical, static handling of dogma. It was then only later, under the influence of the Enlightenment and the triumph of historical thinking even in the realm of theology and the church, that this new understanding, despite occasional reverses, gained the upper hand. The building of the concept "history of dogma" and the acknowledgement of its reality gives evidence to that. Roman Catholicism came to this insight only relatively late,[68] but now is catching up quickly [69] and is in the process, at least in important individual instances,[70] of granting a wide field to the historical understanding of dogma, indeed of attributing an elemental importance for the knowledge of truth to history itself.[71] A book such as Leslie Dewart's *The Future of Belief* [72] shows that a fearless and significant grappling with these problems is not lacking. In as much as Christian theology, encouraged by the fact that it creatively participates in shaping the nature and concept of history, accedes to such a large extent to the historicity of its truth, it must also accede to those other elemental aspects connected with the historical existence of man, namely sociality and the capacity for language, and therefore also to the basic dialogical structure of man and his action.[73] It is not possible to exclude and isolate the one or other matter from that context; with the one elemental aspect the other forms are also given.

Attention must be called in this connection to a not unimportant historical phenomenon. The uneasiness about the dialogic mentioned above is at the same time also a concern that historicity may have as a consequence the relativisation of historical truth. It is not to be denied that the advent of historical thinking soon led to views characterized by such relativism. This was and still is the case with historicism, which became a kind of unarticulated worldview. From its viewpoint, all cats are indeed grey, or better, all flowers bloom in different but absolutely equivalent colors because all that has been in the past and all that is yet to be symbolizes in and through itself one of the infinite rays of the one unfathomable truth. Behind this notion, responsible among other things for the rise of nationalism,[74] stands a Neoplatonic conception of the relation of truth and world, as recent studies convincingly prove.[75] This conception provoked, on the one hand, the awakening interest in history, presenting it with a fascinating philosophical interpretation of history.[76] On the other hand, it is not necessarily identical with this "interest in history." [77] It must thus be emphasized, that although "historicity" and a scheme of history have similar origins and certain material aspects in common, they are not to be made equal. It can be shown for the problem of how value standards become relativized, which is important for our study, where similarities appear and where not. Every theory emphasizing historicity is agreed that "absolute" history in the sense of a material philosophy or theology of history which attributes to historical events the value of final truths, must be rejected.[78] In this rejection they underscore the ambivalence of every historical event, affirming therefore the possibility of interpretation in different directions, and thus for a certain neutrality of historical events. But now historicism takes just this insight of the ambiguity of history and stands on its head, thus making it unambiguous once again. It does this by using the Neoplatonic idea that truth is fully present in every single instance, thus allotting every single phenomenon the value of the presence of the full truth. The whole appears in even the smallest part—that must lead to atomizing the truth, to a special kind of pluralism giving rise to a relativism in principle. Here dialog cannot take place, but only a multitude of successive monologs which fiercely proclaim their equal participation in the truth.

Over against this, the dialog has to do with a kind of historicity which has left the above-mentioned historicism behind. For it emphasizes the particularity of every new situation in order to create, in the act of decision,[79] still a new situation which must be accounted for. Insofar as the situation speaks its own word and through this word provokes the historically responsible person to action, truth cannot be postulated as the self-evident possession of all in equal measure, but is found ever anew in the act of reinterpreting the tradition. Dialog takes place in hearing the voice of the changing situation and giving answer to it. It is then quite obvious that the truth which has already proven itself in the past is brought in its full scope into the dialog there to be remolded in view of the future. This draws attention to a dimension which is already implicit in the concept of historicity, but now requires a more exact explication.

The Dimension of the Future

The eschatological determination of Christian faith also unveils through the certainty of salvation a final meaning of the world and its history and thus sets the future beneath the sign of hope. Faith and hope ignite on the faithfulness of God who keeps his promises and does not revoke his calling. The mystery of history which binds Israel and the church to one another exemplifies the nature of the historical dialog. The seemingly unending dispute over the interpretation of chapters 9-11 of Romans is itself a sign of the futurity of the knowledge of truth which in the present is always hidden and yet already valid; thus it stands beneath the sign of freedom and change.[80] The very fact that in the present Israel and the church have entered into dialog is of greatest importance for the clarification of the real nature of truth. This is the case quite apart from how one evaluates the present state of this conversation.[81] This fact has immense implications, for it signals in principle the end of the past monopolistic and monologistic understanding of truth.

Dialog does not divide the one truth into two or more parts but seeks the one truth ever anew through decision for it, in order to gain the future. It has to do then with the same truth in its ever new and dynamic and future form and not with some other truth; it thus has to do with reinterpretation of the tradition, with reformation and if necessary, with revolution, but not with a change in which one idea is replaced by another. The conviction that in "conversation" truth reveals itself more purely and error is more easily avoided so that through this dialogical method one can approach the pure form of truth—this conviction is paired with the idea of "progress," whereby characteristically immediate problems of social science connect up with problems of epistemology, as has been shown throughout our presentation. Social "well being" and "truth," in which men can participate so that it becomes their own truth, condition each other, both standing in an analogous relation to "salvation." As salvation for faith is always also eschatological hope which determines the historical future, so "truth" and "well being" move forward as well because they are oriented on the future and so are progressive. The conservative-restorative character of Christianity in past centuries was due to a metaphysics principally oriented toward origins, or to a theology which understood the world in terms of the "grace of preservation." The connection between restoration and monologism is again evident here. On the other hand, dialog and progress go together in that both are only conceivable in relation to the certainty and meaningfulness of the future.[82] It is then not accidental but of inner necessity that the rise of dialogical thinking appears connected with ecumenical thinking on the one hand and with the growing social responsibility of the church on the other, and this in the sign of an eschatological consciousness which understands the future as open history.[83]

THE DIALOG OF FAITH

The rather detailed presentation in the first two parts permits us to deal more briefly with those consequences which result for the dialog as the method of faith. We pointed out at the beginning that dialog often appears as an appeal to or wish for dialog in the form of a scarcely articulated expectation.[84] Therefore a special attention was given to its theological grounding which at the same time sought to make clear its philosophical and particularly its anthropological aspects. Here we have to do especially with its importance for faith and the church. These have a role in dialogical thinking as we have just seen.

The Immediate Function of the Dialog for Faith

This has been touched on already under biblical and dogmatic considerations. Now it is necessary to point out that faith in its concrete self-actualization lives from the dialog of God with man insofar as man knows himself addressed as God's partner by the justifying word of promise, and summoned and called to cooperation in the world. Already this knowledge forbids him to act in a monological manner toward his neighbor, as well as his Christian brother. What the assertion of this knowledge could mean for the structuring of the church cannot even be hinted at here. It can only be mentioned that the real problems of present church reform in the individual confessions arise at this point. The importance that even some aspects of the matter could have for church practice can be seen in relation to the problem of education, which has become crucial today. Even beyond the realm of the church,[85] teaching presents one of the key problems of university reform and shows how explosive the question of the institutionalization of conversation[86] can be for the problem of a renewed humanism. It thus becomes clear how from the center of Christian faith, from the conversation between man and God initiated by the Word of the gospel, the dialogical principle permeates the whole realm of the church and reaches even beyond its practice into the realms of society. An incarnational theology which has freed itself from its usual connections with an infusory doctrine of grace and so from theocratic and hierarachic elements, and is decisively shaped by the theology of the cross and the doctrine of justification—such a theology could be the theological basis which on the one hand grounds dialog, and on the other propels it forward on all levels of human and Christian existence. This could also be a meaningful contribution of Lutheran theology for the whole ecumenical movement.

The Conversation of Faith with Other Religious Partners

In dialog faith moves outwards to where it meets conversation partners who confront it as strangers and, in a more or less fundamental difference, not infrequently as foes.[87] In view of the theological existentalia of man through which every interhuman partnership receives its dialogical structure, the differences among these conversation partners are not unimportant, but are given, so to speak, a common denominator under which they can be viewed. Because Christian faith is characterized by its confessional-ecclesiological form,[88] every partner confronts it in the form of the "stranger," the "other"; thus faith experiences "all others" as "separated" from itself regardless of whether it has to do with Christian brothers or representatives of other religious or world-views.[89] That is important for the dialogical method insofar as it involves the basic decision, if faith is willing to recognize the non-confessional and non-Christian world about it as a differentiated group under the common denominator of a conversation partner and to enter into conversation with it accordingly. It has already been said that the other possibility of persisting in monolog allows only a fanatical propaganda of a soliloquy dictated by fear. If the decision is made for the dialog, then it is obvious that the closest partnership is to be found within the Christian churches, even if the confessional controversy is more difficult than all others.

The question of how a "dialogical" church appears within the life and experimentation of the ecumenical movement is extensively discussed in the first volume of this work.[89a] Here however the question of the Christian dialog with the "other religions" needs a special presentation. In this the place of Judaism and Islam represent a special problem of great importance. The association of these two monotheistic[90] religions with the other non-Christian religions is no longer as self-evident today as it was until just recently.[91] Both "religions"[92] have, for their part, a different relation to Christianity and to each other which complicates the Christian dialog with them. This is all the more so as presently these two partners, for different reasons,[93] are not as interested in dialog as the Christians. In view of this theoretically as well as historically complicated situation it is to be doubted that the Second Vatican Council was wise to include the so-called "declaratio Iudica"[94] as one of the five sections in "The Declaration on the Relation of the Church to the Non-Christian Religions," after having dealt with Hinduism and Buddhism[95] and Islam.[96] This inclusion of Israel and Islam among the other religions hardly does justice to the common ground of revelation which Jews, Christians, and Moslems have, although, on the other hand the "Declaratio de ecclesiae habitudine ad religiones nonchristianas" (R.N.) must be seen as a step in the right direction. A closer investigation would show that the council's theology worked with a concept of religion that was not up to the level of the present findings of the science of comparative religion,[97] just as it also appears to be outdated by a new "theology" of the religions.[98] This inadequacy for current problems of a theory of religion originating with the Enlightenment shows that the traditional view of the "absolute nature of Christianity" can no longer be upheld with monologism. Every tempering of this claim, however, necessarily leads to a syncretistic relativism in which the truth is dissolved under the sign of a religious sentimentality or activism. Here tasks arise for dialogical thinking which have hardly been touched upon or solved.

The dialog is in a better position to do justice to the individual forms of the so called religions than was heretofore the case. As the relation Christianity-Judaism-Islam finds new planes of conversation, so the dialog of Christian faith with other past and present religions could also take new forms. Although the radical critique of religion and the religions as carried out by Karl Barth [99] cannot be taken back, and consequently makes a genuine "conversation" impossible, a revised "theology of the question" [100] will confront the religions with the question of truth, while at the same time letting itself be put in question by them. The relation of religion and revelation as well as that of reason and faith will have to be determined ever anew in conversation.

The Conversation with the "Non-Religious" Partners

"Unreligious" has since Dietrich Bonhoeffer [101] signaled for our thinking not only the a-religiosity of individuals or small groups, which in a certain sense always existed, but the broad and deep phenomena within the industrial society which go hand in hand with the historical process of so-called "secularization." But already this term [102] touches on an extremely complex matter which is important to us inasmuch as we must distinguish here between two kinds of profanity. One is to be affirmed and even supported by faith and another is consciously antireligious or antichristian. The second is usually also atheistic and stands in conscious opposition to the first. This distinction must be made even if one does not agree with F. Gogarten's [103] definition of secularization and its contrast to "secularism," and wants to go beyond a mere general world-dialog to which Christian faith is compelled anyway through its own self-actualization. Our final consideration is directly related to the dialog with secular ways of thinking which represent a profanity understanding itself in opposition to faith, or at least its surrogate. One could also speak of an ideological profanity which not infrequently bears pseudoreligious features. In the foreground [104] has stood for a long time now western atheism [105] and the Marxist ideology which, in the form of Marxism-Leninism,[106] is also committed to atheism. In the past few years the "Christian-Marxist dialog" [107] has caused quite a stir along with the accompanying, but in a certain sense independent, "dialog with atheism." [108]

Characteristic of this dialog are certain historical presuppositions forming a common basis from which it could proceed. For although atheism is a phenomenon that appears in all cultures, its western form—the only one to have created a tradition—was conceived from the start in opposition to a theism which to a large extent determined and characterized Christianity. Not only historically, however, but also in view of the matter itself, atheism proves to be an intra-theological problem. Insofar as the theistic idea of God is foreign to the essence of Christian faith, the anti-theistic front of atheism can also call upon certain theological arguments.[109] The dialog originated when both an ideological atheism and an ideologically alienated Christianity came under fire from the critique of ideology and began to call themselves and each other to self-criticism.[110]

The Marxist-Christian conversation currently takes place in many parts of the world and at very different levels, although the first wave of enthusiasm seems to be ebbing. This dialog is sharply criticized by the official groups in both camps, although it can no longer be revoked. It is inevitable first of all because Christians and Marxists continually meet each other as individuals in different positions within their different societies, but secondly because Marxism cannot deny its Christian presuppositions if only as a phenomenon of history. Moreover, there is today a common fate tending to keep the dialog alive. This expresses itself above all in a dilemma in which both are presently involved and which makes the analogies between them even more evident. The theological unrest providing the impetus of the ecumenical departure in the churches corresponds in a certain sense to the ideological unrest in the Marxist realm, wherein powerful political-social processes must naturally also be taken into account. It cannot be denied that a revolution in thinking is making itself known in the realms of historical understanding, ethics, and anthropology, to name only three very important and presently explosive fields in which Christians and Marxists participate. The dialog is a fact even though for many reasons it is officially outlawed and repressed.[111] The dialogical existence of man can indeed lose itself for long periods of time in monological soliloquies and evidently perform remarkable things in this estrangement. But the liberating power of the gospel also calls men out of this self-elected prison and so restores to human history its meaning by drawing man into his responsibility for the other.

—translated by Donald Dutton

NOTES

1. Cf. in Volume I of this *Theology encounters History Series* the study by V. Vajta, "Theology of Dialog," pp. 25-66.
2. Hannah Arendt, *The Human Condition*, Chicago, 1968.
3. Luther, just in his polemical pamphlet against Erasmus on the bondage of the will, underscored the thought of the cooperatio of man with God in world action: W.A.18, 753:12ff.
4. Here lies one of the thorniest theological tasks, the so-called doctrine of the "concursus." It can only be pointed out here that its classical formulation took place within the doctrine of providence, or in connection with the "doctrine of preservation." Over against that, we speak of the "cooperation" of the creature already in the execution of creation and thus put the responsibility of man for creation on a new basis, which has far-reaching consequences.
5. The task encompasses above all the relation of creation and soteriology, or a reformulation of the doctrine of grace after the doctrine of justification has been freed from its previous isolation and made fruitful for thinking about the whole world, for which the Lutheran heritage of the *sola fide—sola gratia* must be viewed as indispensable. Cf. in this volume the contribution by J. Sittler.
6. In the realm of Catholicism with an ecumenical outlook there are presently two periodicals: "Internationale Dialog Zeitschrift," ed. by K. Rahner and H. Vorgrimmler, Freiburg; and "Neues Forum, Internationale Zeitschrift für den Dialog," ed. by G. Nenning and P. Kruntorad, Vienna; I am coeditor of both periodicals.

7. E.g. in some texts of the Second Vatican Council: *Gaudium et Spes* 3, 19, 21, 23, 25, 28, 43, 92; *Unitatis redintegratio* 4, 18; *Declaratio de ecclesiae habitudine ad religiones nonchristianas* (R.N.) 2, 4.

8. E.g. H. L. Goldschmidt, Zürich: "Dialektik oder Dialogik, Eine notwendige geistige Entscheidung," in: *Internationale Dialog Zeitschrift*, Vol. 2, 1969, pp. 194-208. Cf. of the same author: *Dialogik, Philosophie auf dem Boden der Neuzeit*, Frankfurt/M. 1964.

9. The controversy which has flared up again in the present on the question which of the two men first discovered the dialog need not bother us here; the influence of both is so important and manifold that a listing of the literature is not necessary.

10. A good survey of the philosophical problems with their theological dimensions is given by M. Theunissen, *Der Andere, Studien zur Sozialontologie der Gegenwart*, Berlin 1965, esp. pp. 243-373 and pp. 483-507.

11. Cf. note 7.

12. O. Spann, *Kategorienlehre*, 2nd ed. 1939, esp. pp. 274-290; *Gesellschaftslehre*, 3rd ed., Leipzig 1930, esp. pp. 97ff.; id., *Geschichtphilosophie*, Jena 1942, p. 40 et al.

13. As a positivistic naturalism is basic for anthropology in traditional Marxism, so a kind of metaphysical materialism is, in the philosophy of history, rooted in romanticism. Both see man as constituted by his unchanging essence and determine him according to his constant "nature," although in opposite ways. The historical "word" has no anthropological importance here. In like manner, in the one case the word-less eternal essence of God is thought of as the ground of being, while the positivistic opposition to metaphysics negates the word-less God as such.

14. Fr. Gogarten, *Der Mensch Zwischen Gott und Welt*, Stuttgart 1956, pp. 219ff.

15. In place of the wealth of literature: W. Pannenberg, *What Is Man?*, Philadelphia, 1970.

16. It is easily seen that here positive reference is made to Fr. Gogarten's interpretation of secularization, but also to that of D. Bonhoeffer. That is true for the basic question, not necessarily for the details. Many a serious contradiction to that, like that of Hand Blumberg, *Die Legitimität der Neuzeit*, Frankfurt/M. 1966, despite a good total view, does not appear to me to do justice to that alternative.

17. Cf. G. Bauer, *Geschichtlichkeit, Wege und Irrwege eines Begriffes*, Berlin 1963.

18. That can be shown clearly on such an excellent book as *The Ethical Demand*, Philadelphia 1971, by K. E. Løgstrup. However one must be careful of generalizations: Sartre's existentialism, as is known, has another, much closer relation to the field of sociology than is the case in the Scandinavian and German traditions.

19. Consider the disregard for the social dimension by R. Bultmann and in the wide circle of his followers.

20. An old but unfortunately still actual example for that is the dualistic doctrine of the two-kingdoms which in conservative Lutheranism—despite

the historical proof that it once was normal teaching also in Calvinism—appears to be indestructible. Luther's interest was in the difference of God's manner of rule in the dimension of his saving righteousness, which touched the personal center of man, and in the dimension of civil righteousness, in which this person actualized his historical nature. Thus, for him there was also an interrelatedness of the two kingdoms due to the unity of God and the unity of the person of man. Later however a metaphysically structured scheme of two clearly separated realms without functional connection arose which was then reinforced by a word-less juxtaposition of "law" and "gospel." This separation into two realms, which led to a factual fatalism in regard to political action, has obscured for many up to the present the genial insight into the difference of the two realms as taught by the Reformer.

21. Cf. A. Gehlen, *Der Mensch. Seine Natur und seine Stellung in der Welt,* 6th ed. Bonn 1958. Also A. Portmann, *Biologische Fragmente zu einer Lehre vom Menschen,* 2nd. ed., Basel 1951.

22. Gen. 1 and 2 in different reflecting language.

23. Cf. note 1.

24. H. D. Bastian, *Theologie der Frage, Ideen zur Grundlegung einer theologischen Didaktik und zur Kommunikation der Kirche in der Gegenwart,* München 1969, pp. 180ff.; K. Steinbuch, *Die informierte Gesellschaft,* Stuttgart 1966; N. Wiener, *Cybernetics,* Cambridge, Mass., 1961. Present theology forgets in view of the modern concept of "information" that it, for example, has used a related idea in the concept of the "*notitia*" within the dogmatic locus of "*fides.*"

25. J. W. v. Goethe lets Faust speak in this way by the translation of the Johannine prologue, and closes with the words: "In the beginning was the deed." (Our translation)

26. It is sufficient in bringing to mind the biblical word-theology to point to the role of the divine Word in creation in Gen. 1 and to the mighty testimony to the power and function of the human prophetic word as for example in Jer. 1:4-10.

27. The central role of the theology of Martin Luther in this regard should be beyond question.

28. Despite the deep chasm between the Barth and Bultmann schools, a similarity in their Word-theology should not be overlooked which indicates the strength of this tradition in the present. And even beyond the specific Word-of-God theologies, it still has a strong position in the Protestant churches in general and more recently also in renewed Catholicism.

29. J. G. Hamann, *Sämtliche Werke,* ed. by J. Nadler, Wien 1949 ff. Vol. III, pp. 13ff. J. G. Herder, *Sprachphilosophische Schriften,* ed. by E. Heintel, Hamburg 1960. F. Ebner, *Das Wort und die geistigen Realitäten,* 1921. L. Wittgenstein, *Tractatus logico—philosophicus,* London-New York 1922, Frankfurt/M. 1960. M. Heidegger, *Unterwegs zur Sprache,* Tübingen 1959. E. Rosenstock-Huessy, *Speech and Reality,* Norwich, Vermont, 1969. H. G. Gadamer, *Wahrheit und Methode. Grundzüge einer philosophischen Hermeneutik,* Tübingen 1960.

30. Lutheran theology in the famous Rahtmann controversy at the beginning of the 17th century exaggerated the claim of the historical effectiveness of the Word to the utmost in teaching the *efficacia* of the Bible even *extra usum;* characteristic here are the ontological bases of this understanding through which the Bible was attributed a *vis hyperphysica.* The historical word of man disappeared; this show of might caused the real power of the "paper Pope" to be greatly diminished.

31. Cf. G. Ebeling, *The Nature of Faith,* Philadelphia 1961, and: *Word and Faith,* London 1963. K. Rahner, *Hearers of the Word,* London 1969, K. Rahner/J. Ratzinger, *Revelation and Tradition,* London 1966.

32. Cf. H. E. Weber, *Reformation, Orthodoxie und Rationalismus,* 2nd ed., Darmstadt, 1966.

33. C. H. Ratschow, *Das Heilshandeln und das Welthandeln Gottes. Gedanken zur Lehrgestaltung des Providentia-Glaubens in der evangelischen Dogmatik.* Neue Zeitschrift für systematische Theologie und Religionsphilosophie 1 (1959), pp. 25-80. W. Trillhaas, *Dogmatik,* Berlin 1962, 152ff.

34. See also; Arend Th. van Leeuwen, *Christianity in World History. The Meeting of Faith of East and West,* London 1966.

35. Practical theology naturally also belongs here, which today is understood as the "science of action" ("Handlungswissenschaft"), e.g. G. Krause, *Zeitschrift für Theologie und Kirche,* Nr. 64, pp. 467 and 478ff.

36. We refer once again to the book by M. Theunissen, cf. note 10, whose socio-ontological studies deal with the question of the dialogic in principle. The growing literature in peace studies and in the theology of revolution mostly ignore this fundamental problem; through common effort, an ecumenical responsibility for theological ethics in the different confessions could perform an important service in this regard.

37. Such inquiries could of course lead to a radical rejection of ethical responsibility and the dialogical character of existence, as is the theme for example of the monumental novel: *Der Mann ohne Eigenschaften,* by Robert Musil. R. Dahrendorf in his *Essays in the Theory of Society* (tr. by the author, Stanford University Press, 1968, p. 74), took up this question especially in view of Musil's picture of the human person as a washed out hollow and discusses the possibility of preserving human integrity in the face of playing roles which has become homo sapens' fate. Cf. R. Musil, *Man Without Qualities,* New York, 1965.

38. Cf. J. G. Fichte, *Die philosophischen Schriften zum Atheismusstreit,* ed. by S. Medicus, Leipzig n.d. p. 56; J. G. Fichte, *Werke,* ed. by F. Medicus, Leipzig n.d., 3 Vol., pp. 66ff.

39. Schelling, *Werke,* ed. by K.F.A. Schelling, Stuttgart 1856 ff. XIV. 26. Vorlesung, pp. 51-73; G. W. F. Hegel, *Werke,* ed. by G. Hoffmeister, Hamburg 1955, 5th ed. XVIII A, pp. 58ff. G. W. F. Hegel, *Vorlesungen über die Philosophie der Religion,* ed. by G. Lasson, Vol. 2, pp. 173ff.

40. Cf. the article "God" by J. Köstlin in: *Realenzyklopädie für protestantische Theologie und Kirche* 2nd ed. 1879, Vol. V, pp. 289ff.

41. W. Pannenberg, not wholly without due, criticized K. Barth's adherence

to a concept of revelation rooted in the Enlightenment, or in Idealism: *Revelation as History*, New York 1968, pp. 3ff.

42. See also: W. Trillhaas, *op. cit.*, pp. 107-118.
43. W. Trillhaas, *op. cit.*, p. 128.
44. M. Theunissen, *op. cit.*, pp. 506f.
45. F. Ebner, *Das Wort und die geistigen Realitäten*, cit. by: Theunissen, *op. cit.*, p. 183.
46. M. Theunissen, *op. cit.*, pp. 330ff.
47. M. Buber, *I and Thou*, tr. R. G. Smith, Edinburgh, 1944, pp. 80-81, quoted in: M. Theunissen, *op. cit.*, p. 331.
48. M. Theunissen, *op. cit.*, pp. 338ff.; cf. here also the survey of the different uses of this thought by G. Marcel, K. Keim, E. Brunner and K. Barth.
49. K. Barth, *Church Dogmatics*, Vol. III/2, Edinburgh 1960, pp. 203ff. Despite all the differences between Buber and Barth as Theunissen rightly shows, both are related in the dialogical starting-point of their understanding of the Word, which Barth however only partially carries through. Cf. note 41.
50. *Theologisches Wörterbuch zum Neuen Testament*, ed. by G. Kittel, Vol. IV, pp. 69ff.
51. J. Hempel, *Gott und Mensch im A.T.*, *Beiträge zur Wissenschaft vom Alten und Neuen Testament*, Vol. III/2, 2nd ed. 1936. *Theologisches Wörterbuch zum Neuen Testament*, ed. by G. Kittel, Vol. VI, pp. 182ff.
52. E. Käsemann, "God's Righteousness in Paul" in: *New Testament Questions of Today*, London 1969; Chr. Müller, *Gottes Gerechtigkeit und Gottes Volk, Eine Untersuchung zu Römer 9-11*, Göttingen 1964; P. Stuhlmacher, *Gerechtigkeit Gottes bei Paulus*, Göttingen 1965.
53. E. Käsemann, *op. cit.*, p. 185.
54. Cf. W. Dantine, "Rechtfertigung und Gottesgerechtigkeit," in: *Verkündigung und Forschung*, 11.Jg. 1966, Heft 2: Zur Systematischen Theologie, pp. 68-100.
55. Cf. Regin Prenter, *Spiritus Creator*, Philadelphia, 1953.
56. The Latin text of the Large Catechism: *Siquidem haed duo, fides et Deus, una copula conjugenda sunt*, makes that even clearer. Th.G. Tappert (Ed.), The Book of Concord, Philadelphia, 1959, p. 365.
57. E. Bizer, *Fides ex auditu*, Neunkirchen 1958.
58. M. Luther, "Ecclesia enim est filia, nata ex verbo, non est mater verbi," W.A. 42, 334: 12.
59. Even in the developed system of the late Orthodox doctrine of the *ordo salutis*, which began to be understood as a step-wise development of the Christian consciousness and so began to dissolve the Reformation circle of Word and faith, rebirth is set in motion in the concept of the *vocatio*, the calling Word.
60. The concept of the *medium salutis* it is true became objectivized in the course of the doctrinal development so that it no longer also represented

the *fides* which supported a one-sided understanding of the "Word" as an objective entity. Cf. note 30.

61. K. Barth, *Church Dogmatics, The Doctrine of the Word of God,* Edinburgh, 2nd ed. 1949, pp. 418ff and pp. 424ff.

62. Cf. E. Jüngel, *Gottes Sein ist im Werden,* Tübingen 1965.

63. Cf. Joh. 4: 24 and 14: 6 with 14: 16, 26 and 15: 26.

64. Cf. R. Bultmann, *Theology of the New Testament,* Vol. I, London 1952, pp. 329f. and Vol. II, London 1955, p. 89.

65. M. Werner, *Die Entstehung des christlichen Dogmas,* Bern-Leipzig 1941, pp. 302ff. and 337ff. An abridged English version was published under the title: *The Formation of Christian Dogma,* Boston, 1965; G. Kretschmar, *Studien zur frühchristlichen Trinitätstheorie,* Tübingen 1956.

66. Such a statement does not endanger the so-called *"extra nos"* of salvation, or of the divine truth; in the concepts of incarnation and inspiration the initiative in the event of the confrontation of God and man lies with the former. The suspicion frequently raised that the dialogic encourages immanentism is ungrounded.

67. Of the obligatory doctrinal writings it is said: "Other symbols and other writings are not judges like Holy Scripture, but merely witnesses and expositions of the faith, setting forth how at various times the Holy Scriptures were understood in the church of God by contemporaries with references to controverted articles, and how contrary teachings were rejected and condemned." Formula of Concord, *Epitome,* Introduction 8, *The Book of Concord,* Philadelphia 1959, p. 465.

68. Cf. J. Ratzinger, *Das Problem der Dogmengeschichte in der Geschichte der katholischen Theologie,* Köln-Opladen 1966.

69. H. Hammans, *Die neueren katholischen Erklärungen der Dogmenentwicklung,* Essen 1965.

70. K. Rahner, "The Development of Dogma," in: *Theological Investigations,* Vol. I, London 1961, pp. 39-77.

71. K. Rahner and K. Lehmann, "Geschichtlichkeit der Vermittlung," in: *Mysterium Salutis, Grundriss heilsgeschichtlicher Dogmatik,* ed. by J. Feiner and M. Löhrer, Vol. I, 1965, pp. 727-782.

72. New York 1966.

73. Cf. note 34.

74. G. Kaiser, *Pietismus und Patriotismus im literarischen Deutschland. Ein Beitrag zum Problem der Säkularisation,* Wiesbaden 1961.

75. F. Meinecke, *Die Entstehung des Historismus,* 2nd ed., Berlin 1946.

76. That took place, although this philosophical interpretation of history of historicism did not find an important philosophical interpreter, so that it can only be presented in later research.

77. Cf. the book with this title by R. Wittram, *Das Interesse an der Geschichte,* Göttingen 1958.

78. Here belong, among others, also the ideologies such as Marxism-Leninism or the idea of the "Third Reich," but also the "Idee der Heilsgeschichte," as sketched for example in a book with this title by Karl G. Steck, Zürich

1959. Cf. also O. Cullmann, *Salvation in History*, London 1967. It is important that the new Catholic theology of the *Heilsgeschichte* in part moves along other lines. Cf. Adolf Darlap, "Fundamentale Heilsgeschichte," in: *Mysterium Salutis*, vol. I, *op. cit.*, pp. 3-90.

79. Cf. the concept "decision" by Løgstrup, note 18.

80. Rom. 9-11 must be seen together with texts such as 1 Cor. 13:8-13, 2 Cor. 3:17-18 and with the promise of the Paraclete, John 4:16-17, 26; 15:26; 16:7, 13, and at the same time with a reinterpretation of the dogmatic teaching of the "*illuminatio.*"

81. The "*Decretum de Iudaeis*" of the Second Vatican Council, *Declaratio de ecclesiae habitudine ad religiones nonchristianas* 4; "*Der ungekündigte Bund,*" ed. by D. Goldschmied and H. J. Kraus, Stuttgart-Berlin 1962, "*Das gespaltene Gottesvolk,*" ed. by H. Gollwitzer and E. Sperling, Stuttgart 1966; "The Church and the Jewish People. Report on a Consultation," in *Lutheran World* 11 (1964), pp. 264ff.

82. Cf. J. Moltmann, *Theology of Hope*, New York 1967 and G. Sauter, *Zukunft und Verheissung*, Zürich 1965.

83. Cf. the changes in the papal social encyclicals up to *Populorum progressio; Church, Community and State*. The Report of the Conference at Oxford, London 1937; World Conference on Society, Geneva 1966; *The Uppsala Report* 1968, Geneva 1968; *Lumen Gentium* nr. 9 and 13.

84. Cf. note 7.

85. Cf. again here the book by H. D. Bastian, *Theologie der Frage*, note 24.

86. Cf. H. Schelsky, "Ist die Dauerreflexion institutionalisierbar?" in: *Zeitschrift für evangelische Ethik*, Vol. 1 1957, pp. 153-174.

87. The degree of enmity is not at all related to the degree of difference; the manner of the historical confrontation plays a decisive role, so that the fight between the confessional brothers within Christianity is often more bitter than the controversies with other religions.

88. Although the role the confessions play in the churches may vary in individual cases, it has a genuine and necessary relation to truth for the understanding of faith in all Christian denominations and is thus not to be minimized; it is the nature of dialog that every partner brings his understanding of the truth in its full extent into the conversation.

89. That is the logical result of setting Christian faith, or the Christian churches, absolute as the only vehicle of truth in the sense of a monological and monopolistic understanding. It is typical that even the Protestant churches, which never understood the denominations as "*societas perfectae*" seldom react differently than Roman Catholicism and the Orthodox Church: the self-attestation of one's own essence erects a wall against all the "others," which reduces the many different groups on this other side to a wicked conspiracy within which the differences between schismatics, heretics, religious non-Christians and opponents of religion almost disappear. Cf. the parallels between the laws against heretics and those against Jews already in the old church, *Kirche und Synagoge*, ed. by K. H. Rengstorff and S. von Kortzfleisch, Vol. I, Stuttgart 1968, pp. 84ff.

89a. Cf. note 1.

90. The subsummation of Judaism, Christianity, and Islam under the heading of monotheism is a part of western humanistic education since Lessing's *Nathan der Weise*. But the concept of religion behind it has been put in question by the modern science of comparative religions.

91. Cf. "Die nichtchristlichen Religionen," ed. by H. v. Glasenapp, *Das Fischerlexikon*, Vol. 1, Frankfurt 1957.

92. Even the concept "mosaic" religion is hardly acceptable today. It is however further significant—and this fact has been underscored in the antisemitic persecutions in the 20th century—that with Israel and membership in it a circumstance is created which also involves consciously non-religious Jews.

93. Not the least of these because in their historical experience, Christianity has proven itself especially monological, which makes it responsible today for furthering the dialogue.

94. R.N. nr. 4.

95. R.N. nr. 2.

96. R.N. nr. 3.

97. Cf. K. Goldammer, *Die Formenwelt des Religiösen*, Stuttgart 1960; id., *Religionen, Religion und christliche Offenbarung*, Stuttgart 1965; J. Matthes, *Religion und Gesellschaft*, Hamburg 1967; *Intern. Jahrbuch für Religionssoziologie*, ed. by J. Matthes, Köln-Opladen 1965ff.

98. H. R. Schlette, *Towards a Theology of Religion*, London 1963; id., *Philosophie—Theologie—Ideologie*, Köln 1968.

99. K. Barth, *Church Dogmatics*, Vol. I/2, Edinburgh 1956, pp. 280ff.: "The Revelation of God as the Abolition of Religion" (§ 17); H. Kraemer, *Religion and the Christian Faith*, London 1956.

100. Cf. note 24.

101. D. Bonhoeffer, *Letters and Papers from Prison*, London 1953, pp. 122ff., 145ff., 158ff., and 178ff.

102. H. Lübbe, *Säkularisierung. Geschichte eines ideenpolitischen Bergriffs*, Freiburg/München 1965. And H. Blumberg, *Die Legitimität der Neuzeit*. Frankfurt/M. 1966.

103. F. Gogarten, *Despair and Hope for Our Time*, Philadelphia, 1970, pp. 102ff.

104. Naturally a list of analogue phenomena could be named, as for example National-socialism.

105. F. Mauthner, *Der Atheismus und seine Geschichte im Abendlande*, Vol. I-IV, Stuttgart-Berlin 1920-23, Nachdr. Rüdesheime 1963.

106. I. Fetscher, *Von der Philosophie des Proletariats zur proletarischen Weltanschauung*, in: Marxismus-Studien, 2. Folge ed. by I. Fetscher, Tübingen 1957, pp. 26-60.

107. *Christentum und Marxismus—heute (Gespräche der Paulusgesellschaft*, ed. by E. Kellner), Wien 1966; *Schöpfertum und Freiheit in einer humanen Gesellschaft. Marienbader Protokolle. (Gespräche der Paulusgesellschaft*, ed. by E. Kellner) Wien 1969; *Internationale Dialog Zeitschrift* 1968, Heft 1.

108. Cf. B. Bosnjak—W. Dantine—J. Y. Calvez, "Marxistisches und christliches Weltverständnis," Herder-Freiburg-Wien 1966, in: *Weltgespräch, Selbstkritik des 20. Jhdts.*, Schriften Vol. 1.

109. W. Dantine, "Der Tod Gottes und das Bekenntnis zum Schöpfer," in: *Schriften zum Weltgespräch* 1. Cf. note 108, pp. 65ff.

110. Cf. H. J. Lieber, "Art. Ideologie," *Das Fischerlexikon* Vol. 2, pp. 121ff. Frankfurt/M. 1957; *Ideologie, Ideologiekritik und Wissenssoziologie*, ed. by K. Lenk (soziol. Texte Vol. 4), Neuwied/Berlin 1964, 2nd ed.

111. The churches for their part have in fact taken the initiative in entering into conversation with the nonreligious partners. Of especial importance is the fact that Paul VI in 1964 founded a "Secretariate for Nonbelievers" which is led by the Archbishop Cardinal of Vienna, Dr. Franz König. Cf. also note 6.

Chapter 6

Man as Responsible Co-worker with God in a Dynamic World

Modern man feels he is the master and molder of his earthly world. He works incessantly to reshape not only his external environment, nature, but also the structures of his own historical existence, and to use them for his own plans and wishes for a more humane future. This modern attitude toward the world has deep roots in the tremendous scientific and technological advances since the days of Galileo and Bacon and in the comprehensive social changes in the world since the great modern revolutions.

This development in the modern consciousness is irreversible and has important consequences for the Christian faith. "Modern man feels to a great extent that *he* must bring *himself* into a new and entirely different future . . . and this future is conceived not eschatologically—as God's gift which brings temporal history to an end—but rather as something which man creates and conquers for himself." [1] This alleged conflict between enthusiastic world-transforming activity and faith in a creator and Lord of our life is undoubtedly one of the most important roots of the present-day world crisis of traditional Christianity.

Let us not be in too great a hurry to dismiss this idea as utterly mistaken and to reassure ourselves with various biblical and theological arguments. Is it really true that there are no instances of a "religious estrangement" from reality, from the concrete tasks of

178

daily life? Are there really no cases of a "devout" flight from the enormous problems of our present-day world into the past, into inwardness or into the transcendent? Viewing it theologically, is there really no tension between God as the effective cause of everything and human activity in creation and history? Present-day *Christian* theology must take these questions very seriously and scrutinize our faith and our traditional theological ideas under the word of God and in the light of modern secular developments.

But the topic of this study is a relevant theological endeavor from yet another point of view. The "theology of human activity"— to use this somewhat pretentious designation—has always been a critical point of *Lutheran* theology. The "Reformers' one-sided exposition" [2] in their description of justification "by grace alone, without man's cooperation," was questioned repeatedly, sometimes sharply, sometimes gently, from the Roman Catholic side. On the other hand, in the Reformation churches' ecumenical discussions, the weakness of Lutheranism is often seen as lying in the theological treatment of sanctification, in the lack of a fully developed social ethic, and in its "basically conservative" nature. [3] Once again, let us not feel too confident in the face of these kinds of theological reproaches and criticisms! Has our Lutheran theology always taken seriously and so fully elaborated, theologically and with all desirable clarity, man's privilege and responsibility of participating in historical-social processes, the broad social-ethical ramifications of active Christian love, and the living dynamic of God's creative activity in our world? Lutheran theologians have the urgent task of doing this wherever it has not yet been done in sufficient depth and breadth.

In both of these directions, Lutheran theologians can find numerous theological motives for so doing. Reformation theology has already once helped Christendom step out of a spiritualistic desertion of the world into a "sanctified worldliness" and exchange the cloister cell for a secular vocation. Perhaps something similar could happen again today on the strength of Luther's theology! On the other hand, we also must not shrink back in fear from the prospect of extracting from Scripture entirely new insights and their consequences. Abstract theology, isolated from its environment, has always been a mistake. One strong side of the Reformer's theology was precisely the seriousness with which they considered the questions their own time posed to them. But even they could not answer all the questions of Christian theology—not even those of their own age—by themselves. It remains a worthy task of present-day Lutheran theology to think through the questions of the secular world and the ecumenical discussion deeply—all the way down to our own basic theological presuppositions—and, if necessary, also to draw radically new consequences out of the word of God.

But let us return to our topic! Viewed systematically, it is a question of the role of human action in Lutheran theology—human action, that is, in creation and history with regard to the earthly world, or, expressed in good Lutheran terms, in God's secular kingdom. A deeper consideration of man's "participation" in God's redemptive work—the church's ministry in word and sacrament—is not undertaken here and remains a subject for future study.

Here we want first to examine the direction from which Lutheran theology approaches the question of the relationship of human action to divine activity in the world. The remainder of this article then deals with the relationship of human activity to God's activity in the general and in the particular sense, i.e. in the life of all men in the world and in the ministry of the Christian congregation, the life of the Christian.

THE GOSPEL POINT OF DEPARTURE: GOD ALONE CREATES AND RENEWS US TO BE HIS CO-WORKERS IN THE WORLD

God Is at Work Everywhere

God's work of creation does not mean just one divine act in the beginning, but also a continuing creative activity *(creatio continua)* in the dialectical process of the preservation and renewal of the world. God is at work everywhere in the world. "When thou hidest thy face, they are dismayed; when thou takest away their breath, they die and return to their dust. When thou sendest forth thy Spirit, they are created; and thou renewest the face of the ground" (Ps. 104:29-30). God is the one who "himself gives to all men life and breath and everything" (Acts 17:25). Or, as Luther says, God is "an effective power and a constant activity which is constantly in motion and at work" (WA 7, 574: 29), and: "God alone does and works everything in me" (WA 24, 21:35).

This all embracing creating and sustaining work of God does not exclude but rather includes *man's* will and action. "Then God said, 'Let us make man in our image, after our likeness; and let them have dominion over the fish of the sea, and over the birds of the air, and over the cattle, and over all the earth . . .'" (Gen 1:26). As the strongest proof of this privilege of participation, man receives God's energizing blessing: "'Be fruitful and multiply, and fill the earth and subdue it; and have dominion over the fish of the sea and over the birds of the air and over every living thing that moves upon the earth,'" (Gen. 1:28).

It is to this "co-working" and "co-ruling" of man that many theologians look for the meaning of that puzzling statement in the creation narrative: man is the "image of God." "With this saying the Bible may very well have meant that man is the creator's steward on earth and therefore his partner." [4] If we can consider this commission as just the consequence of a deeper meaning of the *imago Dei*—the personal I-Thou relationship between God and man [5]—then this interpretation has something very important to say on our topic. God works incessantly—and his highest earthly creation must demonstrate its nature as his image by participating as well in this creative activity of God. How this happens is our next question.

The Sovereign Action of God and the Cooperation of Man

God created and continues to create a world that is not fixed and static but rather dynamic, constantly changing and ever evolving. The alleged "Lutheran conservatism," the inclination to the traditional and the familiar, does not reckon with this important feature of God's rule in creation and history.

A great amount of God's creative activity takes place through his choosing man to be his co-worker and agent: by letting the possibilities hidden in the world be unfolded through the agency of human hands and human reason—regardless of whether or not man realizes this and thankfully accepts his role as God's co-worker in faith. For examples of "unconscious" cooperation we can mention the familiar Old Testament instances in which God punishes or frees his people through heathen kings as his "servants." The classic example of "conscious" and believing cooperation is Phil. 2:12-13, "Work out your own salvation with fear and trembling; for God is at work in you, both to will and to work for his good pleasure."

The concept of cooperation *(cooperatio)* also occupies an important, though certainly not a central, position in Luther's theology.[6] In the Collected Sermons *(Kirchenpostille)* we meet with the picture of the Christian as a pipe or conduit into which things flow, through faith, from God above, and "are poured out again down below," through love, to our fellowmen. "Luther makes it clear that God's own love reaches out to others through Christians as channels. God is present on earth with his goodness when a Christian directs his service downward to others. God dwells in heaven, but now he is near and working on earth with man as his co-operator."[7]

The question is justified whether Luther's well-known principle of the sovereign action of God in his creatures *(larvae Dei)*, and especially in the believers, does not deprive this *cooperation of man* in the world of any real significance. It is true that some Lutheran theologians did and do formulate the principle that God is the sole effective cause of everything in such a one-sided and misleading way that there really is nothing left over for man other than the role of a mere "means" or performing "instrument," instead of an authentic partnership and relationship of trust in faith One-sided quotations from Luther could very easily lead to this misunderstanding *(e.g.* the example of the sword or saw in God's hand, WA 5, 177: 21; 2, 421: 12ff.). But on the other hand, Luther says often—and for the most part his Roman Catholic critics have passed over these passages in silence—that God does not just work "alone," but also simultaneously "together" with man. God "uses . . . us men in both his physical and spiritual kingdoms to govern the world and everything in it" (WA 23, 9: 3). "Why does God not do it alone and by himself? Indeed, he can, but he does not want to do it alone; he wants us to work with him and he *does us the honor* of wanting to do his work with us and through us" (WA 6, 227: 28-29).[8]

But how is all of this talk about cooperation to be reconciled with the familiar Reformation confession of the redemption and renewal of the sinner "by grace alone," "through faith alone," "without our works?" Here, in the question of justification, lies the key to this complicated, multifaceted, but right now very crucial problem of human action, the problem of Christian ethics.

Creation and New Creation Without Man's Cooperation

God uses man everywhere in the world and works through him and together with him. In his famous work *De servo arbitrio,* Luther says there are only two points at which there is no cooperation —in the creation *ex nihilo* and in justification, the new creation likewise *ex nihilo.*

> (1) Before man is created and is a man, he neither does nor attempts to do anything toward becoming a creature, and after he is created he neither does nor attempts to do anything toward remaining a creature, but both of these things are done by the sole will of the omnipotent power and goodness of God, who creates and preserves us without our help; but he does not work in us without us, because it is for this he has created and preserved us, that he might work in us and we might cooperate with him, whether outside his Kingdom through his general omnipotence or inside his Kingdom by the special virtue of his Spirit. (2) In just the same way (our answer continues), before man is changed into a new creature of the Kingdom of the Spirit, he does nothing and attempts to prepare himself for this renewal and this Kingdom, and when he has been recreated he does nothing and attempts nothing toward remaining in this Kingdom, but the Spirit alone does both of these things in us, recreating us without us and preserving us without our help in our recreated state, as also James says: "Of his own will he brought us forth by the word of his power, that we might be a beginning of his creature" (James 1:18)— speaking of the renewed creature. But he does not work without us, because it is for this very thing he has recreated and preserves us, that he might work in us and we might cooperate with him. Thus it is through us he preaches, shows mercy to the poor, comforts the afflicted. But what is attributed to free choice in all this? Or rather, what is there left for it but nothing? And really nothing! [9]

We have quoted this long passage because it expresses with all due clarity the "Lutheran position" on the most central question of the Christian life and the most important point of the present-day ecumenical discussion. The sinner is justified *sine nobis,* "without our aid" and cooperation, through the gracious working of the Spirit of God alone. In the God-man relationship we can of our own power bring nothing before God: no preparation, no cooperation, no merits—this is the ever necessary shattering of our deep inner human pride *(superbia)*. This is and always remains the first fundamental principle of the truth. But the second half is no less important and necessary, especially in this context and in our age which, as our introduction described it, takes such great pleasure in being active: sanctification, making the sinner righteous and whole, takes place *"non sine nobis,"* not without our aid; for the gracious God who justifies us also draws us in faith into his eternally creative love and puts us to work as "co-workers" in both his secular and spiritual activity (reign). This is the shattering of our laziness, passiveness and hopelessness that is so necessary today; this is being employed from above in the cause of righteousness and love in our world.

The special significance of this Reformation message of justification in the present-day ecumenical dialog is the persistent and biblical way in which it attributes all glory to God alone "in matters of salvation" and safeguards the insight that man never stands in the presence of God as one who is active, but rather only as one who receives in faith. On this point Catholic theology is also much closer to the Reformation teaching today than in the time of the Council of Trent. From Trent we still read that man—awakened and assisted by grace—can assume the posture of "freely assenting to and cooperating with that same grace." [10] But in M. Schmaus' *Catholic Dogmatics* there can be found these sentences which—despite all the dialectics of his statements—stand so near the Reformation's real concern: "In this it (i.e., the Council of Trent) does not intend to say that now man can do something for his salvation, even though God must do most of it," and: "It is no disgrace to man that God has destined him for a goal that he cannot reach through his own strength but only through God's grace." [11]

Here grace reigns supreme, the gospel which forgives sins for Christ's sake, without any cooperation and merits from man's side.

"There Christ rules alone, with his grace and gospel . . . , co-operation is barred from heaven." [12]

The "Lutheran position's" strength for the Christian life consists of its establishing as the foundations of Christian life and action, and the sustaining basis of its theological ethic, not moral laws, principles, or ethical imperatives but rather *a personal relationship* between the gracious God and the man who receives grace: *faith* in God's grace, deep inner trust in the crucified and resurrected Lord Jesus Christ. Therefore the most basic question for Christian action and all Christian ethics can be formulated thus: What is the concrete and theological significance of *Jesus Christ* for the moral life? [13] Here the spirits part in our time, too.

The Good Works of Faith

Let us return once again to the crucial passage, which we have quoted from Luther's *De servo arbitrio*. There it says: the creation and also the new creation of man take place "without our aid," without any synergistic cooperation between God and man. But the realization of this grace *in our lives* takes place "not without our aid." Here God creates us anew by working in us and together with us. Thus the dynamic of the gospel unites us with God not only "in heaven," "in matters of salvation," in the faith that passively receives, but also on earth, "in matters of ministry," in the faith that is actively at work.

This makes it clear that the proper place of God's cooperation with man—and of man's cooperation with God, which always and only results from God's gracious prior condescension—is *the earthly sphere*, where both sanctification and the good works of faith take place. "First for all things hear the word of God. Then believe, then work, and so become blessed" (WA 10 I 1, 329:6). The same faith which God alone works in us through his word and which stands passively before God, trusting fully in the gracious forgiveness of sins, now becomes an inexhaustible fount of love for our fellowmen, good works, and sanctification. Here we must quote the Reformer's famous saying on faith, which does not ask "whether good works are to be done but rather has them done before anyone asks—and is always doing them" (WA 7, 10: 11). That is

the singular and glorious "freedom of a Christian," who is subject
to his neighbor out of love and serves him gladly.

For faith it is obvious that there is a continuing and mysterious
cooperation of God's omnipotence with *all* life and action in this
world. But strictly speaking the *proper* area of this "miraculous
cooperation" is the Christian life, the life of Jesus' community in
the world. This conscious cooperation of the believers is an emana-
tion of God's love out into the world in ministry in both God's
secular and spiritual kingdoms. The Christians' cooperation in
God's creation is always a "fruit of faith." It never becomes an
independent, autonomous activity. Its background is always the
individual's freedom and his dependence in faith on God, God's
unmerited, liberating grace. How is that possible? A cooperation
in which God does everything and nonetheless still does not break
the back of the creature's freedom and responsibility but rather
restores to the creature his joy and freedom through that very
cooperation—this remains a *mystery* even to faith. Faced with this
enigma we can say nothing other than what R. Herman has said
with such touching candor: "I cannot formulate any 'how' for this
'together.'" [14]

The Ethical Message of the Doctrine of Justification Today

It is widely known that a vigorous debate concerning the doctrine of justification flared up as a result of the fourth plenary
assembly of the Lutheran World Federation (1963). The real point
of this dispute was whether the content of this doctrine is relevant
for our life as well, for the active and action-oriented man of the
modern age. As is clear from what has already been said, when it
is delved into a bit deeper this question is easy to answer. For the
justification of the sinner is not only a forensic legal event in God's
judgment but is simultaneously *(uno actu)* also the "*making* righteous" of the sinner, his sanctification in faith through the Holy
Spirit. "In faith justification and sanctification are one." [15] Therefore there is no more monstrous misunderstanding of this biblical
message of justification than to think that justifying faith allows
a person to continue passively and comfortably in his sins. Truly,
"this nominalistic as-if-justification arouses righteous wrath and

scorn among Catholics, Pietists, and Spiritualists of every hue." [16] But, as we saw, this reproach is not justified against the original Lutheran teaching. Justifying faith is always "not only an act of receiving but also a renewing power in the heart and it cannot exist together with sin." [17]

Despite these obvious facts, Lutheran theology has much ground to recover on this point. For Vilmos Vajta is right in saying: "In taking up its polemic positions Lutheran theology devoted less attention to the insight that, quite apart from the divine initiative, the Holy Spirit carries out his sanctifying work *non sine nobis.* Attention was restricted so predominantly to the question of the foundation of salvation that the building itself was no longer given adequate consideration. And so the theology of sanctification remained unexplicated." [18]

The much-discussed "critical point" of the doctrine of justification is right here today. Here it must be made clear that Christianity as an "inner existence of faith" or an active "social Christianity" are false alternatives. Christianity is simultaneously and inseparably both: active, lively existential trust in Christ and a posture of active service toward all areas of personal and social life. But this latter is always and only the fruit and the consequence of the former, the justifying faith in Christ.

The problem of ethics, too, the "theology of human action" as a cooperation with God's all-effecting dynamic love, can be properly handled only from this "Lutheran point of departure." As we said, there are two areas of divine cooperation in our human action: the general area of his divine omnipotence and the particular area of the new creation, the work of the justified. Let us now turn to the first area, in which God "brings about external peace and prevents evil deeds"). (*On temporal authority,* in Luther's Works, American Edition, vol. 45, p. 92, = WA 11, 252: 12).

MAN AS "GOD'S CO-WORKER"—OUTSIDE OF FAITH
God's "Secular Reign"

As mentioned above, the Christian faith in creation sees God at work everywhere. "For 'in him we live and move and have our being'" (Acts 17:28). God's hidden, invisible working and governing extend so far "that it does not lie within my own power to move my hand, but God does and works everything in me" (WA 24, 21: 35). "The world is filled with God" (Luther).

This "secular reign" of God takes place in two ways. One form of it takes place in *nature*. Here life moves within a strict order *(kosmos)*, fixed in natural laws. The eyes of faith see God governing here—from the smallest subatomic particles to the gigantic galaxies—in the eternal immutability of these laws.

But the world of men also stands under the rule of another "divine order." Doubtless man is a part of the material, physical universe. But he is also a part of *history*, the world of the will and ethical decisions. Here God rules "like a father," by giving his creatures a degree of independence to choose alternatives and make decisions along the path of their own lives—but without withdrawing his presence and his all-penetrating omnipotence from them. Man is an "image of God." He either possesses and lives his full freedom in a relationship of creaturely trust to God or else he corrupts it in sin, in his supposed automony from God.

God's instruments in the preservation and evolution of his created world are on the one hand the universal inner law of conscience, written in the heart *(lex cordibus inscripta*, cf. Rom. 2:14-15), and on the other hand the external, natural forms of human life together, the structures of society.

Here we cannot deal in detail with the widely discussed theological problem of the "natural moral law" and its relationship to God's revealed law. But this much must be clear to all thinking Christians: despite all its inner contradictions and ambiguities, this inner "instrument" of God is an inconceivably great gift in the protection of community order from the chaos of human actions.

The "external" instruments of God's secular reign are the basic sociological structures of human life together, the ordained structures of family, state, economic, and cultural life (Luther: *oeconomia et politia*). The Augsburg Confession asserts this, too: "Concerning civil government *(de rebus civilibus)* it is taught among us that all government in the world and all established rules and laws were instituted and ordained by God for the sake of good order." [19] Thus they are good and necessary gifts of God for preserving external order in society—gifts, but simultaneously *tasks* for the man who lives in them. For these structures of society are not immutable. Even under these sociological structures, we still live in God's dynamic world. They are included in a constant process of transformation in time, although their nucleus remains unchangeable, a permanent ordained structure.

Let us take marriage as an example. How many outward forms of marriage and family life are not known to history! And yet one thing remains unchanged: marriage was created and instituted by God for the communion of man and woman and for the propagation of human life (Gen. 1:27 28; 2:18, 23-24). Despite their abiding "nucleus of content," all the other historical social structures of man's world in economic, social, and political life are subject to these same dynamic changes, too. There are two reasons for this: one, because they become outmoded with time, and history flows onward, passing them by in silence; but secondly also, because they can be corrupted through man's sin, egoism and injustice (we will speak of this in still greater detail in the next section). When one or the other of these two happens, and even more so when both occur together, we have the ethical task of exchanging the outmoded and corrupted social structures for new ones—in accord with God's will and law and in keeping with the needs of the time, the evolution of the world. We live in God's dynamic world, where he is constantly preserving and creating anew. "To believe in the immutable determination of society means to fall back into superstition and to look down on man, who has been commissioned by the creator himself to exercise dominion over the earth as the *cooperator Dei* in the world of history." [20]

Therefore a healthy criticism of an inflexible "idea of order" ("immutable orders of creation") is needed also from this point of view. A proper Christian view of the dynamic world of creation and of God's governing of the world never leads to a posture of biased conservatism and a canonization of the social *status quo* for its own sake, but rather obliges us to undertake a responsible, legitimate "reshaping" of the sociological structures and to participate actively in God's hidden creative activity in the world.

Thus the Christian view looks upon human action as participation, "cooperation" in God's action in the continuing historical de-

velopment of the world. It guards man from simply deifying the
historical order and from wanting to escape the God-given task of
building a more just, more humane world.

The Independence and Ethical Determination
of the Social Structures

Owing to the creator's will, the basic sociological structures of
family, state, work, economy and culture have a degree of independence and autonomy in the context of historical life. "These
'orders' are instituted by God to be permanent in the world; they
are supposed to enjoy their own *relative autonomy* under the sovereign law of the creator. Therefore not faith and love, but rather
reason and justice are determinative for the temporal area of
life." [21] Thus it is hopeless to try to sanction for once and for all a
specifically "Christian" economic or social system, as has often
been attempted in the church or in enthusiastic Christian movements since the Middle Ages. God's world does not allow itself to
be governed with the gospel, but rather only through its own God-
given ordained structures, by reason and specialized skills.

But on the other hand we must emphasize very decisively that
this relative independence of the sociological structures in science,
politics, economics and culture *can never mean that these areas of
life are completely independent of ethics* and ethical responsibility.
The structures of the world's life also stand beneath the hidden
rule of God, who has made his will known in the revealed law—
and also in the universal law of the human conscience. The ordained structures of life and life's ethical laws can never be separated from each other without doing serious harm to personal and
social life. This holds true both in the universally human context
and in the specifically Christian sphere. "At the same time, against
the background of the 'German Christians' tragedy . . . it cannot
be emphasized strongly enough that faith can enlighten reason and
love can put justice in the right perspective wherever Christians
perceive their civic responsibility as part of their discipleship of
Christ." [22] Expressed theologically, the separation of society's own
ordained structures from our ethical responsibility before God's
law would be intolerable and disastrous rending of the two "reigns

of God" in the world. For the same Lord has created both "kingdoms" and the same Lord also reigns over them both. To tear them apart would be just as great a mistake as to mix them in a secular or ecclesiastical combination, to draw no distinction between these two modes of God's activity in our historically conditioned world.[23]

"God's Co-workers"—Outside of Faith, Too

If God does not govern man's world and history directly but rather "wraps" his creative and providential activity in the out ward form of human activity, then he uses unbelievers, too, as well as men of faith as his "agents" and "co-workers." We have already mentioned biblical examples such as Cyrus and the role of heathen nations in the history of Israel. But many more examples could be cited, both from the Old and the New Testament. Since God wills to make use of human reason, professional expertise, and the universal law of the conscience in the preservation and evolution of the world, faith in God is not a prerequisite at all.

"For what we assert and contend for is this", Luther says, "that when God operates without regard to the grace of the Spirit, he works all in all, even in the ungodly." [24] Where parents give their children life, nourishment and guidance, where the state and government serve the causes of social order and earthly peace, where the laborer helps the human community faithfully and competently in his occupation, there God is at work, everywhere and in a *hidden* manner. Then they are all "co-workers of God" in his creative activity, his governing of the world—through their own outward works, their participation in the preservation and evolution of the world, independent of the faith or unfaith of their heart.[25] Therefore Luther can say, in just this context: "For that reason government does not require Christians and it is not necessary that the emperor be a holy man. It is enough that he be a reasonable man." [26]

These external "objective good works," which serve the world and human society in the various secular stations and social structures, bring *"civil righteousness,"* honor before men *(iustitia civilis).* Outwardly, human life in society is based on this kind of righteousness. Without it all community life and even our personal existence would perish in a wild chaos. The Christian faith sees the hidden creative activity of God at work everywhere in and behind the external relative ordering and further development of the world through human work, science, social organizations, and culture.

This means that in society there is a common sphere of ethical obligations and tasks shared by Christians and non-Christians. We both live in the realm of God's law, the divinely-created structures of community life, the realm of reason and of the universal moral law—things which are common to all men. Therefore non-Christians, too, can be excellent instruments in God's hand for the preservation and enrichment of human life, and their devotion and faithfulness to their calling can even put Christians to shame. We Christians in the non-Christian society of Socialist Eastern Europe have humbly had to learn this again and again. But on the other hand this means our joint "involvement," in conscious or unconscious cooperation with God, in the preservation of his creation; this means we must work together with all honest and well-meaning men of other faiths and ideologies in the humane endeavor for peace and justice in the world and against hunger, ignorance, immorality, exploitation, and all forms of inhumanity. God's hidden universal rule in the world unites us in this work "from above." But the distress of our suffering fellowmen and concern for the common good of the society in which we all live together obligate us "from below" to do this work together.

Consequences for a "Theology of the World"

An important task for Lutheran ethics today is the re-evaluation of God's hidden rule in secular events, in human society. In Lutheran theology today we urgently need a biblically based, clear and realistic "theology of the world." We need a clearly explicated theological view of history, society, economics, culture and politics —based on theological reflection on the two different modes of God's rule in the world and in his community within this world. But any application of the Lutheran teaching of the "two kingdoms" requires great caution. Not everything that is "traditional" is true. And not everything that today sails under the "Lutheran flag" is truly biblical and Lutheran. We see two consequences of what has been said up to this point that are especially important for this new theological view of the world.

a. As we have already stated more than once, God's creative-providential action does not exclude but rather includes man's thought and action. For us Christians a hydroelectric plant is no less God's work than a waterfall; a heart transplant is no less God's work than a birth. Therefore there is a pressing need for a new theological evaluation of nature, reason, science, technology, and of the economic and social activity of Christians and non-Christians.

It cannot be denied that our much-lauded and oft condemned "Lutheran faith-piety" has very often brought along with it a depreciation of and a disregard for this other "mode of God's rule" and its instruments in the world, a contempt for the secular, reason, universal morality, and the external structures of social life. For centuries we have—rightly and necessarily—concentrated our theological efforts on Christ's work of redemption, the church and the "spiritual ministry" in the church. But in so doing we have often—and this was by no means right or necessary—neglected far too much the other sphere of God's loving activity in which we as Christians and the church also must live and serve, namely the world, society; we have "looked down our noses at it" theologically and sometimes have even treated it with outright contempt.

Recently—most recently and very decidedly in the Lutheran World Federation's Commission on Theology—Lutheran theologians have turned their attention much more to this set of questions. Ever since the time of the great change in their social environment, our Lutheran churches in the Socialist countries have also felt themselves obliged to re-think these problems theologically, in order to work out the fundamentals of Lutheran social ethics in a non-Christian secular society. But here there is still much more to be done than has as yet been done, to meet both the demands of the present time and the challenge of a similar theological endeavor in ecumenical theology and the work of Vatican II.

b. Another important task of Lutheran ethics in this context is renewed concern for the Christian doctrine of sin, both in the personal and the social areas of life. On the one hand it is important to guard against a naive optimism about nature and the future of mankind—as can often be found in the so-called "social theology." But on the other hand it is just as important not to try to derive from the Lutheran Reformation's radical doctrine of sin an "incapability of moral life and a distrust of reason." This "pessimistic understanding of man" [27] is no less a danger for us than a neglect of the menace of sin in the created world. Therefore we want to turn to this problem.

MAN'S SIN AS A MENACE TO GOD'S CREATION
Misused Freedom

Among all earthly creatures, God gave a "creaturely freedom" only to man. This freedom enabled man to cooperate, consciously and responsibly, with God in his world. But its negative side was *man's fall into sin,* which has subsequently been repeated a millionfold and continues unceasingly to be repeated in all areas of personal and social life.

The fact that he is a created being means that man cannot have any absolutely free will—free from God and free from the evil one; on the contrary, it means he can have only either a freedom in obedience to God or a freedom as "autonomy of the will" over against God—in which he must then fall into the bondage of sin. "For although they knew God they did not honor him as God or give thanks to him, but they became futile in their thinking and their senseless minds were darkened" (Rom. 1:21). After man's fall from God there followed inevitably the *revelation of the wrath of God* against "all ungodliness and wickedness of men . . ." (Rom. 1:18).

This "tragedy of man," who seeks his freedom in sin and disdains the true freedom in obedience to God, can in no way be charged to "God's account" through any kind of eternal divine predestination.[28] It is the mystery of human rebellion against God and it shows how little the original communion with God, the "image of God-relationship," meant any form of divine compulsion for man. God never forces man into communion with himself. He calls man and gives it to him as a gift through the power of his grace and love. Despite his creatureliness, man can—this is the deep mystery of sin—at any time reject God's grace and its freedom in communion with God. This is what happened in the fall and has been repeated ever since in every concrete realization of man's original sin.

A Menace to His Own Existence

The most immediate consequence of the fall into sin appears for man on the one hand in his alienation from God, the loss of his ethical responsibility *coram Deo,* and on the other hand in the ruin of every aspect of his personal life.

The first consequence of sin that the biblical fall narrative speaks of is man's fear of and flight from God (Gen. 3:8ff.). But this flight soon turns into a charge against God, the creature's accusation of the creator (Gen. 3:12f.). That is a visible symptom of the utter ruin of his relationship to his creator (G. von Rad). He thereby draws God's just judgment upon himself, the threat of the loss of his temporal and eternal life.

In sin man falls out of the relationship that was the most important and helpful relationship also for his action in the world. He loses his "response-ability" before God, his conscience, the God-given inner "touchstone" for life's crucial question: "What am I supposed to do?" As long as he hears and responds to the word of God in a relationship of trust, he has in this "word-response" relationship a firm basis for his ethical decisions, the judgment of the ethical propriety of his action. But here the fall into sin means man's absolute "alienation," a flight into the unknown, the loss of his reliable inner compass for his conduct. And so "having to make choices" in ethical decisions without that inner assurance and joy becomes a torment for him.

Then there is no lack of immediate consequences in other areas of his personal and social life, either. The fall narrative describes these consequences paradigmatically. For man the world is no longer a place of true harmony with himself, his fellowmen and nature. In the awareness of his sin man comes into conflict *with himself* (Gen. 3:7). The human community turns into the place of his betrayal of his *fellowman*—Adam's accusation of his wife before God (3:12)—and soon, as the most extreme consequence of this intra-human alienation, the scene of fratricide (4:8). Sin breaks into the third dimension, too, man's direct relationship to *nature*, and causes catastrophic confusion. "And here, too, is a cleft, a mutual recalcitrance that now breaks into creation as a profound disorder: man was taken from the earth and so was directed to it; she was the material basis of his existence; a solidarity of created existed between man and the ground. But a break occurred in this affectionate relationship, an alienation that expresses itself in a silent, dogged struggle between man and soil." [29] And the narrative closes with the most frightening form of human alienation: the appearance of death (3:19), as the "wages of sin" (Rom. 6:23), which threatens to annihilate man's entire created existence.

In this way man's sin is an ominous menace to human existence in its innermost essence, God's creation in us.

A Menace to the Created World

Now that we have considered sin's immediate consequences for our relationship to God and for our own existence, let us turn our attention to sin's indirect consequences in the created world.

It is customary to weigh the consequences of our own and others' sins only in an individualistic sense, in *interpersonal relationships*. Here sin appears as egoism, the denial of solidarity, the damaging of our fellowman's life, property, honor, etc. Here sin is, so to say, in its most easily recognized form, because it takes on a "personal shape" and meets us in this or that individual person.

It is much more difficult to recognize the "impersonal form" of sin, the *social dimension* of the misuse of man's God-given freedom. We are thinking of the *"sinful structures"* of society which, however, are not sinful and corrupt in and of themselves but are misused by sinful and corrupt human egoism—both personal and corporate egoism. The state, for example, is a good and necessary form of human life together, "instituted by God" (Rom. 13:1). But this emphasis on the divine institution would be one-sided if we could say nothing about how disastrously human sin had also corrupted the various forms of civic life, how in the course of mankind's history they had become the instrument of collective egoism, means for exploiting whole social classes and oppressed peoples. Human sin takes on similar "impersonal form" in egoistical economic systems and unjust social systems or unjust forms of the political relationships between nations.

Not only are these "impersonal" forms of sin more difficult to uncover, but also their most immediate consequences are more dangerous. The personal form of murder destroys perhaps only one single life—we do not say this in order to minimize the guilt of this gross sin in any way! But the institutionalized, structured form of murder, war, destroys millions of human lives and corrupts the moral and material life of society. And yet it was a general practice until very recently to glorify war, and even the church did not withhold its blessing from it! The misused "sinful" structures of social life destroy not only the immediate victims of their injustice— as one would automatically think—but they also corrupt those who benefit from the injustices. In his early writings Karl Marx gives a profound analysis of "alienated work," unjust labor structures. He points out that it is not only that the exploited worker is alienated from his own work, himself, and his whole environment. The employer, meanwhile, also loses his own humanity—even if this is not as conspicuous and visible as the suffering of the victims of the unjust economic structures.[30]

Here we must bring into view yet another form of "social sin": sinful man's attempt to extend his God-given dominion over nature to include his fellowmen, his desire to "manipulate" his fellowman completely and so rob him of his humanity. Fantasizing authors describe a society in which the scientists can turn every single ordinary man into a walking mechanism of unconscious reflexes and where human personality is extinguished in an "externally-controlled human mechanism." This picture of a "brave new world" may still just be a nightmare of science fiction literature today, but tomorrow it may present a serious danger. Already now there exists the possibility of manipulating man extensively with medical-biological methods. "Man's prenatal life was previously inaccessible to external manipulation. Now even this sphere of reality is gradually moving into the realm of human planning. Perhaps medical science will soon find effective ways to plan the sex of the unborn child. Above all: it is becoming possible to influ-

ence all human hereditary factors."[31] "Chemical stimulants alter
the functions not only of the body but also of the mind. With
drugs and pills man can escape worry, fear, loneliness, feelings of
guilt and consciousness of responsibility and can find a chemical
short-cut to joy, happiness, harmony, even metaphysical knowledge
and mystical rapture."[32] Today the waves of sex and violence in
the mass media of highly industrialized societies, as well as the
excesses of the most insidious forms of the advertising industry,
in which "advertising mass-produces consumers just as the factories
mass-produce goods,"[33] all signify this same danger of manipulation for the human mind.

As 20th century man's tremendous power has increased almost
to infinity, the dangers of the misuse of that power have grown
right along with it. Today "sin no longer walks, it flies in a jet."
Last but certainly not least, let us refer to the unimaginable threat
hovering above our world in the form of a *nuclear war*. Mankind
has reached a point in its historical development at which it can,
through a sinful, irresponsible misuse of the power of its science
and technology, completely annihilate not only itself but also the
entire created world, with all its life and all its treasures.

All this shows us clearly what a real threat human sin is today
not only to us ourselves but also to all of creation.

Naive Humanistic Optimism and Despairing Nihilism—
No "Christian Alternatives"

Faced with the tremendous progress of human civilization and
the equally enormous dangers lurking in our world, the man of
today is exposed to two kinds of temptations.

On the one hand, many people today are still inclined to minimize the dangers to the future evolution of human history in their
adherence to a naive and unrealistic *optimism* about the evolution
of human civilization. Many people do not reckon with the seriousness of human sin and place their full trust in reason. Karl Jaspers,
for example, sees in reason the unifying bond for the many modes
of existence of being. Where reason is at work, he says, everything
that exists seeks links to every other.[34] This philosophy—to name

a concrete example—sees no other help against the atomic bomb except the hope that "common sense" will still finally eliminate this deadly danger. The two world wars have shaken this humanistic optimism to its foundations and raised serious doubts about it, but they have not been able to eliminate it completely from the minds of many men.

But today the *opposite* temptation is an even greater danger. In his above-cited essay, Aukrust mentions a novel written by Dostoevski after his visit to the first technical exhibition in London (1852) in the crystal palace. In a vision of horror, Dostoevski portrays modern technology as a demonic threat to man's integrity; he has the main character of his novel retreat into a "celler-hole" in helpless protest against the surrounding inhuman civilization. For many men today this "celler-hole" is a nihilistic-pessimistic kind of existentialist philosophy, in which they hope to entrench themselves in a self-contained existence, outside of society, away from human social obligations and without concrete contacts with their fellowmen.

Neither of these two attitudes is a *Christian* alternative. Fortunately many other people of non-Christian faiths or ideologies also do not see them as the only possible alternatives!

A Christian can never lose sight of the reality of sin, in himself and in others, and so stay stuck in a shallow humanistic optimism. For many the Lutheran teaching of the "bondage of the will" appears to be a dark, pessimistic conception of man. It can, as we said, even be misunderstood in this sense. Then it can easily lead to a one-sided disdain of and flight from the world, to a mistrust of science, technology and culture, to a "celler-hole existence" in the world. But this is certainly not the right way to understand what Luther meant! On the contrary, this oft-criticized teaching points to the real dangers lying in the corrupt, irresponsible human will. It indicates the utter incapability of man to save himself from God's righteous wrath and from the fateful threats to himself in his own sin.

But on the other hand our lack of freedom before God does not mean a dark pessimism and hopelessness about this world of man. As can be clearly seen from Article XVIII of the Augsburg Confession and Apology,[35] this does not mean the equivalent of a denial of "civil righteousness" *(iustitia civilis)*, honest and humane conduct and the humane struggle against the crude, visible forms of sin in human society. For in his "secular kingdom" God has erected strong "dams against the evil one" in the universally human law of the conscience and the ordained structures of secular life. In fact, the obviation of this danger of the destruction of the creation through sin is precisely the purpose of human cooperation in God's "secular reign." And here we Christians work together with non-Christians.

The "Christian Alternative"

For us the true reason for rejecting every doubt and all pessimism about the future of man and his world is the gospel. The "Christian alternative" to shallow, humanistic optimism and doubting, dark nihilism and hopelessness in the face of the dangers of human sin is—Jesus Christ.

He is "God's solution" for the world: ". . . that your faith might not rest in the wisdom of men but in the power of God. . . . 'What no eye has seen, nor ear heard, nor the heart of man conceived, what God has prepared for those who love him,' God has revealed to us through the Spirit" (1 Cor. 2:5, 9-10).

And from this there opens up for man a new, second way in which he may be "God's co-worker" *(cooperator Dei)* against all forms of sin, visible and invisible.

THE CHRISTIAN AND THE CONGREGATION AS "GOD'S CO-WORKERS" IN THE WORLD
The "New Center of Life" that Comes with Faith

God sent his son into the world not only to free the world of men from the immanent consequences of sin, but also to rescue them from the just judgment of God and renew their lives completely (Jn. 3:3ff., 36; Rom. 5:9f.; 2 Cor. 5:17). To see the purpose of Jesus' advent and incarnation *only* in the restoration of intramundane relationships, the healing of the inwardly torn condition of human existence, "man's self-consciousness," and in the liberation to a "new understanding of existence," is to miss the Bible's real meaning. Jesus proclaimed not a new kingdom of man, but rather a new kingdom of God, which is now present still in a hidden manner and whose future consummation is now only hoped for (Mk. 1:15; 14:62; Mt. 26:29).

But it would be absolutely wrong to want to conclude from this that the gospel of Jesus has nothing to do with this *earthly* world and life. God's saving act in Christ brings not only a "transcendent salvation" from wrath and eternal damnation but also rescue from the immanent consequences of sin, both in the world and in our own existence. Jesus gives us the forgiveness of sins. But in faith he also graciously heals the internal and external ruin of human society, alienation from ourselves, our fellowmen and nature, and also rescues us from the "sting of death" (Mk. 2:5ff.; Lk. 4:18ff.; Jn. 13:34ff.; 14:27ff.; Mk. 16:17ff.; 1 Cor. 15:54ff.). In him, the grace and love of God incarnate, all the wounds of sin are healed.

This renewal has its center inside man. It is a "meta-noia." "And be renewed in the spirit of your minds" (Eph. 4:23). Its first consequence is a *new center* for our innermost life. Just as the first consequence of the fall into sin was the loss of communion with God, alienation from the creator, so now the first, inward fruit of salvation is the restoration of this original communion, reconciliation with God. Now *God* becomes the center of our life instead of our own ego. But since man, including our fellowman, is the "image of God" in this world, with this change our *fellowman* also comes into the center of our life. Now, in faith, our selfless love of our fellowman replaces our egoistic self-love. In faith the otherwise unfulfillable requirement of the "great commandment" now comes to fulfilment through the Holy Spirit: "'You shall love the Lord your God with all your heart, and with all your soul, and with all your mind.' This is the great and first commandment. And the second is like it, 'You shall love your neighbor as yourself'" (Mt. 22:37-39).

This is the link between heaven and this world. The consequences of faith touch upon not only our relationship to God but also our relationship to the world. This demonstrates the absolute inseparability of the "vertical" and "horizontal" lines in the Christian life and the life of the church. This is the ultimate source of Christian secular responsibility before God.

Proclamation of the Word and Ministry to the Fellowman— The Mission of Jesus' Community

One of the most striking descriptions of Jesus' community is the apostle's statement about it as the "Body of Christ" (Eph. 1:23ff.; Col.1:18ff.). Present-day exegesis universally holds that for Paul this "image" is much more than a mere image or symbolic expression. K. L. Schmidt, for one, asserts: ecclesiology is always simultaneously Christology. For when we speak of the church we also speak of its head, Christ, and his presence and activity. And so today, too, the mission of the corporate body of Jesus can be nothing other than what the ministry of Jesus was 2000 years ago. "If Christ is in fact the Head and the church his body, then its thought and activity must be determined by him and he must be allowed to use its members as the head uses the members of the body. Then its life must be none other than Christ himself going forth to achieve his redeeming purpose. Its voice must be the voice of Christ proclaiming his eternal gospel. Its hands must be Christ's hands doing his works of love. Christ himself must look through our eyes, walk in our steps, love through our hearts." [36]

It follows from this innermost unity of Jesus' ministry and his church's ministry that the basic forms of the church's ministry, its "cooperation with God," are the same as in the life of Jesus' proclamation of the word and deeds of love. The church performs its ministry of testifying to God's laws and to his forgiving, renewing grace in a twofold manner: its proclamation of the word (including its administration of the "visible" word, the sacraments) and its works of love for the fellowman, its *diaconia* in this world. We would exclude ourselves from the kingdom of God, says Werner Elert, "if we only proclaimed it, *i.e.* if the church were to be only a 'church of the word.' This reign is really in effect only where forgiveness is received and also practiced. In forgiveness God reveals himself as that powerful love which draws us, too, into the *allelous agapan* (loving each other)." [37]

With this we have again arrived at the problem of God's "co-operation" with men and man's "cooperation" with his creator. In his hidden governing of the world God uses unbelievers, too: all who work against the chaos of sin according to the inner law of their conscience and who carry out their secular calling faithfully in the ordained structures of society. But that is an unconscious cooperation with the omnipotence of the creator and preserver of the world. However, Christians are conscious and responsible "co-workers of God" in this world. They are not only renewed inwardly in faith, but they are also drawn into the active power of God's love in the world. For Jesus' truth must always be put into action.

Luther says that after receiving the forgiveness of sins man should and can "hasten to works." [38] His more detailed description of these works takes three directions. The first is to kill one's own fleshly lusts and other sins. Here the reformer almost never speaks of cooperation but rather only of the work of the Holy Spirit, so as not to give an opening to any idea of merit. But the second task of "cooperation" is to practice love toward one's fellowman. For Luther this is the proper place to speak of a "cooperation" between God and man: service to others. The third direction is that of "humility and awe before God." But later this is absorbed entirely into the other two, for a man can serve God only in his fellowman, and only in self-denial. [39]

The distinguishing marks of the "cooperation" of God and the justified, renewed man are on the one hand the inner joy of the union with God, and on the other hand the service-nature of his work in the world, diaconia. The main characteristic of the inner Christian life is, according to Luther, "the freedom of a Christian," a clear conscience. This in turn comes from the inner assurance that our works of faith are in harmony with God's work, in fact, that in the last analysis they are not our own works but God's works through us and with us. "The gospel . . . does achieve happy, willing and free consciences." [40] But the main characteristics of the outward Christian life is its service-nature, its diaconia. Just as Jesus did not come to be ministered unto but to minister (Mk. 10:45), so also the life of the justified sinner and of the congregation must be a life of continuing service in this world. In Luther's opinion, a man receives his station, his vocation—and in the last analysis we live our entire earthly life, with all its various areas of relationships, in such "stations"—in order to serve others in it. "Married people must serve others than just themselves, and a secular government must in some way be of use to its citizens. Servants and all common people must work for and serve others." [41]

What Is Specifically "Christian" About Our Works?

This also yields an answer to the much-debated question: what makes our works and life Christian? Are there definite distinguishing marks of these works and this life?

Yes and no. The dialectic of this answer finds it resolution in the point from which we look at the good works of a Christian or a congregation. If we look at these works from the outside, we must answer this question with "No." The specifically "Christian" thing about them cannot be ascertained externally. Often to the shame of many Christians, non-Christians can and also do these same good works for the good of both individuals and society—all the way to the sacrifice of their own life for the sake of others, the highest measure of love according to Jesus (Jn. 15:13). For the works of the general-humanistic love and of Christian love both share in this "service-nature." Jesus' well-known saying (Mt. 7:16) does not refer to his disciples but rather to the false prophets.

But if we look from the inside at these "objective good works" of neighborly love, which are done by both Christians and non-Christians, the situation is entirely different. Here there are essential differences in the intrinsic content, the motivation, and the goal of the works. The specifically "Christian" element in the *content* of ethical good works can be defined as follows: where the full divinely-created humanity of man (i.e. his physical and mental well-being as well as his salvation) is taken seriously—in the interest of all men, without any differentiation of faith, ideology, class, nation or race—there a Christian ethical deed is done. We can establish a second and still more important dimension of the difference in content by recalling something we have already mentioned: we believe that these works are always God's work and our work, Christ's activity through the Holy Ghost and our own responsible activity in a mysterious unity—a deep, hidden, real "partnership"; for the Christian this unity and responsibility before God is conscious and desired. Seen from the viewpoint of its inner motivation and its goal, a deed is "Christian" only when it is done as an act of obedience to God's command, in discipleship to Christ, and to the praise and glory of God the Holy Spirit who works in the Christian's own works and life. We act as "Christians" when in our activity the "penultimate goals" on this earth are encompassed and "surpassed" by the ultimate eschatological goal in the kingdom of God and by thanksgiving and praise to the glory of God.

Briefly summarized: our works share their objective servicenature, the hidden cooperation in God's rule of the world, with the ethical good works of non-Christians. But they differ in their inner faith-nature, the conscious and responsible "complete" cooperation with God's activity.

Areas of "Cooperation" with God

What are the most important focal points of our Christian ministry today, our "cooperation" in the dynamic divine process of creation? There are as many such areas, the "loci of cooperation," as there are components of humanity in the divinely created human life. For God loves the whole man. Therefore Christian diaconia must also be directed at the whole man.

Let us first mention life's *personal* relationships. Here there are the thousands of "little" good works of every day life, in the family, at work, in society. Think of "the least of Jesus' brethren" (Mt. 25:40): the hungry and thirsty, the widows and orphans, the weary and heavy laden of the Gospel. But think also of society's lonely and forgotten, hungry and thirsty for human company and understanding; think of those who have lost the meaning of their lives under a heavy blow of fate or beneath an inner "boredom." They are all our neighbors, our fellowmen, for our personal diaconia today. Jesus wants to come to them through us. And likewise he also wants to meet us in them.

But Christian ministry in society does not end with just personal assistance to the needy. It is inevitably also help for the healthy:

an all-around enrichment of their lives and of the whole *society* with everything that we have received from God. A second and very extensive area of Christian "cooperation" with God's creative activity is the influence of the believers' Christian life and of the Christian community's life on the other patterns of society, families, labor organizations, social and national life. What works flow from us Christians out into our everyday environment, the world around us? It is regrettable that the significance of this kind of "social diaconia" for society is generally perceived and regarded so little in ecclesiastical praxis. This kind of Christian ministry is no longer a self-understood matter of course where our Christian conduct testifies daily before the non-Christians for or against Christ, where it portrays authentic humanity or its opposite every day in the various circles of society. This is also the purport of the "diaconic theology" and the "diaconic life style" envisaged by churches in Socialist societies.

Today we must place also the *broader social relationships* into the light of Christian responsibility for the world and a "universal" Christian diaconia much more than we have in the past. Today the world-embracing community of Christians is confronted by the needs and cares of the entire family of man. Today the especially burning problems of the Third World stand before us: the threat of wide-spread famines, the danger of an even more violent outbreak of the race problem, the global problem of education, the universal diffusion of a truly humane culture. But far and away the most comprehensive aspect of this "great humane help for the world" is still the preservation of world peace—primarily from the danger of a nuclear holocaust which could well be the last war of world history, mankind's suicide. Wars are not natural catastrophes but rather are the consequences of combinations of human decisions; accordingly they are also ethical questions and tasks, for whose answers and solutions all men and specifically Christians are responsible. Christians, according to Jesus' saying, must be *eireno-poioi,* trail-blazers of peace in both senses: eschatological peace with God in Christ and earthly peace among the nations in all areas of life.

As we saw above, despite their irreconcilable contradictions in matters of faith and ideology, *believers and unbelievers are obligated to ethical cooperation* in all these areas of the humanization of our world, from the smallest deeds of personal assistance all the way to the Christians' "great world-embracing love." In fact, in their humanistic activity in the preservation and evolution of the world, both are, consciously or unconsciously, "God's co-workers" in his hidden "secular reign." In societies where the co-existence of Christians and non-Christians is becoming an increasingly pressing problem—and with the wider diffusion of secularization in the future this problem will come to the fore not just in Socialist coun tries and the "third world"—the thorough consideration and the concrete practice of various forms of social-ethical cooperation is an increasingly urgent, indeed, unavoidable task. But it is also an important practical presupposition for a—not merely abstract, but realistic—dialog on the common ethical tasks in society.

These are just a few spotlights on the most varied dimensions of the Christian ministry, the universal Christian diaconia, in the world of today. The Christians' other broad area of "cooperation with God" would be their participation in God's "spiritual reign," their ministry in the church's life. God wants to use us—as we heard in Luther's words—in "both of his kingdoms": in service to our fellowman but also in the ministry of the gospel. Paul speaks of our being "God's fellow workers" (1 Cor. 3:9) in precisely this context of ministry of the gospel. But this other broad area of Christian cooperation in "God's spiritual work" in this world must remain a special topic for a more detailed future study.

The Christian in the Social Revolution

In this context it is absolutely necessary to include the Christians' "ministry to the structures of society" in our consideration. We have already spoken briefly of the significance of social structures. It has also been emphasized how human sin corrupts these vital, ordained structures of family, state, economic, labor and cultural life and so can make them a source of unspeakable suffering for millions.

Benevolent assistance and charitable aid will certainly help very much here, but it will not accomplish everything that is necessary. Indispensable as this personal and institutional charity may still be, it nonetheless must let countless others of the world's suffering and needy human beings perish or continue to suffer without being able to help them. What other possibilities for real help are there? To help a hungry man, I can share my bread with him. But to be able to help the world's millions of hungry people, we must reshape the outmoded and unjust structures of the economic and social system. "Ascetic Christianity called the world evil and deserted it. Mankind is waiting for a revolutionary Christianity that will call the world evil and change it" (W. Rauschenbusch).[42] Karl Marx rightly criticized the church of his time for trying only to alleviate the consequences of the unjust structures, the physical and intellectual-moral needs of the working class, but for having neglected or even defended the root of the evil, the injustice of the economic and social systems.

Today there is almost full agreement within Christian social ethics on this: even the theologians acknowledge the concrete significance of "structural assistance" and openly admit that they have learned much about it from Marx and other social theoreticians. "This reshaping stands under the humane principle: what best serves the cause of freedom and justice for man? Thus every institutional reform must be for man's sake, and the whole system of society must be measured against this yardstick: does it guarantee a dignified human life to individual men and groups of men? The principle of 'societas semper reformanda' must be linked with the principle of 'ecclesia semper reformanda.' " [43]

The most hotly discussed problem in this area is still whether there is a place in theological social ethics for a revolutionary reshaping of the structures and Christian support for it. The over-all negative answer of the social encyclical *Populorum progressio* and of many Christian social ethical theoreticians is well known. At the other extreme there is a view which wants to embrace "revolution" —also in the social sense—as the "essence of Christianity" and so consider the church of Jesus as the "avante-garde of the world revolution."

In our opinion, this question finds a satisfactory theological solution only when approached from the direction of our topic. Then the crucial question reads: can we believe in God's hidden activity in history not only in gradual evolutionary changes but also, in explosive revolutionary reshapings of the rotted, sinful and unjust socio-economic structures? May we, must we recognize *ex post facto* and support those humane revolutionary changes of social life which have come about without our participation? These are vital questions today, not only for Christians in a Socialist society, who have experienced the sudden complete change of their socio-economic environment, but also for the many millions of Christians in the Third World, where, in the opinion of the best qualified experts (Raoul Prebisch *et al.*), such revolutionary changes appear to be inevitable.

It is our conviction that *both* evolutionary and revolutionary forms of the just and humane necessary alteration of society are just two different modes of the one and the same hidden, believed, reign and activity of God in history. Both belong in his "secular kingdom." Thus they are not "ecclesiastical tasks" but rather tasks of the "secular vocation"—and this holds also for men of faith. Where, after a conscientious and objective evaluation of all the concrete possibilities for change in the direction of eliminating outmoded and unjust structures, there is still no other alternative than a revolutionary break with the conservative and the traditional, there Christians can and must contribute responsibly to this reshaping. They must do this either in a "non-violent way"—as far as they possibly can—or, when it appears absolutely unavoidable, also with the application of force—but without hatred or a spirit of revenge and only in the interest of oppressed and suffering humanity. The final decision on this question is always made in each Christian's conscience before God: can this conscience believingly understand active participation in a revolutionary reshaping or an *ex post facto* support of it as "cooperation" in God's hidden rule in history? This is a severe test of a Christian's ability to make ethical decisions; in the last analysis it can be resolved only in the context of the concrete situation. But Christians can escape this severe ethical test of their conscience *coram Deo* neither in theology nor in their lives.

Consequences for Lutheran Theology

In concluding this important section let us summarize briefly a few of the consequences which seem especially significant for current Lutheran theology.

a. In the past—especially in the last 150 years, since Wichern's time—much effort has been expended in Lutheran circles in developing a "theology of diaconic action" in the traditional sense, as the diaconia of the good works of faith in the interpersonal sphere. But the broad and vital area of Christian responsibility for society's socio-economic structures, i.e. the theological problems of a *universal diaconia,* the good works of faith in the broader social contexts, were for the most part not considered. This often appeared to confirm the accusation that Lutheran theology "has not developed any social ethics" or "was incapable of" doing so.

Of course we know that this is not consistent with the truth. In Luther's teaching of the "two kingdoms"—in its original sense and according to the renewed understanding of it—we have a theological foundation for Lutheran social ethics that is simultaneously biblical and modern and that is better than anything else in illuminating many of the difficult problems of current social-ethical thought.

What must be done now is to draw the consequences of this theological foundation for all the areas of life in man's atomic and space age. This means making a clean sweep of any one-sided inclinations to desert the world and any predilection for an outmoded individualism or the strictly traditional; it also means the end of an ecumenism and an ecclesiocentricity which deal only with intra-ecclesiastical problems and are neither sensitive nor responsive to society's problems in the present-day world.

b. Lutheran theology has concentrated its efforts on the gospel and its work in the world—and must continue to do so in the future, too. But since law and gospel are inseparably bound together in God's activity, the theological problems of the law in both personal and social life must not be slighted. It is true that there is only one law of God for our entire life and work. But to determine how this law should be applied ethically in the extremely complicated situations of our own social and personal life is a never-ending theological task at which we and every generation must work with all our resources. Our Lutheran position on this is clear and unambiguous: detailed rules for the areas of economy, labor, culture and political and international life cannot be erected on the basis of the biblical word. Holy Scriptures provides only the most important ethical "guidelines," the ethical norms of action for all these areas. But joint work, with a reason enlightened by faith and a regenerated conscience, on the concrete, universally human problems and tasks of our society in our modern world is a never-ending task.

c. We confess that in the final analysis God is placing us before a decision and calling us to action as his "co-workers" in the world's economic, social, cultural and political problems. This is the very highest honor that can be given to this kind of Christian work for transforming the world. For this means that our own solitary or joint, modest and imperfect work in our vocation, in public life, and in the so-called "secular areas" of the Christian life, becomes a part of God's hidden work in the world (Jn. 5:17) and that it is indeed pleasing to God and signifies a sort of "reasonable" or "worldly" worship of God (cf. Rom. 12:1). Therefore our place in the world and society is always where God is: standing at the side of those who are poor, weak, oppressed and suffering. The old patristic quotation is true also in this context: *Gloria Dei vivens homo.*[44] We honor and love God by honoring and loving his "image" *(imago Dei),* our fellowman.

In another direction, this means that in no area of human activity does modern man's dynamic ability for, and great pleasure in, activity jeopardize God's honor and activity in the world. On the contrary, man's activity is an objective and/or subjective "good work," an unconscious or, in faith, conscious "cooperation" in God's service. The greater the power of modern man becomes, the greater also his responsibility becomes. It is our Christian task to express this responsibility of man before God in his action for his fellowman and for the world with an ever increasing clarity and decisiveness.

OUR CHRISTIAN "COOPERATION IN THE WORLD" IN ESCHATOLOGICAL PERSPECTIVE

The Necessity of Viewing Our Christian Activity in the World "Eschatologically"

We have now arrived at the point where we must place our activity as "God's co-workers" in its ultimate context, namely in its eschatological framework. We do not add this eschatological appendix at the conclusion of our theological discussion just to be theologically fashionable. On the one hand, this theological outlook comes out of the biblical theological view of these problems; on the other hand it is a systematic theological necessity; and lastly we can also mention the turn toward the future in current thought.

Holy Scripture views all of our earthly activities in the double perspective of "already now" and "not yet." The Christian life consists of "the new life of the spirit" (Rom. 7:6) and "newness of life" (Rom. 6:4). But at the same time life in the full sense, without sin and death, is only given in the coming kingdom of God (1 Cor. 15:42-44; Rev. 7:16-17). The New Testament emphasizes that the "new earth," the consummate kingdom of God, does not grow out of this earthly world and is not ever realized in earthly history, but rather will come to us at the end of time with an "inbreaking of the kingdom of God."

Viewed systematically, it is necessary when speaking of man's responsibility for the world and his secular action to keep in view the fact that the goals which lie before us on our earthly path are always "penultimate" goals. They must never hide from our eyes the ultimate goal in the kingdom of God, eternal life with God. Jesus' parable of the wise and foolish virgins warns us against this (Mt. 25:1-13). But it is just as important that in hoping and waiting for the transcendent we never lose sight of our earthly tasks and become lazy in our vocation—which Jesus' parable of the unfaithful servant warns us against (Mt. 24:45-51).

Finally, it is a characteristic mark of present-day thought, as well as of current Christian thought, that it is turned toward the future. "Man's ideological and organizational center of gravity has been in the past—the way things have always been, the laws which were learned by our fathers, the social structures we have inherited.

But the mood today has shifted radically; man today is future oriented in a manner and degree heretofore unknown. It is a mood fully consistent with the Christian expectation and hope. . . . But the Christian perspective is not mere "futurology"; it is future oriented because of its expectation and hope and faith that God is making all things new. . . ." [45] Even if these forms of "future-orientation" are very different in content, nonetheless, in this context this tendency of modern thought cannot be considered entirely insignificant.

The "Eschatological Perspective" as Critique of Our Christian Activity

The eschatological framework of our Christian ecclesiastical activity in the world preserves us from an unrealistic, enthusiastic "ecclesiastical avant-gardism," as can be found especially among the representatives of a one-sided, world-oriented "social gospel." On the other hand it also clears our heads about all the "Christianization programs," which were especially fashionable with our liberal forefathers and sometimes can still be found today. Jesus' message of the end of the world nowhere speaks of a "Christian society" or a "Christian world."

Eschatology also helps us to look upon our goal and expectations for the future with a *Christian realism* which is serious about both the real presence of the crucified one and the realities of this world. An "eschatological view" can never disregard the reality of human sin, neither our own nor others', in our earthly goals. Eschatology—and in the last analysis this is its happiest "critical function"—gives our earthly existence an inextinguishable and unfailing hope. But the *perspective of hope* gives our activity, our ministry and "cooperation" in the world an as yet unequalled dynamic, an undefeatable force that renews itself again and again despite all failures. Here every small or large deed of Christian love in service to our fellowman and the human community becomes a sign, a "guarantee" of the coming of God's kingdom, where the relative goals of this Christian ministry in the world find their ultimate consummation.

What is this Christian hope of ours based on? For faith this question is not hard to answer. It is based on the believing experience of the presence of the resurrected Lord. It is based on the visible signs of the new life, the "new creation," in our personal life and in the life of Jesus' community (Col. 1:27; 2 Cor. 5:17; Eph. 1:14). Above all it is based on faith's unfathomable trust in the triune God and his word (Rom. 4:1ff.). For where these three things: *faith* based on Jesus' crucifixion and resurrection, *hope* for the future perfection of life, and active *love* busy with the concrete tasks of this earthly life in God's created world, all are found side by side, *there* is the Christian life and *there* the corporate body of Jesus Christ is present in this world.

Translated by Jonathan Grothe

NOTES

1. K. Rahner, *Theological Inquiries*, Vol. V., tr. by Karl H. Kruger (Helicon Press, 1966), pp. 135-153.

2. Cf. M. Schmaus, *Katholische Dogmatik* III:2, 5th ed., Munich, 1956, p. 259.

3. M. Honecker, "Zwischen Planung und Revolution. Theologische Sozialethik von der Verantwortung der Zukunft." In: *Evangelische Kommentare*, 1968, nr. 10, p. 575.

4. P. Smulders, "Das menschliche Schaffen in der Welt," in: *Die Kirche in der Welt von heute*, ed. by G. Barauna, Salzburg, 1967, p. 208 (our translation).

5. Man as "God's counterpart," cf. Karl Barth's exegesis of this passage, *Church Dogmatics*, tr. and ed. by G. W. Bromiley, Edinburgh, 1961, pp. 182-205.

6. A detailed analysis of this important concept of Lutheran theology was published a few years ago: M. Seils, *Der Gedanke vom Zusammenwirken Gottes und des Menschen in Luthers Theologie*, Berlin, 1962, p. 202. This book is indispensable for any detailed examination of this question.

7. G. Wingren, *Luther on Vocation*, tr. by Carl C. Rasmussen, Philadelphia, 1958, p. 126. It is important to point out that in Wingren's book the chapter "Cooperatio" appears not in Part III (Man), but rather in Part II, under the activity of God; this strikes upon a typical impulse of Lutheran thought on where this concept belongs.

8. Cf. Seils, *op. cit.*, pp. 9ff., 89ff., and 156ff.

9. *Luther and Erasmus: Free Will and Salvation,* LCC, Vol. XVII, tr. ed. Philip Watson, SCM Press, London, 1969, p. 289 (= WA 18, 754: 1ff.).

10. eidem gratiae libere assentiendo et cooperando. Tridentinum, Sessio 6, Cap. 5, in: Denzinger, Enchiridion Symbolorum, 33rd ed., Freiburg, 1965, nr. 1525 (= 797).

11. Schmaus, *op. cit.,* pp. 266, 275.

12. Wingren, *op. cit.,* p. 128.

13. Cf. the excellent book by J. Gustafson, *Christ and the Moral Life,* New York-London, 1968.

14. R. Hermann, *Von der Klarheit der Heiligen Schrift,* p. 124, quoted in Seils, *op. cit.,* p. 17.

15. W. Dantine, *Die Gerechtmachung des Gottlosen,* Munich, 1959, p. 140. On this same subject cf. "Christus heute—Rechtfertigung heute. Ein Studiendokument der Lutherischen Kirche in Ungarn." In: *Ung. Kirchl. Nachrichtendienst,* Vol. XV, nr. 12, Budapest, 1963, p. 20.

16. Dantine, *op. cit.,* p. 140.

17. E. Schlink, *Theology of the Lutheran Confessions,* tr. by Paul F. Koehneke and Herbert J. A. Bouman, Philadelphia, 1961, p. 105. Cf. also Augsburg Confession and Apology, art. IV, VI, XII, XX; Smalcald Articles C III, XIII; Small and Large Catechism, Third Article; Formula of Concord, art III-IV.

18. V. Vajta, "Sine Meritis. Zur kritischen Funktion der Rechtfertigungslehre," in: *Oecumenica* 1968, pp. 146-197, p. 193. Cf. also: V. Vajta, *Gelebte Rechtfertigung,* Göttingen, 1963, pp. 39ff.

19. Th.G. Tappert, (ed.), *The Book of Concord,* Philadelphia, 1959, p. 37, Art. XVI, 1.

20. H.-D. Wendland, *Die Kirche in der revolutionären Gesellschaft,* Gütersloh, 1967, p. 178 (our translation).

21. W. H. Lazareth, "Luther's 'Two Kingdoms' Ethic Reconsidered," in: *Christian Social Ethics in a Changing World,* London-New York, 1966, p. 125.

22. *Ibid.*

23. The "DC (Deutsche Christen) Theology" tried to make history and national life an independent source of revelation next to the revealed law and gospel and so to tear apart the two "kingdoms." That was its tragic mistake, which must never be repeated. It is partially understandable that the theological reaction of Karl Barth's dialectical theology desired to do away with the difference between law and gospel and between a "secular" and a "spiritual reign of God." In his Christological conception of the state he wanted, with the help of the analogical method, to pattern the life of secular communities, too, after the Christ-revelation and the church's life (cf. esp. *Church and State,* tr. by G. R. Howe, London, 1939; "The Christian Community and the Civil Community," in: *Against the Stream: Shorter Post-War Writings,* tr. by E. M. Delacour & St. Godman, London, 1954). This attempt, too, was destined to fail. Therefore we retain Luther's biblically based teaching of the two modes of God's

activity in the world (two-kingdom-teaching)—purified as much as possible of all historical misinterpretations and preserving the unity of God's rule in both areas of the earthly life—as the theological foundation of the Christian teaching of history and society and thus of our theological social ethics. Cf. also the lecture given at the 5th World Assembly of the Lutheran World Federation on "Creative Discipleship in the Contemporary World Crisis," in *Lutheran World,* Vol. XVII, 1970, pp. 318-329, esp. pp. 325ff.

24. *Luther and Erasmus: Free Will and Salvation, op. cit.,* p. 238 (= WA 18, 753:28).

25. "As for co-operation in office, we need not decide to what extent the fellow-worker God uses is or is not made new in heart by the Spirit. . . . The matter of the heart's purity or impurity is relevant to heaven . . . on earth the prime consideration is that our works do good to others, whether they come from willing or unwilling hearts." Wingren, *op. cit.,* p. 133.

26. WA 27, 418: 2 (our translation).

27. "The 'Two Kingdoms' and the Lordship of Christ." A Working Paper of the Commission of Theology of the Lutheran World Federation, *Lutheran World* (1967), nr. 1, pp. 79-88, p. 83.

28. Cf. The Augsburg Confession, art. XIX, De causa peccati. Luther sees the fall into sin of Judas, Pharaoh, and of all men from Adam on as happening only under God's "permissio," but not under his "determinatio." Therefore there is a "contingentia, quae omnino statuenda est, ne constituatur Deis autor mali" (WA Tr. 5, 396: 5). Cf. Seils, *op. cit.,* p. 123.

29. G. von Rad, *Genesis. A Commentary* (Old Testament Library), tr. by John H. Marks, London, 1961, p. 91f.

30. K. Marx, *Die Frühschriften,* pp. 181ff. Cf. A. Rich, *Glaube in politischer Entscheidung,* Zürich, 1962, pp. 67ff.

31. T. Aukrust, "Human Freedom and Manipulated Man," in: *Faith and Society. Toward a Contemporary Social Ethic,* Geneva, 1966, pp. 21-33, p. 25.

32. *Ibid.*

33. *Ibid.,* p. 30.

34. Cf. K. Jaspers, *Philosophical Faith and Revelation,* tr. by A. G. Ashton, New York, 1967, pp. 9-10.

35. Th. G. Tappert, (ed.), *The Book of Concord, op. cit.,* pp. 39ff., 224ff.

36. T. A. Kantonen, *A Theology for Christian Stewardship,* Philadelphia, 1956, p. 79.

37. W. Elert, *The Christian Ethos,* tr. by Carl J. Schindler, Philadelphia, 1957, pp. 407-408.

38. festinari ad opera, WA 57, Heb. 143:5.

39. WA 2, 145: 38ff., 147: 2ff., cf. Seils, *op. cit.,* pp. 80ff.

40. Luther's Works, *Selected Psalms II,* Vol. 13, tr. Martin Bertram, ed. J. Pelikan, p. 10 (= WA 8, 11: 14); cf. WA 13, 577: 13ff., 18ff.

41. WA 10, I, 1, 656: 9-12; cf. 43, 68: 22 (our translation).

42. Quoted in J. Moltmann, "Gott in der Revolution," in: *Evangelische Kommentare*, 1968, nr. 10, p. 568.

43. H.-D. Wendland, *op. cit.*, pp. 177-178 (our translation).

44. Irenaeus, *Adversus Haereses*, IV, 20, 7 (PL VII, 1037); (The Anti-Nicene Fathers, American Edition, Vol. I, p. 490).

45. R. Dickinson, *Line and Plummet. The Churches and Development*, Geneva, 1968, p. 40.

Chapter 7

Political Responsibility as the Obedience of Faith

This is a time for the church to listen. If ever men needed guidance of the Word of God to face a political crisis, it is now. The major ethical dilemma faced by Christians is clear and unmistakable. We must find a way to resist ruthless tyranny while at the same time avoiding the horrors of total nuclear war. God wills both peace and justice for our political life together. Amid all the tensions and frustrations of a "cold war," however, men are continually tempted to settle for one at the expense of the other. In such a dangerous situation, it is the urgent duty of the church to nurture its members in the faith to make difficult decisions, the love to carry them out, and the hope to live with their morally mixed results.

Equally sincere Christians often view the church's political responsibility very differently today. Some would have the church avoid political discussion and action altogether, insisting that as Christians we are concerned exclusively with the gospel. They forget that the church is commissioned to proclaim God's law as well as his gospel. It is just because of our passion for the gospel that we should be concerned to hold the political world accountable to God's sovereign law. On the other hand, there are many in the church who would welcome the enunciation of a definitive "Christian foreign policy" on the strength of their faith in the universal lordship of Jesus Christ. But these people forget that an unregenerate world cannot be ruled by the gospel. The Lord of the nations exercises a hidden lordship outside the church by means of the law and the rule of civil authorities.

In the face of such erroneous views, this chapter is written in the hope that it might stimulate more informed thought and action on some of the crucial political issues of our day. Lutheran Christians must learn to view political responsibility as an integral expression of their obedience of faith.

Two ecumenical documents provide valuable raw materials for the churches' answer to the pleas of modern men for a more "worldly Christianity." The first is the *Pastoral Constitution on the Church in the Modern World* promulgated at the Second Vatican Council (1965) of the Roman Catholic church.[1] The second is the *Official Report* prepared by the Protestant, Anglican and Orthodox participants of the World Conference on Church and Society (1966) under the sponsorship of the World Council of Churches.[2] Their impact has already demonstrated that they will likely be among the most important ecumenical social statements of this generation. Our limited aim here is twofold: (1) to outline and evaluate the theological and political ethics of both these ecumenical documents; and (2) to propose an alternate position based on the Pauline theology at the heart of the Lutheran Reformation.[3]

CHRISTIAN FAITH AND SOCIAL ACTION

The popes of the 20th century have issued a stream of encyclical letters dealing with modern social problems. They range from Leo XIII's *Rerum Novarum* ("The Condition of Labor," 1891) down to John XVIII's influential *Mater et Magistra* ("Christianity and Social Progress," 1961) and *Pacem in Terris* ("Peace on Earth," 1963). Never before Vatican II's *Pastoral Constitution*, however, did a council of the Roman church address "the whole of humanity" with its theological understanding of "the presence and activity of the Church in the world today" (art. 2).

Recent non-Roman social thought on an ecumenical level can be traced back to the first Universal Christian Conference on Life and Work held at Stockholm (1925). Christian ethics received major attention at the succeeding Conference on Church, Community, and State in Oxford (1937). Major documents on social issues were also prepared in connection with the assemblies of the World Council of Churches in Amsterdam (1948), Evanston (1956), New Delhi (1961), and Uppsala (1968). A series of explosive regional conferences on "rapid social change" culminated in the call of the Geneva Conference on Church and Society under review here. High were its original aims: "to consider the bearing of the Christian gospel on social thought and action."

The Pastoral Constitution

The opening chapters of Part One are addressed to the basic questions, "What does the Church think of man? . . . What is the ultimate significance of human activity throughout the world?" (art. 11).

In response to these questions each chapter begins with man in the world and ends with man in Christ. We have here the beginnings of a Christian humanism of cosmic dimensions. That is, the *Constitution* seeks to combine a christological view of man's nature (as fulfilled in communion with God) and a christological view of man's activity (as transfigured into the kingdom of God).

First, "the dignity of the human person" is based on man's creation in the image of God (art. 12) and is to be fulfilled in the revelation of Christ as God's perfect image, the New Man (art. 22).

To be created in God's image means that man is "capable of knowing and loving his Creator, and was appointed by Him as master of all earthly creatures that he might subdue them and use them to God's glory" (art. 12). But man rebelled against God and "sought to find fulfillment apart from God." Cosmic disorder has resulted: man has disrupted his relation to his ultimate goal, fallen out of harmony with himself, with others, and with all created things. This has resulted in man's individual and collective bondage. Hence, "sin has diminished man, blocking his path to fulfillment" (art. 13).

Although "wounded," "damaged," and "blocked" by sin, man's inherent dignity still remains. It demands the acknowledgment that "by his interior qualities he outstrips the whole sum of mere things"; that man "recognize in himself a spiritual and immortal soul"; that "by his intellect he surpasses the material universe, for he shares in the light of the divine mind"; that in the depths of his conscience, "man has in his heart a law written by God"; and that "authentic freedom is an exceptional sign of the divine image within man." Even his anxiety about death witnesses to the fact that man "bears in himself an eternal seed . . . and that God has called man and still calls him to an endless sharing of a divine life beyond all corruption" (arts. 14–18).

It is only in Jesus Christ as the final Adam that the mystery of man is illumined. Christ "fully reveals man to man himself and makes his supreme calling clear." It is in Christ that "all the aforementioned truths find their root and attain their crown" (art. 22). By his revelation as "the image of the invisible God" (Col. 1:15), Christ "restores the divine likeness which had been disfigured from the first sin onward." Indeed, by his incaration, Christ has "united Himself in some fashion with every man," so that "all this holds true not only for Christians, but for all men of good will in whose hearts grace works in an unseen way" (art. 22).

Second, "the community of mankind" is based on man's social nature (art. 13) and is to be consummated in the redemptive work of Christ for the whole human race (art. 32).

Technical progress has promoted the interdependence of men in modern society. This welcome development must be seen against the background of God's fatherly will that "all men should constitute one family and treat one another in a spirit of brotherhood" (art. 24). It is stressed that "social life is not something added on to man" (art. 25); only in community with his fellow men is man able to "develop all his gifts" and "rise to his destiny" (art. 25).

The vital links between man and society are being intensified today by the growth of socialization. The resultant need is to build a worldwide community on the demands of the common good.

By "socialization" (not socialism) is meant "the increasing development of reciprocal ties and mutual dependencies that give rise to a variety of associations and organizations, both public and private" (art. 25). This trend in technological societies, despite inherent dangers, can greatly benefit mankind. It requires, however, that the common good "takes on an increasingly universal complexion and consequently involves rights and duties with respect to the whole human race" (art. 26).

What are these "universal and inviolable" rights and duties of every man? The *Constitution* enumerates the following:

> . . . everything necessary for leading a life truly human, such as food, clothing, and shelter; the right to choose a state of life freely and to found a family, the right to education, to employment, to a good reputation, to respect, to appropriate information, to activity in accord with the upright norm of one's own conscience, to protestion of privacy and to rightful freedom in matters religious too (art. 26).

Coming down to "practical and particularly urgent consequences," the council lays stress on reverence for all men based on their essential equality.

> . . . whatever is opposed to life itself, such as any type of murder, genocide, abortion, euthanasia, or willful self-destruction, whatever violates the integrity of the human person, such as mutilation, torments inflicted on body or mind, attempts to coerce the will itself; whatever insults human dignity, such as subhuman living conditions, arbitrary imprisonment, deportation, slavery, prostitution, the selling of women and children; as well as disgraceful working conditions, where men are treated as mere tools for profit, rather than as free and responsible persons; all these things and others of their like are infamies indeed (art. 27).

Furthermore, with respect to the fundamental rights of the person,

> . . . every type of discrimination, whether social or cultural, whether based on sex, race, color, social condition, language, or religion, is to be overcome and eradicated as contrary to God's intent (art. 29).

The chief point is clear: more than an individualistic ethic is required today. "It grows increasingly true that the obligations of justice and love are fulfilled only if each person, contributing to the common good, according to his own abilities and the needs of others, also promotes and assists the public and private institutions dedicated to bettering the conditions of human life" (art. 30).

This "communitarian character" of man's destiny is seen most clearly in God's saving acts among men, culminating in the work of Jesus Christ. From the beginning of salvation history, God made a covenant with persons in community. Then Jesus Christ, the Word made flesh, "willed to share in the human fellowship . . . revealed the love of the Father in terms of the most common social realities . . . sanctified those human ties, especially family ones, from which social relationships arise." He also commanded the gospel to be preached "so that the human race might become the Family of God." Hence, the brotherly community of faith and love which is his body, the church, "must be constantly increased until that day on which it will be brought to perfection" (art. 32).

Third, "man's activity throughout the world" is based on God's mandate for him to exercise dominion over the earth (art. 34) and is to be transfigured into the kingdom of Christ and God (art. 39).

Through science and technology, "man has extended his mastery over nearly the whole of nature and continues to do so" (art. 33). This is in keeping with God's will, "for man, created to God's image, received a mandate to subject to himself the earth and all that it contains." Modern progress is to be welcomed as part of man's joyous vocation as God's responsible steward of creation.

> Thus, far from thinking that works produced by man's own talent and energy are in opposition to God's power, and that the rational creature exists as a kind of rival to the Creator, Christians are convinced that the triumphs of the human race are a sign of God's greatness and the flowering of His own mysterious design (art. 34).

It must be clear, however, that human activity is to be ordered for the good of man. Technological progress is not an end in itself; it cannot be compared with the efforts of men to attain greater justice, wider brotherhood, and more humane social relationships.

> Hence, the norm of human activity is this: that in accord with the divine plan and will, it should harmonize with the genuine good of the human race, and allow men as individuals and as members of society to pursue their total vocation and fulfill it (art. 35).

If human progress can serve man's true happiness, why does Paul warn, "Be not conformed to this world" (Rom. 12:2)? The

Constitution explains, "By the 'world' is here meant that spirit of vanity and malice which transforms into an instrument of sin those human energies intended for the service of God and man" (art. 37). For when "the order of values is jumbled," as in our day, the world "ceases to be a place of true brotherhood" and "the magnified power of humanity threatens to destroy the race itself."

There is one answer to man's dilemma. "All human activity, constantly imperiled by man's pride and deranged self-love, must be purified and perfected" in Jesus Christ (art. 37).

By Christ's incarnation, "He entered the world's history as a perfect man, taking that history up into Himself and summarizing it" (art. 38).

By Christ's teaching, "He taught us that the new command of love was the basic law of human perfection and hence of the world's transformation."

By Christ's resurrection and present lordship, "He arouses not only a desire for the age to come, but, by that very fact, He animates, purifies, and strengthens those noble longings too by which the human family strives to make its life more human and to render the whole earth submissive to this goal" (art. 38).

The *Constitution's* new vision of the world concludes dramatically with the promise of a sacramental transfiguration of creation into a new earth and a new heaven. The meaning of all man's earthly activity is to be found in the paschal mystery, the Holy Eucharist, "where natural elements refined by man are changed into His glorified Body and Blood, providing a meal of brotherly solidarity and a foretaste of the heavenly banquet" (art. 38).

So it will also be with "the consummation of the earth and of humanity." We do not know when and how this cosmic transformation will take place. But certainly, "the expectation of a new earth must not weaken but rather stimulate our concern for cultivating this one. For here grows the body of a new human family, a body which even now is able to give some kind of foreshadowing of the new age" (art. 39).

> Earthly progress must be carefully distinguished from the growth of Christ's kingdom. Nevertheless, to the extent that the former can contribute to the better ordering of human society, it is of vital concern to the kingdom of God.

For after we have obeyed the Lord, and in His Spirit nurtured on earth the values of human dignity, brotherhood, and freedom, and indeed all the good fruits of our nature and enterprise, we will find them again, but freed of stain, burnished and transfigured. . . . On this earth that kingdom is already present in mystery. When the Lord returns, it will be brought into full flower (art. 39).

This is the church's hope for Christian social action: the city of man is even now being purified and perfected into the city of God.

The Geneva Conference Report

The working group on "Theological Issues" (pp. 195-207) concentrated on three themes of general relevance to the conference as a whole: (1) a Christian approach to the intelligibility of nature in light of the advances of modern science and technology; (2) a theological understanding of social change in view of the relation of God's kingdom to political affairs; (3) some theological issues in racial and ethnic relations as seen in terms of needed changes in social structures as well as personal attitudes.

In approaching the problem of nature's intelligibility, it is first affirmed that "nature is under both the providence of God and the mastery of men" (para. 3). This biblical view of nature as God's creation saves us from two common errors.

On the one hand, we avoid a false divorce between nature and history. It is through the ongoing activity of God and men in history that the processes of nature find meaning in continual creation. On the other hand, we do not falsely identify God with his creation. Men may engage in scientific research "without fear of being impious, or guilty of desecration" (para. 6). In fact, the Bible's "desacralization of nature" is an essential starting point of all scientific technology.

Modern man's capacity to acquire scientific information is indisputable. This massive data, however, must be viewed from the biblical perspective on "the meaning of facts in relation to man's God-given destiny" (para. 9). God's lordship and man's mastery are both involved in the divine ordinance, "Subdue the earth and have dominion" (Gen. 1:28). Hence man's mastery must be understood in terms of responsible stewardship. "His dominion over nature, considered as God's creation, is that of a keeper and transformer, not of a conqueror" (para. 11).

The working group turns next to examine "the relation of God's history of salvation to the events of human history." A new situation has been created in our day by the convergence of widespread "ideological ferment" and a strong disposition to "revolutionary thought and action" in opposition to the inequities of the status quo (paras. 14-15). Prominent also are strong feelings of nationalism among the recently liberated former colonies at a time when technological development poses serious questions about man's ability "to control the dynamism he himself has created" (paras. 16-17).

The *Report* goes on to insist, however, that "the Christian who turns to the biblical source of his faith for guidance finds there a remarkable parallel to this modern temper" (para. 18). In opposition to the static and meaningless worldview of classical philosophy, existence in the Bible, as in our world, is intensely historical.

> It is concerned, not with abstract and timeless structures of thought, society and the physical world, but with the truth which can be known and the good that can be done in living relation with God to whom the future belongs. . . . Therefore, in secular technology and revolution, man in the context of faith differs fundamentally from man in a non-believing context, in his understanding of the power of God to whom he is responsible, the human sin with which he must reckon, and the vision of true humanity which he finds in Christ. He is by this very token a part of the struggle in our time to achieve a responsible society of justice and peace among men, and to discern and realize relative meanings in history (para. 18).

Four principal ways are suggested which express both the solidarity and the difference of a Christian's calling and witness in the world.

"First, the Christian knows by faith that no structure of society, no system of human power and security is perfectly just, and that every system falls under the judgment of God in so far as it is unable to reform itself in response to the call for justice of those who are under its power" (para. 19).

This means that there is no "divinely ordained social order";

there are only "relative, secular structures" that are periodically in need of the Christian's radical "No." His task consists of "bringing about effective social change" and "discerning in the protest of the poor and oppressed" the demands of historical justice.

"Second, the Christian lives in the world by the hope of the final victory of Christ over the powers of this age. He therefore sees the struggle for justice and true humanity in our time under the sign of this hope" (para. 21).

The conviction is expressed that "human life itself will be transformed in a way beyond imagination." God's kingdom has broken into history with Christ and "it will extend over all men and over the whole creation." Even now, signs of the Messiah's rule over the demonic powers "break into our time and transform the world."

> This transformation is, of course, never a simple completion of human plans and desires. . . . Nor can we speak of a continuing transformation of this world until it becomes the Kingdom of God. The world faces judgment and destruction in the future as well as progress and development. But because the Messiah who is God and Man has risen from the death to which perverted human power put him, Christians are called to work to transform human society at every point in the hope that God will use their work for good whether they succeed or fail (para. 21).

"Third, the discernment by Christians of what is just and unjust, human and inhuman in the complexities of political and economic change, is a discipline exercised in continual dialog with biblical resources, the mind of the Church through history and today, and the best insights of social scientific analysis" (para. 23).

The aim of this disciplined study is "action in human society." Its object is "to respond to the power of God" which is recreating the world. "Christian theology is prophetic only in so far as it dares, in full reflection, to declare how, at a particular place and time, God is at work, and thus to show the Church where and when to participate in his work" (para. 23).

"Fourth, the Church is called, in the world, to be that part of the world which responds to God's love for all men, and to become therefore the community in which God's relation to man is known and realized" (para. 26).

The church may be looked upon as either the world's center or servant, either its present fulfillment or the witness to its future hope. In either case, "it is called to the community in which the world can discover itself as it may become" (para. 26).

Since this viewpoint did not reflect the unanimous position of the working group, "a Norwegian theologian" was requested to append a minority statement to the *Report*. While granting the central importance of the New Testament concept of the kingdom of God, the second position challenges the view that men help to bring in God's kingdom through their political activity.

> The contemporaries of Christ understood the Kingdom as such in political terms, and the role of the Messiah was conceived in the image of a revolutionary leader. In refusing to be a Messiah of this pattern, the Master clearly demonstrated for all times that his Gospel neither will nor can conquer the world by political means. Therefore, Christians should frankly distinguish between the activity of promoting Christianity through proclaiming the coming of Christ, and the kind of social commitment in which they themselves—under the obligation of a Christian responsibility—choose to engage (para. 28).
>
> A man who is justified by faith in Christ no longer needs to struggle to justify himself. He is free to face his sin, admit his guilt, and enter into a life of never-ceasing departure and renewal, and he is free and—by virtue of this freedom— obliged to love and serve his neighbor in accepting himself as loved and served by Christ (para. 29).

This view does not mean that the Christian may avoid political involvement as a crucial arena in which his neighbors can be served. But it does mean that "in the field of secular activities a Christian is primarily concerned with his neighbor, and that his dealings with ideologies, programmes and organized movements are subject to this primary concern" (para. 30). Because of the moral ambiguity in all political decision-making, moreover, particular choices that are obeyed as a divine imperative by a particular Christian "cannot be launched as a general obligation for all Christians."

The church has an obligation to encourage its members to "take a stand" on controversial social issues, but "without prescribing this or that type of engagement as the only possible one." In addition, the minority statement concludes, the church as a body is also called to "speak to society on behalf of the oppressed" in situations when "the humanity of man is . . . clearly at stake" (para. 31).

Such a situation is clearly present, agrees the entire working group, in the current crisis in racial and ethnic relations throughout the world. "This idolization of race has in some cultures become the basis for one race seeking to oppress and dominate others whom they consider inferior." Non-biblical myths that root racial distinctions in creation must be exposed as false and dangerous. "Such idolatry, or group self-deification which is the consequence of human sin, oversteps creaturely limitations and defies God" (para. 33).

> Reconciliation in this context cannot be mere sentimental harmonizing of conflicting groups. It demands sacrifice. It demands identification with the oppressed. It demands determination to break down the unjust pattern. It should restore the dignity of the oppressed. Changes in personal attitudes and reconciliation of individuals are of fundamental importance, but nothing less than structural change can create a pattern of justice in which the dignity and freedom of all will be assured (para. 35).

"For Christians to stand aloof from this struggle," the *Report* concludes, "is to be disobedient to the call of God in history."

Ecumenical Theological Ethics

In light of the New Testament's witness to the righteousness of God and man, the theological foundations of the Vatican Council's *Pastoral Constitution* must be questioned on two grounds. First, its christological view of man and history results in a qualified "theology of glory" that one-sidedly minimizes the sin of man, the cross of Christ, and the eschatological origins and judgment of God's kingdom. Second, there is no organic unity between the theology of Part One of the document (Teilhard De Chardin's cosmic redemption) and the social ethics of Part Two (Thomistic natural law). Evangelical Christians can only regret the "peaceful coexistence" of these two wholly incompatible dominant motifs.[4]

Cosmic Redemption

By combining an incarnational theology with an evolutionary cosmology, the dominant motif of Part One is the sacramental transfiguration of creation into the likeness of the kingdom of God. As grace "purifies and perfects" nature, so the whole of creation is being renewed and recapitulated in Christ. As the eternal Word mediated the creation, so the incarnate Word mediates the new creation (arts. 12, 22, 34, 36, 38, 39, 45, 57). Eschatologically, this cosmic vision stresses the "already" of the kingdom's inauguration (Matt. 28:18; Col. 1:15-20; Eph. 1:10; John 20:23), at the expense of the "not yet" of its final consummation (1 Cor. 15:24; Heb. 2:8, 10:13; Rom. 8:23-24; Col. 3:3-4).

Hence, all our cultural advances are said to "prepare men to accept the gospel" *(praeparatio evangelica)*, for the gospel is "in harmony with the most secret desires of the human heart" (arts. 57, 21). But is such a humanly appealing gospel compatible with the apostolic message that enraged Jews as a stumbling block, and offended Gentiles as folly? In the New Testament, Paul proclaims "Jesus Christ and him crucified"; in the *Pastoral Constitution,* the church "courteously invites atheists to examine the gospel with an open mind" (art. 21).

Natural Law

Along with the *Constitution's* major theme of "cosmic transformation" through the gospel, there is also the minor theme of "cultural penetration" through the law. In the final chapters of Part One, it is suddenly and incongruously affirmed that "the earthly and the heavenly city penetrate each other" (art. 40). Although "Christ gave His Church no proper mission in the political, economic, or social order," the council asserts that the church's religious mission will nevertheless result in "a function, a light, and an energy which can serve to structure and consolidate the human community according to the divine law" (art. 42).

Ironically, with the exception of the chapters on culture and (partially) marriage, it is the natural law orientation of the papal social encyclicals (especially John XXIII's *Mater et Magistra* and *Pacem in Terris*) that is actually determinative for the ethical chapters in the *Constitution's* Part Two (economics, politics, international affairs), as well as for the council's *Declaration on Religious Freedom.* Wholly apart from any notions of "cosmic transformation," the church seeks to "penetrate the earthly city" by appealing to such varied grounds of non-redemptive ethical authority as man's creation in God's image (arts. 3, 12, 18, 23, 68), God's moral law written on man's heart and conscience (arts. 8, 16, 33, 78), philosophical values and ideals (arts. 4, 7, 11, 16, 37, 57, 66, 77), along with the chief one based on divine and natural law, human rights, and the common good (arts. 26-30, 48, 50, 51, 65, 68, 74, 79, 84).

The section of the *Geneva Conference Report* dealing with theological issues reveals two similar weaknesses: limited consensus on the relation of God's creative and redemptive activity in the world, and, consequently, only limited direction from biblical and theological criteria for guiding the churches' involvement in society.

Political Theology

What is the relation of the righteousness, peace, and freedom of the kingdom of God to the justice, peace, and liberty in men's political affairs? Do Christians (and non-Christians) help to bring in God's kingdom through their political involvement? Can we not still validly distinguish (without separating) what Christians are expected to render to Caesar and to God?

These unanswered questions from the Geneva Conference were later reviewed at the World Council's Hague Consultation of the Commission of the Churches on International Affairs in April, 1967. The report of a working group there provides us with a succinct summary of the present state of theological ethics in non-Roman ecumenical circles: unity in social commitment, but diversity in the grounds and goals of that commitment.

> The biblical message of God's love for all men, and His taking upon Himself of human nature and history in Jesus Christ, impels the churches to be of service to mankind in every aspect of life including international relations. Particularly today when international relations open new prospects of enriching human life even while they are also full of menace, this aspect of our service is of great and growing importance.

We are all agreed that this service and witness is an essential part of the Church's mission.

Another view has sometimes been found in the churches, that the responsibility of the Church is confined to the spiritual and personal life of the individual, and ought not to be extended to social, political and economic questions. We do not share this view.

Different theological accents emerged as we reflected on this acknowledged responsibility. The main approaches were:

1. Starting from the biblical testimony to the creation of the world by God and the divine providence in ordering it, the oneness of all mankind under the law of God is emphasized.

2. Starting from the creative and perfecting activity of God's grace in human history, the dynamic element in history, moving to a glorious consummation is stressed.

3. Starting from the message of the coming kingdom of God in Jesus Christ, the inspiration to action and the challenge this presents to our present imperfect and sinful world are revealed.

4. Starting from the Church's participation in the continuing threefold ministry of Christ in the world, the emphasis falls on priestly intercession, prophetic judgment, the arousing of hope and conscience and pastoral care for mankind.

All these accents and some others emerged in our deliberations. But the variety of these theological approaches in dialectical tension, far from concealing our common Christian convictions, enriches ecumenical thinking.[5]

Ecumenical Study

The highly pragmatic and ideologically tainted judgments made throughout the section reports of the Geneva Conference reveal the high price the churches are paying for their lack of theological clarity in social ethics. For instance, the critical need for meaningful dialog between theologians and social scientists is still badly frustrated by mutual fears of irreverence and irrelevance.

It might well be argued that this is the price the church has to pay if it wishes to begin to speak relevantly to a revolutionary age in more than pious platitudes (as in many of the economic and political sections of the *Pastoral Constitution*). Nevertheless, the *Report* of the Geneva Conference indicates the need for the ecumenical churches to be as courageously committed to theological study as they are to social action. The key issue is, What makes social action "Christian"?

PEACE AND THE COMMUNITY OF NATIONS

As the council fathers opened their debate on the *Pastoral Constitution's* final chapter on international affairs, Pope Paul VI was engaged in a pilgrimage of peace at the United Nations. Addressing the world through a major speech at the U. N.'s General Assembly, he dramatized the irenic message of Vatican II by warmly endorsing the United Nations and its worldwide efforts for peace with justice. At the heart of his address, Paul declared:

> You are expecting us to utter this sentence, and we are well aware of its gravity and solemnity: not the ones against the others, never again, never more! It was principally for this purpose that the organization of the United Nations arose: against war, in favor of peace!
> It suffices to remember that the blood of millions of men, that numberless and unheard of sufferings, useless slaughter and frightful ruin, are the sanction of the past that unites you, with an oath that must change the future history of the world: no more war, war never again! [6]

In much the same spirit, some of the liveliest debate at the Geneva Conference took place in connection with the report and conclusions of Section III on "Structures of International Cooperation." After the conference and armed with its findings, the World Council's General Secretary, Dr. Eugene Carson Blake, delivered a scathing indictment of American foreign policy in Vietnam. He based his critique on what he termed "the new and growing consensus on peace of the ecumenical movement." Its five major components:

> . . . (1) that the peace which ecumenical Christians support is not merely the absence of war but is a peace based upon justice and freedom . . . (2) that war among the nations is no longer a live option . . . (3) that a world of independent sovereign nations under no enforceable law and no morality but their own safety and prosperity must give way to one worldwide community of all humanity . . . (4) that worldwide community can be built only upon the foundation of full justice

and equality among all men . . . (5) that Christians must give up the old triumphalist hope of dominating the world and must win men to the authentic way of Christ to serve the world.[7]

The Pastoral Constitution

The theme of chapter 5 is "The Fostering of Peace and the Promotion of a Community of Nations." Following a descriptive introduction, the material is structured under two headings: (1) "The Avoidance of War"; and (2) "Building Up the International Community."

The council begins by asserting that "the whole human family has reached an hour of supreme crisis in its advance toward maturity" (art. 77). There is on one side the promise of a genuine world community; on the other, the threat of new and more horrible wars. Confident of the Christian gospel, "which is in harmony with the loftier strivings and aspirations of the human race," the *Constitution* aims "to summon Christians to cooperate with all men in making secure among themselves a peace based on justice and love, and in setting up agencies of peace" (art. 77).

Since peace is not merely "the absence of war," it cannot be achieved by dictatorial imposition or a precarious balance of power. Genuine peace is actualized only as men "thirst after even greater justice" and trustingly share in neighborly love. "Insofar as men are sinful, the threat of war hangs over them. . . . But to the extent that men vanquish sin by a union of love, they will vanquish violence as well. . . ." (art. 78).

The destructive power of modern weapons is such that their use would "lead the combatants to a savagery far surpassing that of the past" (art. 79). Contemplating this "melancholy state of humanity," Section 1 of the *Constitution* recalls

> . . . the permanent binding force of universal natural law and its all-embracing principles. Man's conscience itself gives ever more emphatic voice to these principles. Therefore actions which deliberately conflict with these same principles, as well as orders commanding such actions, are criminal. Blind obedience cannot excuse those who yield to them (art. 79).

Having reaffirmed the inviolable nature of the universal natural law and man's duty and responsibility to obey its principles, the council fathers proceed to make some moral judgments on current problems in military life.

First, genocide is vehemently condemned as a "horrible crime." Men are called to "openly and fearlessly resist" any leaders who design plans for "the methodical extermination of an entire people, nation, or ethnic minority" (art. 79).

Second, there is strong approval of international agreements that aim at "making military activity and its consequences less inhuman." Conventions concerning the handling of wounded or captured soldiers, etc., should be "honored and strengthened" (art. 79).

Third, there is an appeal for humane treatment of conscientious objectors by civil laws and public officials. While neither praising nor condemning the practice as such, the council pleads for equitable laws to protect those "who for reasons of conscience refuse to bear arms, provided however, that they accept some other form of service to the human community" (art. 79).

Fourth, there is prudent support for the legitimate right of self-defense on the part of governments. This right cannot be denied so long as "there is no competent and sufficiently powerful authority at the international level." Military power may be used, however, only after "every means of peaceful settlement has been exhausted" (art. 79). Clearly distinguishing the "just defense of the people" from "the subjugation of other nations," members of the armed forces engaged in just warfare should regard themselves as "agents of security and freedom" who are making a "genuine contribution to the establishment of peace" (art. 79).

Fifth, there is a flat rejection of the kind of total war that is threatened by any extensive use of modern scientific arms. Nuclear weapons are capable of inflicting "massive and indiscriminate destruction far exceeding the bounds of legitimate defense." Their ready availability demands that men now "undertake an evaluation of war with an entirely new attitude." Consequently, the council issues the following declaration: "Any act of war aimed indiscriminately at the destruction of entire cities or of extensive areas along with their population is a crime against God and man himself. It merits unequivocal and unhesitating condemnation" (art. 80).

Sixth, the arms race is strongly criticized as "an utterly treacherous trap for humanity, and one which injures the poor to an intolerable degree." Whatever may be said for the deterrent value of a government's "capacity for immediate retaliation against an adversary," the council puts no hope in the precarious "balance of terror" now existing among the great nations. "Rather than being eliminated thereby, the causes of war threaten to grow gradually stronger" (art. 81).

The ultimate goal calls for a time when "all war can be completely outlawed by international consent" (art. 82). For the long run, this requires the replacement of sovereign national states with an international government and police force. It demands "the establishment of some universal public authority acknowledged as such by all, and endowed with effective power to safeguard, on behalf of all, security, regard for justice, and respect for rights" (art. 82).

In the meantime, public officials must continue to strive "to put an end at last to the arms race, and to make a true beginning of disarmament." It ought not to be a unilateral arrangement, "but one proceeding at an equal pace according to agreement, and backed up by authentic and workable safeguards" (art. 82). Public officials should be supported and encouraged along these lines by Christian citizens and others who have experienced a "change of heart" in their fervent commitment to international peace and justice.

Section two examines ways in which the emerging international community can be firmly established. In the conviction that wars thrive on "the causes of dissension between men . . . especially on injustice," the *Constitution* highlights two especially grievous social evils: "excessive economic inequalities" and "contempt for personal rights" (art. 83). The council fathers rejoice at the "spirit of true fraternity flourishing between Christians and non-Christians" as they work together in regional and international organizations and agencies for the "relief of the world's enormous miseries" (art. 84).

Four norms are suggested to guide the expansion of international cooperation at the economic level:

(a) Developing nations should strongly desire to seek the complete human fulfillment of their citizens as the explicit and fixed goal of progress.

(b) . . . advanced nations . . . have a very heavy obligation to help the developing peoples in the discharge of the afore-mentioned responsibilities.

(c) The international community should see to the coordination and stimulation of economic growth . . . [honoring] the principle of subsidiarity. [The principle of "subsidiarity" formulated by Pope Pius XI in the encyclical letter *Quadragesimo Anno* (1931) reads: "Just as it is wrong to withdraw from the individual and commit to the community at large what private enterprise and endeavor can accomplish, so it is likewise unjust and a gravely harmful disturbance of right order to turn over to a greater society of higher rank functions and services which can be performed by lesser bodies on a lower plane." Quoted by Pope John XXIII in the encyclical letter *Mater et Magistra* (1961), p. 414.]

(d) In many instances there exists a pressing need to reform economic and social structures. But nations must beware of technical solutions immaturely proposed, especially those which offer men material advantages against his spiritual nature and development (art. 86).

As if by way of implementing these norms, the *Constitution* turns once again to the unresolved "burdens and difficulties stemming from a rapid population growth." International study and cooperation is urgently recommended in order to help overpopulated nations (1) "to abandon ancient methods of farming in favor of modern techniques"; (2) "to establish a better social order and regulate the distribution of land with greater fairness"; (3) to support, "within the limits of their own competence," the rights and duties of government officials with regard to "social legislation as it affects families, migration to cities, and information relative to the conditions and needs of the nation" (art. 87).

While denying the right of any government to interfere with the "honest judgment of parents" on the question of how many children should be born, the educational efforts of family-planning clinics are endorsed. "Human beings should also be judiciously informed of scientific advances in the exploration of methods by which spouses can be helped in arranging the number of their children. The reliability of these methods should be adequately

proven and their harmony with the moral order should be clear"
(art. 87).

In connection with a recommendation to establish a "social
agency of the universal Church for the worldwide promotion of
justice for the poor," the *Pastoral Constitution* concludes this chapter with an appeal for ecumenical charity and collaboration.

> Christians should collaborate willingly and wholeheartedly
> in establishing an international order involving genuine respect
> for all freedoms and amicable brotherhood between all men.
> This objective is all the more pressing since the greater part of
> the world is still suffering from so much poverty that it is as if
> Christ Himself were crying out in these poor to beg the charity
> of the disciples.
> Without being inflexible and completely uniform, the col-
> lection and distribution of aid should be conducted in an order-
> ly fashion in dioceses, nations, and through the entire world.
> (Wherever it seems appropriate, this activity of Catholics
> should be carried on in unison with other Christian brothers)
> (art. 88).

The Geneva Conference Report

The members of Section III also concentrated attention on the
subject of "Structures in International Cooperation." Their report
(pp. 122-52) is presented under the following headings: (1)
"General Affirmations"; (2) "International Peace and Security";
(3) "World Social, Economic, and Political Development"; (4)
"The Church's Involvement"; (5) the Conference-adopted "Conclusions."

Life and peace are the two distinctive notes struck in the introductory theological affirmations. The church's mission is to witness
in word and deed to this message: "God wills life, he gives life, he
loves the life of men, and he will guide men to his kingdom. . . .
Jesus Christ died and rose again for all. The Gospel gives man the
peace of God, and it is the God of peace who equips us with
everything, that we may do his will. . . . We are called to serve
God's peace among our fellow men. Although God's peace and
peace in the world of nations are not identical, he who serves
because he has been given the peace of God will seek peace
among men" (paras. 1-3).

Turning directly to the current threat of nuclear warfare, the *Report* asserts that the development of military technology, and especially of atomic, radiological, biological, and chemical arms, and the means to deliver them, "marks a decisive turning point in the history of mankind, of states and their wars" (para. 6). An indiscriminate nuclear war could now involve the massive extermination of civilian populations, "the impossibility of self-defense by smaller nations, the danger of annihilation of human cultures, and the continuing danger for future generations from radiation" (para. 6).

The conference participants conclude that this new and terrible situation "forces Christians to re-examine previous thinking in the churches concerning war." Their verdict: nuclear war is now impossible for Christian pacifists and non-pacifists alike.

> In Amsterdam in 1948, the First Assembly of the World Council of Churches declared, "War is contrary to the will of God", and at the same time distinguished three possible atti tudes towards the participation by Christians in the evil of war [one of the three attitudes being that war might at times be a lesser evil]. Today the situation has changed. Christians still differ as to whether military means can be legitimately used to achieve objectives which are necessary to justice. But nuclear war goes beyond all bounds. Mutual nuclear annihilation can never establish justice because it destroys all that justice seeks to defend or to achieve. We now say to all governments and peoples that nuclear war is against God's will and the greatest of evils. Therefore we affirm that it is the first duty of governments and their officials to prevent nuclear war (para. 7).

Four long-range steps are later recommended which could help to end the "old history of the international jungle." First, "the changing of a mere balance of power into a community with institutions for the prevention of escalation of conflict between the main powers." Second, "the embodiment in a code of conduct of the discipline necessary to prevent war; step-by-step agreements concerning limitations on the use of war; the development of a new international law for the nuclear dimension." Third, "control and inspection of armaments by international agencies to ensure an equilibrium of power and regulate the different phases of disarma-

ment." Fourth, "an increasing role for the smaller powers in de-
polarizing international affairs" (para. 97).

In discussing the relations of the major nuclear powers to the
other nations, the *Report* makes special mention of the tragic situation in Vietnam, and of matters relating to the People's Republic
of China. Concrete proposals on foreign policy are made for the
consideration of the member churches to whom the conference
findings are addressed.

With regard to Vietnam, the Geneva participants advocate "stop-
ping the bombing of the North by the United States and South
Vietnam and the military infiltration of the South by North Vietnam." They particularly deplore "the massive and growing American military presence in Vietnam and the long-continued bombing
of villages in the South and of targets a few miles from cities in
the North. . . ." Fearing an "escalation of the war into a world
conflict," the *Report* urges a negotiated peace "through the United
Nations, or the participants in the Geneva conference, or other
international agencies" (paras. 23-25).

The admission of the People's Republic of China into the United
Nations is also favored. The fact that Red China is outside the
UN is "unanimously deplored." Her isolation is judged to be a
"growing danger to world peace." Also, "disarmament negotiations
cannot be satisfactory without her participation" (para. 26).

The United Nations is strongly endorsed as "the best structure
now available through which to pursue the goals of international
peace and justice" (para. 37). The conference members therefore
call upon the churches of the world "to defend it against all attacks
which would weaken or destroy it," as well as to seek out ways in
which the UN can be "transformed into an instrument fully capable
of ensuring the peace and guaranteeing justice on a world-wide
scale" (para. 37)

It is freely acknowledged that the United Nations still has obvious limitations. For example, it can exercise little influence in con-
flicts between the great powers, and the process of decision-making
in the General Assembly is weakened by lack of agreement (para.
38).

Nevertheless, the United Nations does have many resources
which are recommended for fuller use:

(1) UN debates offer a corrective for national self-righteousness and unilateral action in world affairs;

(2) the UN offers a forum for continuous diplomacy, conciliation and mediation:

(3) the UN can contribute to peacekeeping operations and the elimination of local conflict;

(4) the UN machinery can be used as an instrument for the promotion of dynamic justice;

(5) the work done by the UN and its specialized agencies in the fields of human rights, labor relations, and social and economic conditions may form the basis for an international ethos in these fields;

(6) the churches should make use of their consultative status with the UN to bring their influence to bear (para. 114).

At the same time, the *Report* also favors the formation of regional organizations of states "which are closely linked geographically, and which have the same level of economic and technical development, or a similar civilization and culture" (para. 50). By pooling resources and working together to regulate the competition between enterprises and states, such regional organizations can promote more equitable international trade, provide more help to underdeveloped areas, and play a more responsible role in international politics, especially with regard to problems of national sovereignty (paras. 50-53).

Turning to international economic development, the delegates reiterate their contention that "technological, economic and social developments now make possible the achievement in our generation of true freedom from hunger, misery and poverty for all people." Progress toward this noble goal is being frustrated, however, by a host of factors: private oligopoly and public restraints in international trade, inadequate and unpredictable support of development by the wealthy nations, and inept administration of financial grants and technical assistance in the developing countries (para. 71).

Christians should arouse the conscience of all men to a recognition of their human solidarity and their obligation to support the increase of development assistance. The doubling of such assistance would begin to make it adequate for the world's present needs. The transfer of resources should not impose undue burdens on the recipients, and should be made on terms which support creative development and social justice. This aid must be disinterested in the sense that it should never be used to further the donor's ideological or selfish interests. It should be given only where there is a real possibility for regional or national development, but the enforcement of such conditions is more properly a function of a regional or international institution than of a donor country (para. 79).

As the conference members turn to view the political role of the developing nations, they find it difficult to offer more than a few generalizations about the peoples of the so-called Third World (Africa, Asia, and Latin America). Yet in at least two important respects, the political dynamics of these nations display some marked similarities.

First, "Though the developed nations have made political development possible in Africa, Asia and Latin America, the fact remains that they have also contributed heavily to political conflict, injustice and corruption" (para. 82). Pointed illustrations include "the attempt to use 'Third World' nations as instruments of Cold War politics, for example . . . Korea and Vietnam," the support given by developed countries, particularly those of the North Atlantic area, "to ruling *élites* in the developing nations whose rule is oppressive," and the "indiscriminate use of an ideology of 'anti-communism' to resist change of any sort" (para. 82).

Second, "A revolutionary mood pervades the thought of many of the more active and influential groups in public life in many of the nations of the 'Third World' and is an important factor in their politics" (para. 84). Plans concerning national independence and economic development are interpreted as revolutionary, "not only because of the magnitude of the changes which they seek, but also because of their concern for *rapid* change, accomplished, if necessary, by the use of violence" (para. 85).

While the *Report* records the inability of the Geneva Conference participants to resolve this critical debate, it also points to the emergence of certain conclusions about the way Christians ought to approach these problems. With regard to the policies of the developed nations: (1) their involvement should be shaped as far as possible by concern for the promotion of the welfare of peoples in the Third World; (2) they should also consistently give attention to the views of the peoples in these areas (para. 88).

Two more controversial judgments are offered with regard to the approach of Christians to the reorganization of the structures of power in the Third World. One is that, "wherever small *élites* rule at the expense of the welfare of the majority, political change towards achieving a more just order as quickly as possible, should be actively promoted and supported by Christians" (para. 90).

> The second is that, in cases where such changes are needed, the use by Christians of revolutionary methods by which is meant violent overthrow of an existing political order—cannot be excluded *a priori*. For in such cases, it may very well be that the use of violent methods is the only recourse of those who wish to avoid prolongation of the vast covert violence which the existing order involves. But Christians should think of the day after the revolution, when justice must be established by clear minds and in good conscience. There is no virtue in violence itself, but only in what will come after it. In some instances significant changes have been made by non-violent means, and Christians must develop greater skill and wisdom in using these (para. 90).

In conclusion, the members of Section III have five things to say to their fellow Christians:

> We thank God that a nuclear holocaust has not occurred. . . . It is our belief and experience that in suffering God's grace abounds. . . . We urge Christians and the churches, by every means at their disposal, to join those who seek to arouse the conscience of their fellow men concerning peace and justice. . . . The witness of radical non-conformity has always been part of the Christian tradition. . . . We ask Christians to bear constant witness to their faith in the life of their nation in the world (para. 91).

Ecumenical Peace Ethics

When viewed against the background of the New Testament's teaching on the civil righteousness of Christian citizens, the chapter on international affairs in the *Pastoral Constitution* can be praised as a responsible effort to speak to the whole world on behalf of the whole (Roman) church on two of the most pressing issues of world politics: nuclear warfare and international justice.

Nuclear Warfare

Employing the most vigorous language in the entire *Constitution*, the central declaration of this chapter condemns unequivocally as "a crime against God and man himself," any act of war that is "aimed indiscriminately at the destruction of entire cities or extensive areas along with their population" (art. 80).

Commentators have noted, however, that this seemingly straightforward prohibition is open to at least three possible interpretations. Acts of war should not be aimed at the destruction of entire cities because this would (1) violate the moral immunity of noncombatants from direct attack, thus violating the principle of "discrimination," or (2) cause greater evil than any good resulting from such strikes, thus violating the principle of "proportion," or (3) be tantamount to the "subjugation of peoples," and therefore in violation of the proscription of "aggressive wars" by recent Popes even though the war had its origins in legitimate defense.

Hence advocates of the classical "just war" and more recent "nuclear pacifist" positions have both claimed support from the *Constitution*. The unresolved ethical question: Is nuclear warfare different from conventional warfare in form or in kind?

International Justice

The council fathers demonstrate the kind of political realism that is appropriate for Christian citizens in the realm of civil righteousness. They point both to long-range goals and to realistic interim strategies. The ultimate political goal is described somewhat grandiosely as "the establishment of some universal public authority acknowledged as such by all, and endowed with effective power to safeguard, on the behalf of all, security, regard for justice, and respect for rights" (art. 82).

In the meantime, however, man's chief hope for peace lies in eradicating political injustice and excessive economic inequalities, the two great causes of war among men. Periodic displays of charity to the suffering millions of the world are not enough. Radical structural reforms and massive redistributions of the world's power and goods are called for on a scale unprecedented in human history. Men in a revolutionary age are called to implement the parable of the Good Samaritan "with a universal outlook—something certainly appropriate for Catholics" (art. 90).

The section group on international affairs at the Geneva Conference approached these same areas with such similar convictions that a number of key passages in the *Official Report* and the *Pastoral Constitution* are virtually interchangeable. However, in recognition of those few pointed recommendations that are not so easily substituted for one another, it might be appropriate to direct a few concluding remarks to the ethics of Christian ecumenical relations themselves.

Ideological Partisanship

The Geneva Conference demonstrated that non-Roman ecumenical churches still have a lot to learn from their "separated brethren" when it comes to "speaking the truth in love" *as Christians* on political, economic, and social affairs. Their lack of theological agreement can easily lead to ideological partisanship; their inexperience in ecclesiastical discipline can suddenly prompt irresponsible, *ad hoc* pronouncements on virtually all the major problems of the world. (Note, for example, the aggressively anti-western, especially anti-American, spirit dominating many of the polemical floor debates and public resolutions at the Geneva Conference.)

The forms of the church's involvement in society will vary, of course, according to the situation. At different times and places, Christians will be called on to make a prophetic witness of protest against the cruel and the unjust, a pastoral witness of service to the suffering and the oppressed, or a priestly witness of intercession for the good and the evil alike. Certainly the church must speak and act; equally needful, however, is the distinctively *Christian* character of its speech and action.

Ecumenical Partnership

"Our final word to the churches must be a call to *repentance* and to the recognition of God's judgment upon us, and of the reality of the new humanity in Jesus Christ offered to us all. It is also an urgent appeal for more effective and vigorous action, as an expression of our *witness* to the Gospel in the world in which we are living" ("Geneva Conference Message," p. 50).

The world's social needs are so urgent that Christians must now try to meet them together as fellow servants if they are to be faithful to their common Lord and effective in their common calling. Even as we turn now to offer a distinctively Reformation-oriented alternative to the theological and political ethics of both the *Pastoral Constitution* and the Geneva Conference *Report,* we do so in the earnest conviction that Lutheran Christians can best demonstrate their obedient faith in loving service to the world, standing shoulder to shoulder with all the rest of the people of God.

A LUTHERAN THEOLOGY OF POLITICS

The personal and corporate exercise of our Christian social responsibility will be strengthened by a clearer understanding of both the faith of the church and the facts of modern political and military life. We therefore turn first to Holy Scriptures in the conviction that the church does have a relevant word to speak to our confused and frightened world.

The Biblical Foundations

Ever since New Testament times, Christians have had to face the dilemma of living "in but not of" this world. The shaky balance required in this ambiguous situation has provided a peculiar boundary-line quality to all biblically-grounded approaches to political ethics.

Paul reminds us that "our commonwealth is in heaven" (Phil. 3:20), but that we nevertheless must "be subject to the governing authorities, for there is no authority except from God" (Rom. 13:1). Peter addresses the followers of Christ as "a chosen race, a royal priesthood, a holy nation, God's own people" who are merely "aliens and exiles" here on earth (I Peter 2:9-11), but who are still enjoined to "be subject for the Lord's sake to every human institution" (I Peter 2:13). And it was Christ himself who warned,

"My kingship is not of this world" (John 18:36), even as he proclaimed, "The kingdom of God is in the midst of you" (Luke 17:21), and admonished his followers, "Render to Caesar the things that are Caesar's and to God the things that are God's" (Mark 12:17).

There is little wonder that such paradoxical assertions have provided Christians with ammunition for centuries of theological strife and political struggle. In searching for what light the Bible can shed on the realm of politics, therefore, it will not do for us to proceed in literalistic fashion by piling proof-text upon proof-text. What is needed instead is a key to the whole biblical drama of salvation which will reveal to us the nature and purpose of political life in terms of the creative and redemptive activity of God. Fortunately, Christians have been provided with this indispensable key in Paul's Epistle to the Romans.

> Therefore, since we are justified by faith, we have peace with God through our Lord Jesus Christ. Through him we have obtained access to this grace in which we stand, and we rejoice in our hope of sharing the glory of God. . . . If, because of one man's (Adam's) trespass, death reigned through that one man, much more will those who receive the abundance of grace and the free gift of righteousness reign in life through the one man Jesus Christ. Then as one man's trespass led to condemnation for all men, so one man's act of righteousness leads to acquittal and life for all men (Rom. 5:1-2, 17-18).

With the authority of an apostle of God, Paul encompasses all human history here in his dramatic contrast of Adam and Christ. In and through Adam, we are all fallen creatures in the "old age" of sin and death. In and through Christ, on the other hand, all who believe in him are incorporated into the "new age" of righteousness and life. The fall of Adam stands at the head of the "old age" and subjects all creation to the wrath of God. The cross of Christ stands at the head of the "new age" in which men are justified by grace through faith and come to know the peace of God. The "two ages" of Adam and Christ stand in radical opposition to each other. By birth all creatures are "in Adam," but only by rebirth are all Christians "in Christ."

248   *William H. Lazareth*

The Christian as Righteous and Sinful

There are at least four ethical consequences of these theological affirmations which are of great importance for political life. In the first place, *the Christian belongs to both ages at the same time.* "God shows his love for us in that while we were yet sinners Christ died for us" (Rom. 5:8). In the providence of God, the new age does not supplant the old but interpenetrates it. The Christian does not cease to be a sinful creature even though he receives forgiveness and new life in Jesus Christ. He is simultaneously righteous in Christ and sinful in Adam.

It is because of his dual citizenship in both realms of creation and redemption that the believer can be admonished by Paul, "Do not be conformed to this world (age) but be transformed by the renewal of your mind" (Rom. 12:2). Any slackening of this life-long Christian tension leads to disastrous political results. Secularists are generally those who live as if the new age in Christ had not yet begun; clericalists are most often their opposites who live as though the old age in Adam had been completely abolished. Both views are unbiblical distortions of the Christian's dual status as a forgiven sinner under God.

God's Word as Law and Gospel

In the second place, *the law and the gospel have very different functions to perform in the two ages of Adam and Christ.* The gospel belongs to the new age of Christ and is "the power of God for salvation to every one who has faith" (Rom. 1:16). The law belongs to the old age of Adam "since through the law comes knowledge of sin" (Rom. 3:20). The gospel is the good news which promises men a share in the saving benefits of the righteousness of Christ. The law is the holy will of God which demands the perfect righteousness of which sinful men are incapable.

Important for us is the conclusion that the Christian is related both to the gospel insofar as he is already righteous, and to the law insofar as he still remains sinful. The civil function of the law is to compel all sons of Adam to govern their political affairs with due regard for peace and justice. The ethical function of the gospel is to empower all followers of Christ to serve their fellow men in the body politic by working to make peace more wholesome and justice more loving. As justice gives love its political form so love gives justice its ethical content. This denies, in principle as well as in practice, the naive notion that Christians should guard against "mixing religion and politics."

God's Rule Through Church and State

This leads to our third affirmation, namely, that the *church is primarily the agency of the gospel in the new age of Christ, while the state is primarily the agency of the law in the old age of Adam.* Since the two ages interpenetrate, however, the church also has an obligation to support the civil law, just as the state is likewise obliged to sustain the kind of open society in which the gospel may be proclaimed.

This interaction of both law and gospel in both church and state permits of no divorce between the realms of the so-called "sacred" and the "secular". All of life is sacred civil as well as ecclesiastical—when lived in obedience to God's loving will. In contrary fashion, all of life is secularized—ecclesiastical as well as civil—when lived in rebellion against God's loving will. Consequently, Christians exercise their dual citizenship in the two ages of Adam and Christ by means of their responsible participation in both church and state. This fundamental Christian belief has received classical formulation in a later chapter of Romans.

> Let every person be subject to the governing authorities. For there is no authority except from God, and those that exist have been instituted by God. Therefore he who resists the authorities resists what God has appointed, and those who resist will incur judgment. For rulers are not a terror to good conduct, but to bad. Would you have no fear of him who is in authority? Then do what is good, and you will receive his approval, for he is God's servant for your good. But if you do wrong, be afraid, for he does not bear the sword in vain; he is the servant of God to execute his wrath on the wrongdoer. Therefore one must be subject, not only to avoid God's wrath but also for the sake of conscience (Rom. 13:1-6).

Before analyzing some of the profound implications of this passage for our theology of politics, we should also recall the lurid description of the state in the 13th chapter of Revelation. For if Romans describes the divine side of the state, Revelation balances this realistically with some of its more demonic features. The same Roman government which Paul lauds as a "servant of God" is denounced in Revelation as a satanic "beast" which blasphemes against God, makes war on his saints, and engages in imperialism against other nations (Rev. 13:6-8). This parallels the Old Testament portrayal of the tyrant as one who "shall do according to his will; he shall exalt himself and magnify himself above every god, and shall speak astonishing things against the God of gods" (Dan. 11:36).

In contemporary language we may say that *the state ("civil authority") is depicted in the New Testament as a divinely ordained institution which has been delegated its power by God for the establishment and maintenance of peace and justice in a fallen and sinful world.*

The state is divinely ordained. No matter what historical forms its particular governments or governors may happen to take, the undergirding "governing authority" as such is to be respected and obeyed as an expression of the sovereign will of God the Creator. This means very practically that there is nothing inherently sacred about the particular pattern of nation-states which we have come to take for granted in recent centuries. That which is divinely ordained, for example, is not the United States or the Soviet Union, but rather civil *exousia,* meaning political authority or power. In a rapidly shrinking world in which our warring nation-state system seems to have reached the point of diminishing returns, it is important for Christians to note that there is absolutely no biblical objection to the development of regional or even international systems of political sovereignty if they can fulfill the civil purposes of God more effectively. On the contrary, it is to be highly encouraged.

The state's power is delegated to it by God. The state is accountable to God under his sovereign law for the ways in which it uses, abuses, or neglects to use its powerful civil "sword." This means, realistically, that the backbone of the state is might. Whether employed by Satan or against him, all politics is "power politics"— our unbiblical sentimentality notwithstanding. However, this in no way justifies any state's self-deification. The state's power is not inherent. It is delegated by God to be used responsibly for the attainment of beneficial social goals. This means that no state is worthy of the Christian's uncritical loyalty and unquestioning obedience. The state is in continual need of the prophetic guidance and judgment of the law of God—as proclaimed by the church—in order to be reminded of its secular limits and potentialities.

The purpose of the state is to establish and protect men's peace and social justice in this sinful world. In other words, its might must be enlisted in the service of right. But Christians should not thereby expect love to replace justice in the operations of a secular government. Civil authorities are not elected to run a pseudo-church on the basis of a culture-religion. The state's limited goal is earthly preservation under the law and not heavenly salvation under the gospel. There is consequently no "Christian" form of the state, its political parties, or its foreign policy. While persons can be transformed by the gospel, impersonal institutions can only be reformed by the law. We can "Christianize" politicians and statesmen but not politics and the state. It is therefore not justification before God but justice among men that Christians expect from the civil realm. For coupled with the law's theological struggle against sin is always its civil campaign against injustice. This means, for example, that political tyranny is both a sin against God and a crime against men. Especially in an age of martyrs like our own, we dare never forget—nor let Caesar forget—that there are times when the civil laws of men are in such conflict with the moral law of God that "we must obey God rather than men" (Acts 5:29).

The Conflict of War and Peace

Finally, *along with famines, earthquakes, sickness and death, wars are regarded in the New Testament as sinful expressions of the old age in Adam.* Wars belong in principle to "the form of this world which is passing away" (1 Cor. 7:31). "Wars and rumors of wars . . . nation rising against nation and kingdom against kingdom" are all foretold by Christ as signs of his second coming at the end of history (Matt. 24:6-7). At best—in defense—wars are very ambiguous remedies against grosser forms of evil; at worst—in aggression—they are very vivid expressions of man's sinful inhumanity to his fellow men.

The New Testament, while always careful to distinguish the religious "peace of God" from the political "peace among the nations," takes it for granted that believers in the new age of Christ will be in the vanguard of those fighting against all forms of human sinfulness. Among the chief of these is the corporate lust for power we call war. Sin is inevitable, but its particular expression in aggressive warfare is not. Along with attacking the plight of the hungry, the sick and the destitute, as well as the elimination of infanticide and chattel slavery, the humanizing if not final abolishment of warfare is certainly an essential part of the merciful mission of the people of God.

Though the New Testament says very little about wars as such, it does speak a great deal about sin. It speaks even more about sin's victor, the Prince of Peace, who called the peacemakers blessed. When Christians work for the establishment of political peace and justice, they do so in faithful witness to the kingdom of God in which "men shall beat their swords into plowshares, and their spears into pruning hooks; nation shall not lift up sword against nation, neither shall they learn war any more" (Isaiah 2:4).

The Heritage of the Reformation

The classical Lutheran answer to the problem of living "in but not of" this world has been formulated in Luther's doctrine of the "two kingdoms" and reaffirmed in the Augsburg Confession. Now it is no secret that this doctrine, especially as misinterpreted and misapplied by the *Deutsche Christen* in Nazi Germany, has been a source of keen concern and embarrassment to evangelical Christians throughout the free world. The wartime propaganda attacks linking Luther and Hitler need not concern us here since they were generally refuted as quickly as they were spewed forth. Of far more importance are those persisting theological attacks which root the traditional political quietism of Lutherans in the alleged "cultural defeatism" of Luther.

It is commonly charged that the Reformer advocated an "ethical double standard" which limited the impact of Christianity strictly to personal relationships, thus permitting social institutions such as the state to flourish in godless autonomy. If this indictment were true, Lutherans would be incapable of making any discriminate judgments in the controversial area of the current international political power struggle and the problem of armaments in the nuclear age. Since the purpose of this study is to lay the theological groundwork for such judgments, it is first necessary for us to disavow this mistaken "dualist" interpretation of Luther's theology of politics as part of the unfortunate historical mortgage passed on to us by late 19th century German Lutheranism.

At this point we need only recall the unflinching testimony of those like Norway's Bishop Eivind Berggrav who answered both the Nazis and traditional German "Lutheran" servility—with Luther himself!

> Luther became the liberator for the Norwegian Church. . . .
> I do not say that Luther was our only source of strength in our battle against Nazism and all that it implies. The most important source was the New Testament. But Luther's words were current; they showed us very clearly and powerfully what we should do. Above all, he was the very best remedy to expel all "Lutheran" servility to the state and secular authorities.[8]

Our case rests upon the conviction that Luther's doctrine of the "two kingdoms" is an authentic restatement of Paul's doctrine of the "two ages." Luther's intention was to demonstrate God's twofold rule of the whole world by law and gospel, and not to divide the world into two divorced realms of the "sacred" and the "secular." This has been carefully documented in many theological studies of the recent Luther Renaissance.

Neither Paul nor Luther advocate any "rigorous dualism" between the two ages or kingdoms of creation and redemption. Both insist that these two realms must first be distinguished by Christian theology in principle and then interpenetrated by Christian ethics in practice. We have already shown this to be the case in the political ethics of Paul and we must now do the same for Luther.

Luther on the "Two Kingdoms"

The foundation is laid carefully in *Secular Authority: To What Extent It Should Be Obeyed* (1523).[9] On first glance, the title might suggest that Luther found it necessary to protest against the godless inroads of a secularized state so soon after he had challenged the clericalism of an overzealous church. Actually, the very opposite is closer to the truth. *Weltlich* meant civil, temporal, nonecclesiastical authority for Luther and his medieval contemporaries. If we translate this today as "secular," we should disavow as anachronistic any of the irreligious and antireligious associations which this ambiguous word currently suggests to us.

In attempting to translate Luther's theology into the 20th century, we must always carefully shift the accent in the central thrust since his chief enemy was clericalism whereas ours is secularism. Over-simply, Luther had to put the church back under God's gospel; we have to put the state back under God's law.

Luther's basic task was to re-establish the theological coordination of civil and religious authority which he found in Paul's doctrine of the "two ages" of Adam and Christ. He therefore devotes the first part of this study to an emphasis on the divine character of the establishment and maintenance of civil authority. He does so in conscious opposition to the views of both Roman Catholics and the sectarian radicals who alike depreciate the civil realm as religiously inferior and contaminating to a truly Christian life.

While Luther believes that "if all the world were composed of real Christians, that is, true believers, no prince, king, lord, sword, or law would be needed," his biblical realism convinces him that "Christians, however, are few and far between." Even one who confesses Christ as Lord remains simultaneously sinful while "on the road" to becoming a true Christian. As a remedy against the sin of the world, therefore, God has ordained secular authority "for the punishment of the wicked and the protection of the upright."

In order that "no one may doubt that secular law and the sword exist in the world by God's will and ordinance," Luther quotes approvingly the now-familiar verses of Rom. 13:1ff. and 1 Pet. 2:13. He contends that its validity is continually reaffirmed throughout biblical history by God (Gen. 9:6), the law of Moses (Exod. 21), John the Baptist (Luke 3:14) and Christ himself (Matt. 26:52).

It would be difficult for us to overemphasize the decisive role which these biblical passages played in the formative stages of Luther's political ethics. The more Rome neglected them, the more Luther stressed them, often forcing both into rigid positions which did not always take the totality of the biblical witness (e.g. Rev. 13) into balanced consideration. Nevertheless, Luther's central attack on Roman clericalism was devastating: "For I might boast that, since the time of the Apostles, the temporal sword and temporal government have never been so clearly described or so highly praised as by me."

Yet parallel with all these biblical affirmations, Luther recognized that certain passages in the Sermon on the Mount (Matt. 5-7) "would make it appear as though in the New Testament there should be no secular sword among Christians." Luther's classical reconciliation of this abiding Christian dilemma is grounded in his masterful delineation of the "two kingdoms" in which God reigns both as man's Creator-Preserver and Redeemer-Sanctifier. Luther boldly drives the mystery of the tension between the "two ages" of Adam and Christ in Scripture back into the diversified activities of the triune God. Since the Christians live on earth by faith and not sight, this doctrine is intended as a confession of faith in the lordship of God over all creation.

Luther charges that it is blasphemous for man to designate some realm of God's creation as "secular" or "profane," if we thereby judge it to be unworthy of his divine activity or self-sufficient in its own autonomy. God alone rules everyone and everywhere. It is he alone in whom "we live, and move, and have our being" (Acts 17:28). And yet, because not all of God's creatures acknowledge his lordship, he rules men differently as their Creator and as their Redeemer. In Luther's words:

> We must divide all the children of Adam into two classes; the first belong to the kingdom of God, the second to the kingdom of the world. Those belonging to the kingdom of God are all true believers in Christ and are subject to Christ . . . and the gospel of the kingdom. . . . All who are not Christians belong to the kingdom of the world and are under the law. Since few believe and still fewer live a Christian life, do not resist evil, and themselves do no evil, God has provided for non-

> Christians a different government outside the Christian estate
> and God's kingdom, and has subjected them to the sword. . . .
> For this reason the two kingdoms must be sharply distin-
> guished, and both be permitted to remain; the one to produce
> piety, and the other to bring about external peace and prevent
> evil deeds. Neither is sufficient in the world without the other.

The key points in Luther's position are these: 1) God is the
Lord of *both* kingdoms, although he rules each by different means
(law and gospel) for different ends (a just peace and personal
piety); 2) every Christian lives in *both* kingdoms simultaneously
—in the kingdom of God insofar as he is already righteous, and in
the kingdom of the world insofar as he is still sinful; 3) the two
kingdoms are sharply to be *distinguished* from each other, which
means that the realms of law and gospel are to be neither separated
(in secularism) nor equated (in clericalism). They ought rather
to co-exist in harmonious interaction and coordination as comple-
mentary expressions of God's creative and redemptive activity
among men. Absolutely no "rigorous dualism" is advocated here
either in the gracious action of God or in the faithful and loving
responses of men.

Man's Twofold Righteousness

In more concrete terms, this means for Luther that the ethic of
the Ten Commandments is enjoined upon all of God's rational
creatures, while the ethic of the Sermon on the Mount is addressed
primarily to faithful Christians. It goes without saying, of course,
that insofar as Christians remain sinful, they fall with all other
men under the "Thou shalt nots" of the Ten Commandments. It is
of the greatest importance for our understanding of the totality of
Luther's political ethic that we clearly distinguish this twofold
righteousness of man which corresponds to the twofold rule of God
in the two kingdoms of redemption and creation:

1) *Christian righteousness* is the personal piety generated by
   the Holy Spirit in the hearts of Christians in the form of
   faith active in love;
2) *civil righteousness* is the social morality of which all God's

rational creatures are capable—Christians included—in the form of law-abiding political justice.

Required of the Christian citizen, therefore, is *both* a calculating love which takes the form of justice ("wise as serpents") *and* a sacrificial love which "exceeds" the demands of the law ("gentle as doves"). In the struggle for civil righteousness, we may join with other men of good will—whatever their faith—in seeking to translate the moral law of God into the civil laws of the nation. But God always asks more of us as Christians than Caesar demands of us as citizens. Consequently, in the exercise of Christian righteousness, the man of faith also goes "the second mile" in offering love beyond justice and sacrifice beyond service to his needy neighbors.

Once again it is the interaction of God's law (in justice) and gospel (in love) which is central. Just as men cannot be saved by reason and the law, neither can society be ruled by faith and the gospel. But as the demands of the law break into the consciences, of the redeemed (in the church), so too the fruits of the gospel break out to nourish the lives of the unredeemed (in society).

Luther's primary concern in *Secular Authority*—as is ours—is with the interpenetrating Christian righteousness which believers exercise for their neighbors' benefit in the realm of civil and temporal affairs. Significantly, it is not as though they were necessarily to perform different functions or to engage in different activities from their non-believing fellow men. The decisive difference between the "stations" or "offices" *(Staende)* which all men hold, and the "callings" or "vocations" *(Berufe)* which only Christians have, is that of inner motivation. The saints are always hidden. It is not what we do or where we do it, but rather why and how it is done, that pleases God. In the universal priesthood of believers, the ethical fruits are always judged by the religious roots.

Christians and a "Just War"

Luther applies his political ethic concretely to the issue of warfare in *Whether Soldiers, Too, Can be Saved* (1526).[10] He teaches that Christians are voluntarily to submit themselves to the authority and demands of rulers and civil officials for the sake of the general welfare of the community. Believers and non-believers alike are all children of God whom Christians are to look upon as "neighbors" in need of personal love and social justice. The question of bearing arms on behalf of the civil community—in the light of the non-resistance demands of the Sermon on the Mount—is thereby settled for Luther in terms of the "two kingdoms."

Privately, in the realm of redemption, no man may take up the sword on his own behalf as one Christian among others (under the gospel). But officially, in the realm of creation, he may bear arms as a Christian citizen acting on behalf of others in the larger community of Christians and non-Christians (under the law). In a sinful world, Christian love—like God's love—will often have to express itself remedially in strange ways in order to protect the good and punish the wicked. Luther writes:

> When I think of the office of soldier, how it punishes the wicked, slays the unjust, and creates so much misery, it seems an un-Christian work and entirely contrary to Christian love. But if I think of how it protects the good and keeps and preserves house and home, wife and child, property and honor, and peace, then it appears how precious and godly this work is, and I observe that it cuts off a leg or a hand, so that the whole body may not perish. . . . When men write about war, then, and say that it is a great plague, that is all true; but they should also see how great the plague is that it prevents.

A "just" war, then, is a necessary evil in the world as a means of restraining and punishing those who would challenge and disrupt God's created order of peace and justice. However, it is strictly a remedial instrument to be employed only as a last resort after everything else has failed on behalf of a just cause and in fear of God.

Wars of aggression or preventive wars are inherently wrong. Since "princes are rare birds in heaven," Luther warns, "It is not right to begin a war whenever any crazy lord takes it into his head. . . . Worldly government has not been instituted by God to break peace and start war, but rather to maintain peace and repress the fighters." God is not mocked, and rulers accountable to him and his law are further reminded, "You must not consider your own interests and how you remain lord, but your subjects, to whom you owe help and protection, that all may be done in love."

Subjects must also be sure that theirs is a just cause. Luther's repudiation of pacifism in principle does not free Christian citizens from ethical decision in any given situation. If they are convinced that a proposed war is actually for conquest or self-aggrandizement, they must conscientiously refuse to fight. "For it is no one's duty to do wrong; here we ought to obey God who desires the right, rather than men." But if they are truly persuaded of the necessity and (always relative) rightness of their cause, Christians should enter the struggle as loyal soldiers and get the dirty job over with as quickly as morally possible.

Yet even here the political end does not justify any military means. (This insight is crucial, as we shall see below, for a Christian approach to the moral dilemma posed by the threat of nuclear warfare.) All is not fair in either love or war for Christian non-pacifists. Even in the simpler days of 16th century feudalism, Luther sharply distinguished between justifiable and unjustifiable forms of warfare. He taught, "In such a (just) war, it is a Christian act and an act of love confidently to kill, rob, and pillage the enemy, and to do everything that can injure him until one has conquered him according to the methods of war. Only one must beware not to sin, not violate wives and virgins, and when victory comes, offer mercy and peace to those who surrender and humble themselves."

The Augsburg Confession

To conclude this brief survey of our Reformation heritage in the area of politics we shall quote from two articles of the Augsburg Confession in which Luther's restatement of the central thrust of Paul's social ethic is afforded normative authority by the Lutheran church.[11] First, Article XVI guards effectively against secularism. It insists that Christians are not to espouse a "rigorous dualism" between the two kingdoms, but are rather to permeate all of society with personal love and political justice in the exercise of their Christian social responsibility.

> It is taught among us that all government in the world and all established rule and laws were instituted and ordained by God for the sake of good order, and that Christians may with-

out sin occupy civil offices or serve as princes and judges, render decisions and pass sentence according to imperial and other existing laws, punish evil-doers with the sword, engage in just wars, serve as soldiers, buy and sell, take required oaths, possess property, be married, etc.

Article XXVIII then complements this with a rejection of clericalism. It sharply distinguishes the functions of the two kingdoms and refuses to permit the church to prescribe any specific program or legislation which falls properly within the domain and competence of the state. The church (as an institution) must proclaim God's moral law over the state but it should not attempt to legislate man's civil approximations of that law within the state.

Therefore, the two authorities, the spiritual and the temporal, are not to be mingled or confused, for the spiritual power has its commission to preach the gospel and administer the sacraments. Hence it should not invade the function of the other, should not set up and depose kings, should not annul temporal laws or undermine obedience to government, should not make or prescribe to the temporal power laws concerning worldly matters.

The Church's Political Responsibility

We have attempted to outline an evangelical theology of politics based upon the teachings of the New Testament, Luther, and the Augsburg Confession. To be sure, this has not provided us with a moral handbook with specific answers to all the concrete political and military problems which beset us on every side today. When men seek this kind of legalistic casuistry from the church, they demonstrate their complete misunderstanding of the nature of Christianity. Even worse, they display their distrust in the ongoing counsel of the Holy Spirit in the hearts of God's people.

The liberating power of Christian faith as a life-transforming commitment to a personal Savior—rather than to some static and impersonal ideology, moral code, or institutional structure—militates against any social ethic which would subject men once again to the yoke of self-righteous legalism. All church traditions have been tempted to betray men's Christian liberty by denying in practice that "Christ has set us free for freedom" (Gal. 5:1). Let it therefore be said clearly and unequivocally: Christians do not have "merits to earn," or "principles to apply," or "ideals to realize," or "rules to obey." We have rather a crucified and risen Lord who calls us to personal discipleship in all areas of life. In his loving service we find perfect freedom.

Neither Quietism Nor Activism

If taken seriously, the Christ-centered orientation puts an evangelical church in a perennial quandary as to how far it should go in the ethical guidance of its own people and of society at large. At the risk of unfair caricature, we may cite two inadequate approaches to this vexing problem.

On the one hand, Lutheranism has tended to say that the church should "preach the gospel and administer the sacraments," and strictly limit its social witness to the everyday lives of the laity. This concentration on the gospel has energized a sound evangelical *personal* ethic: "faith active in love." But the whole vast realm of corporate structures and institutional life has thereby often been deprived of the normative judgment and guidance of God's law by the church's neglect of any corresponding *social* ethic: "love seeking justice." Though responsible for the proclamation of the whole Word of God, Lutherans have traditionally been much stronger on the personal appropriation of the gospel (for politicians and statesmen) than on the social demands of the law (for politics and the state). What is desperately needed today is a prophetic counterpart to the priesthood of all believers.

On the other hand, the modern advocates of a liberal "social gospel" are too ready to have the church of Christ identify itself with any secular program, political legislation, or judicial decision which happens to meet the approval of the majority of the church's delegates gathered at a particular convention. Here the remedy proposed for the church's political quietism is even more dangerous than the sickness itself. The gospel is distorted into a "new law," the church is prostituted into a political pressure group, and the kingdom of God is secularized into a human utopia. Yet, paradoxically, one theological error in liberalism is precisely the same as that of traditional Lutheranism. It is the inability to recognize that in *social* ethics, the main bridge from the church to an un-regenerate society is not the gospel but the sovereign law of God.

We may now confidently reject both of these false alternatives on the authority of our re-won theology of politics. For Paul and for Luther, it is fundamental that God rules the whole of his creation by the power of his holy Word. This Word includes both law and gospel. By the law he rules men as their Creator and Judge; by the gospel he rules them as their Redeemer and Sanctifier. This means that all of God's sinful creatures are subject to his law, while only Christians—as both righteous and sinful—are responsible under God's law and gospel alike.

Thus the church is given its twofold social ethical mission in this world. On the one hand, it must perform a *prophetic* function by calling all of society to account for its conduct in keeping with the universal law of God. On the other hand, it must perform a *priestly* function by empowering and guiding the social action of Christians in keeping with the ethical fruits of the gospel of God. In its speech and by its actions, the church of Christ dare not proclaim less than this whole Word for the whole world.

Priestly Service and Prophetic Judgment

We have seen that there is biblical authority for the church to speak and to act boldly on controversial social and political issues. It must speak authoritatively for God even though it cannot speak infallibly as God. Like any individual Christian, the church lives solely by faith in God's forgiving and life-giving grace, and not because of its own superior moral perfection or political wisdom. It speaks God's Word, therefore, in tones mixed with both confidence and humility. Whatever light it does possess it offers freely to those floundering in greater darkness.

Following what "has seemed good to the Holy Spirit and to us" (Acts 15:28) is the prayerful way in which the early Apostles solved their problems and also the best way in which we should seek to solve ours. By employing that means of grace which the Reformers called "the mutual conversation and consolation of the brethren," the church has four real contributions to make today toward a just and lasting peace among the nations.

The church can encourage qualified and consecrated laymen to make government service the occupational expression of their Christian vocation. In a church which insists that there is only a functional difference of services between the clergy and the laity, this is one very concrete way of implementing the Christian righteousness of the priesthood of all believers. Empowered by the Holy Spirit to activate their faith socially in terms of love and justice, Christians engaged in making the crucial decisions of public life must be strengthened in the conviction that as they speak and act the church is also speaking and acting through them.

On the political frontiers of the world, the ministry of the laity in their daily pursuits is still the most important arm of the church in society. The church does not have to construct any artificial bridges to society as long as the communion of saints is acting as a leaven in the body politic by nourishing its common life with deeds of mercy and justice.

The church can conduct serious discussions among its members in the analysis of domestic affairs and international relations from a distinctively Christian perspective. Composed ideally of men and women representing different economic levels, races, political parties, and walks of life, the local congregation is in a particularly strategic position to act as a community of reconciliation within the community at large. In the midst of their hurried and hectic lives, few people have the time to grasp all the facts behind the headlines. Even fewer are then capable of evaluating those facts critically from a distinctively Christian (rather than merely patriotic) point of view. By providing local congregations with the theological and technical resources necessary for responsible Christian citizenship, the church helps to implement its members' discipleship in all areas of life.

The church can strive to create a moral and legal climate of opinion at home and throughout the world in which solutions to vexing political problems can take place more easily. Certain of the peace and righteousness of God through faith in Jesus Christ, Christians are free both personally and corporately to join with other men of good will—whatever their faith—in working for more just civil approximations of the moral law of God.

Some form of that law, however corrupted by sin, is to be found written upon the hearts of all of God's creatures (Rom. 2:15). Building on that foundation, our active participation in a political party provides a fruitful point of contact for Christian and non-Christian cooperation in the extension of civil righteousness among the nations. While fully aware of the relative and non-redemptive character of all political life, Christians will strongly champion human rights, equality under the law, and the strengthening of democratic processes and institutions as part of their public service to all men created in the image of God.

The church (or one of its official agencies, such as the Commission of the Churches on International Affairs) can proclaim the general norms and guidelines of Christian political ethics in order to provide judgment and guidance for those responsible under God for the peace, justice, and freedom of the world. This must always be done in a manner which is both reverent to God and relevant to the contemporary situation. The ethical and technical alternatives in a given situation might even be clear enough to justify a definite stand on a specific policy of the government in relation to a domestic or international issue. Unpopular as this may sometimes be, the church should fearlessly prick the conscience of the state by holding it accountable to the sovereign law of God. States as well as churches fall under God's holy lordship and judgment.

An evangelical theology of politics permits us to respect the institutional separation of church and state without neglecting the vital functional interaction of religion and politics in the free exercise of the priestly and prophetic functions of the people of God. Whenever the church is true to its nature as the body of Christ, it will empower its "watchmen of God" to "let justice roll down like waters, and righteousness like an everflowing stream" (Amos 5:24).

Christians and a Nuclear War

By way of illustration, what does the Lutheran Church's traditional recognition of "just wars" mean for us in the 20th century? Certainly the vast political differences between the medieval Christendom of Luther's day and the secularized democracies and dictatorships of our own make any simple historical analogies impossible. In addition, technological advances during the last four centuries have made atomic, biological and chemical warfare something completely different from anything known to churchmen in the past. To recall some of Luther's 16th century limits on a "just war," loyal soldiers are now expected—in their line of duty—to employ nuclear weapons, incendiary bombing and radioactive fallout to help "rape" and "violate" not merely individual wives and virgins, but whole cities full of helpless civilian victims of both present and future generations.

Nevertheless, in at least two very important respects, underlying Christian ethical considerations would seem to be fairly constant. In the first place, Luther strongly championed national order for peace and justice to check the periodic local uprisings of the knights and the peasants. Today when much worse military chaos has reached the national level, it is imperative that we likewise become champions of international order, peace and justice. As the most effective instruments available to carry out the growing rule of international law, the United Nations and its varied humanitarian agencies deserve to be supported and strengthened in their valiant efforts to wage peace and prevent war among all the children of God throughout the world.

In the second place, Luther's basic distinction between "conventional" methods of war and other means of retaliation so inherently and indiscriminately evil that they dare not even be considered by Christian soldiers, sheds light on the most agonizing question faced by evangelical non-pacifists today. Most simply stated: Even if we grant that "just wars" against aggressors are permissible in principle, would nuclear retaliation be justifiable in practice?

War has always been hell, but in a nuclear age it could easily become a suicidal exercise in mutual annihilation. For the first time in history, the military means could completely nullify the political ends for which even a "just war" might be fought. Neither side would emerge victorious from a total nuclear war. Moreover, any limited nuclear operation could rapidly "escalate" into an all-out nuclear holocaust which no Christian ethic could possibly sanction as a "just war." The urgent conclusion should be obvious to all men committed to the reconciling mission of the Prince of Peace: "We must work the works of him who sent me while it is day; night comes when no one can work" (John 9:4).

Selective Conscientious Objection

In view of the suicidal character of most forms of warfare in a nuclear age, 20th century Lutherans dare not mechanically recite the sixteenth century rationale for Christian participation in a "just war." Indeed, the contextual character of Christian ethics demands that governments now grant Lutheran Christians the right to refuse to participate in a particular war which they consider to be inherently unjust. Against the background of widespread American opposition to the Vietnam War, the Lutheran Church in America has officially endorsed the right of "selective conscientious objection." [12] Because of its pioneering role on Lutheran soil, the social statement is deserving of full citation:

"War and military service are and always have been a cause of division among men of conscience. Many choose to bear arms, recognizing that in a sinful world force is often required to restrain the evil. Others, unable to reconcile the inhumanity of war with the demands of love and justice, refuse to participate in particular wars or in any armed conflict. Still others either enter the military or seek deferred status without having resolved the basic ethical dilemmas facing them.

"Lutheran teaching, while rejecting conscientious objection as ethically normative, requires that ethical decisions in political matters be made in the context of the competing claims of peace, justice, and freedom. Consequently, a man need not be opposed to participating in all forms of violent conflict in order to be considered a bona fide conscientious objector. It is in responsible grappling with these competing claims that he should consider participation or nonparticipation in the military.

"Consistent with this, the responsible, conscientious choice of the individual to participate or not to participate in military service or in a particular war should be upheld and protected. The office of soldier, like all other temporal offices, is to be held in esteem by all. At the same time, the conscientious objector should be accorded respect and such freedom as is consistent with the requirements of civil order.

"Governments have rightly seen fit to provide legal status for conscientious objectors, allowing them the privilege of performing alternative service in lieu of military duty. In granting such status, governments recognize that conscientious objectors may make a more valuable contribution to their nation in alternative service than they would if imprisoned or otherwise penalized.

"Furthermore, the moral considerations which underlie the stand of the conscientious objector can have a salutary influence upon a nation. The ethical sensitivity and human concern represented in conscientious objection have a value that far outweighs any potential risk to security involved in granting legal exemption. It is better for the general wellbeing that the conscientious objector be given more than the stark choice between compromised integrity and imprisonment.

"However, legal exemption for the conscientious objector is a privilege, not a right, which a just government grants in the interest of the civil good. This does not imply that governments are required to exempt men from any legal obligation. Governments must reserve the right not to grant, or to revoke, the privilege of legal exemption in situations of clear danger to the public order.

"The fact that some persons may falsely exploit conscience to defend irresponsible disregard for the obligations of citizenship does not excuse the church from its responsibility of defending the bona fide conscientious objector. The church must exercise special care in judging the spirit and motives of those who may call upon the church for safeguarding in such a position.

"Recognizing both the heart-searching of many persons confronted with the possibility of military conscription and the broader considerations of justice and public order, the Lutheran Church in America adopts the following affirmations:

1. "This church recognizes its responsibility of assisting its members in the development of mature, enlightened and discerning consciences. It calls upon its pastors and agencies of Christian education and social ministry to continue in their efforts to cultivate sensitive persons who can act responsibly amid the complexities of the present day.

2. "This church stands by and upholds those of its members who

conscientiously object to military service as well as those who in conscience choose to serve in the military. This church further affirms that the individual who, for reasons of conscience, objects to participation in a particular war is acting in harmony with Lutheran teaching.

3. "Governments have wisely provided legal exemption for conscientious objectors, allowing such persons to do other work of benefit to the community. While such exemption is in the public interest, the granting of its does not imply an obligation on the part of government to provide legal exemption to anyone who finds a law to be burdensome.

4. "In the best interest of the civil community, conscientious objectors to particular wars, as well as conscientious objectors to all wars, ought to be granted exemption from military duty and opportunity should be provided them for alternative service, and until such time as these exemptions are so provided, persons who conscientiously object to a particular war are reminded that they must be willing to accept applicable civil or criminal penalties for their action.

5. "All conscientious objectors should be accorded equal treatment before the law, whether the basis of their stand is specifically religious or not. It is contrary to biblical teaching (cf. Romans 2:15f) for the church to expect special status for the Christian or religious objector.

6. "This church approves provisions whereby persons in the military who become conscientious objectors are permitted reclassification and reassignment. This church urges that these provisions also be extended to the conscientious objector to a particular war.

"Consistent with these affirmations, the Lutheran Church in America directs a member who is a conscientious objector to send a written statement of his convictions to his pastor and to the president of his synod and the secretary of the church. Pastors of the church are directed to minister to all in their care who are conscientious objectors."

Conclusion

Our nuclear weapons have attained such an awesome destructive capacity that controlled arms reduction has now become the most moral (as well as the safest and cheapest) means of national defense. At a time when every cent is desperately needed to combat hunger, poverty, disease and ignorance among the teeming masses of Africa, Asia, and Latin America, it is ethically reprehensible to spend billions of dollars to continue to overstock a mammoth military arsenal whose power already far exceeds the nation's basic needs for either an adequate nuclear defense or an effective nuclear counter-attack ("megadeaths in overkill").

Therefore, above and beyond the deterrence value of sufficient stockpiles legitimately maintained against totalitarian threats as "a terror not to good conduct, but to bad," biblical realism would clearly guide all Christian citizens to work in the direction of 1) multilateral phased reduction of all armaments; 2) multilateral cessation of all kinds of nuclear weapons testing; 3) the protection of both policies by effective international inspection and controls.

In conclusion, we might say that the Christian reaction to the advent of the nuclear-space age is one of hopeful realism. Acknowledging the universality of man's sin, we must recognize the very real possibility that rebellious nations will only employ these vastly-expanded sources of power for their own selfish and destructive ends. Power has always corrupted already-corrupt men, and nuclear power will probably be no exception.

Nevertheless, in confession the universality of God's lordship, we are also confident that men of faith will be empowered by the Holy Spirit to fulfill his will for our day. If there is anything mightier than the nuclear power latent in creation, it is the evangelical power promised to his witnesses by Jesus Christ, the Lord of that same creation. The living and active Word is the far greater power of God for the salvation and service of mankind. Therefore, in the face of a future which will bring tribulation as well as triumph, Christians will do best to remain firmly grounded in the body of Christ whose living head has told us to be of good cheer, for he has overcome the world.

NOTES

1. Cf. *The Documents of Vatican II*, edited by W. M. Abbott, S.J., and J. Gallagher, New York, 1966, pp. 199-308. The location of quotations from the *Pastoral Constitution* will be identified directly in our text: e.g., (art. 73).

2. Cf. *Christians in the Technical and Social Revolutions of Our Time: World Conference on Church and Society*, Geneva, July 12-26, 1966, 232 pages. The location of quotations from the *Report* will also be identified directly in our text: e.g., (para. 14).

3. Further background documentation may be found in the author's studies in *A Theology of Politics*, New York, Lutheran Church in America, Board of Social Ministry, 1965, and *Righteousness and Society; Ecumenical Dialog in a Revolutionary Age*, Philadelphia, 1967.

4. Cf. these evaluations with the critical analysis of Ed. Schlink, "The Theological Basis of the Pastoral Constitution and the Church in the Modern World," in: *Challenge . . . and Response. A Protestant Perspective of the Vatican Council*, ed. by W. Quanbeck, Minneapolis, 1966, pp. 161-185.

5. The printed report is available in *The Ecumenical Review*, 19 (1967), pp. 317-19; the quotation is from p. 317.

6. X. Rynne, *The Fourth Session*, New York, 1966, p. 288f.

7. *The New York Times*. April 27, 1967.

8. Cf. Introduction to *Luther Speaks*, London, 1947, p. 11. See also Berggrav's "Experiences in the Norwegian Church in the War," in: *The Lutheran World Review*, I, 1 (1948); and his *Man and State*, Philadelphia, 1951.

9. Quotations are taken from the American Edition of *Luther's Works*, Vol. 45, Philadelphia, 1962, pp. 75-130.

10. Quotations are taken from the American Edition of *Luther's Works*, Vol. 45, Philadelphia, 1967, pp. 87-138.

11. Cf. Th. G. Tappert, ed., *The Book of Concord*, Philadelphia, 1959, pp. 37 and 83.

12. Adopted by the Fourth Biennial Convention, Atlanta, Georgia, June 19-27, 1968.

AUTHORS

WILHELM DANTINE, Th.D., professor of systematic theology at the Protestant Theological Faculty in Vienna, Austria.

ROY A. HARRISVILLE, Th.D., professor of New Testament at Luther Theological Seminary, St. Paul, Minnesota.

WILLIAM LAZARETH, Th.D., professor of systematic theology and academic dean at the Lutheran Theological Seminary, Philadelphia, Pennsylvania.

GYULA NAGY, Th.D., professor of systematic theology at the Lutheran Theological Academy, Budapest, Hungary.

JOSEPH SITTLER, Th.D., professor of ethics at the University of Chicago, Chicago, Illinois.

LARS THUNBERG, Th.D., assistant professor at the Theological Faculty at Uppsala and director of the Ecumenical Institute at Sigtuna, Sweden.

CLAUS WESTERMANN, Th.D., professor of Old Testament at the Theological Faculty in Heidelberg, Germany.